Beatrice Leathers

88 Canora St.

Wpg.

EMILY

EMILY

The Moroccan Princess from the Elephant and Castle

UNITY HALL

SOUVENIR PRESS
London

First published 1971 by Souvenir Press Ltd.,
95 Mortimer Street, London, W1.
and simultaneously in Canada by
J. M. Dent & Sons Ltd., Toronto, Canada.

ISBN 0 285 62010 X

Printed in Great Britain by
Northumberland Press Limited
Gateshead

CONTENTS

ILLUSTRATIONS

Chapter One

THE IMPOSSIBLE MARRIAGE

Tangier, January 17th, 1873, on a bright and windy North African morning. The town, always a noisy, changing confusion of race, colour, bargaining, selling and quarrelling, was for once united in one topic. Moslem, Catholic, Protestant and Jew all speculated; obsessed with the same subject—the marriage that would take place that morning at the British Legation.

Morocco's holiest man, the Grand Shereef of Wazan, keeper of the Moslem faith in the Maghreb (land of the furthest west) was to marry a Nazarene (a Christian girl) and had divorced three wives of his own faith to do so. In the markets, the streets, the mosques and in the cool, luxurious homes of the European community all agreed that the alliance could only result in trouble.

The Moslems were bewildered and angry. Holy men said that the Koran allowed such a union, even though Moslem women were not permitted to marry Christian men. Nevertheless, they believed that their holy Shereef had lost his senses and prayed for him. The people of the town also knew that even if the Prophet, by the will of Allah, had laid down that such a marriage was proper, the Sultan of Morocco himself disapproved of the ceremony that was to take place that morning. They feared civil war, for already relations between the family of his Sherifian Highness, Muhammed XVIII and the Prince and Grand Shereef of Wazan were strained. The marriage would further widen the gap between the country's two most powerful families.

Not only the Moslems were concerned about the implications of the marriage. The European residents wondered uneasily what the reactions of the Moroccan community would be and were dismayed by the disgrace that the bride, young Emily Keene was bringing on the small British stronghold who determinedly kept up Victorian British standards under considerable difficulties.

Most disapproving of all was John Keene, the father of the bride. At the Victoria Hotel, in a room overlooking the great blue Atlantic bay sweeping around Tangier, Mr. Keene, a big, clean-shaven man, hot and unhappy in his dark frock coat, was trying without success to persuade his eldest child to change her mind about marriage to a Moroccan.

Even as he argued in a last attempt to stop the ceremony he had little chance of winning. All the previous clashes over the years with his daughter had ended with her the victor while he fumed that she always left him powerless to act as he felt was correct.

On the question of the marriage he did not wish to concede. He would have given much to be able to say a final and unshakable 'No.' But even without the Keene family's blessing, the ceremony would still go on. In fact, a Moroccan ceremony had already taken place.

Emily Keene was twenty-three years old on the day of her wedding—a tall, well-built girl with a dignified carriage and magnificent chestnut brown hair, similar in colour to her father's, but with grey eyes while his were blue, and with the same high forehead. She was also very much like him in temperament and they had always clashed. John Keene's eldest daughter was as strong-willed as he was himself, but loving her, he was always at a disadvantage. However difficult she proved, he always lost.

'Emily,' he said, 'please listen to me. We can precure a disguise for you. We can take you back to Gibraltar and away from here without any difficulty if you will only agree to go. I have made all the arrangements.'

'There was no need to make arrangements, papa,' she told him. 'I have made a promise and I must keep to it. Besides, you forget that in the eyes of the Moroccan people, Sidi and I are already married.'

Sitting in the room with them was Emily's mother, Emma Keene. An authoritative, dark-haired woman she could at times be more implacable than her husband, but her arguments were having no more effect on the daughter than those of the father. Emily was polite and loving to her parents, but she could not be persuaded.

John Keene took a couple of harassed turns up and down the room, finishing with his hands behind his back, looking out over the bay. As concerned as he was, he must have noted its beauty and for a moment understood the seductive qualities of the country. But as seductive as the place might be, his attitude to both Morocco and his daughter was one of resentment. She had no right to embarrass her family so. At 47 he was too old to go gallivanting around the world, leaving his seven other children to his second eldest daughter's care, in a fruitless effort to persuade a daughter not to marry some foreigner. He was deeply concerned as to the effect upon the Keene family's reputation when the news broke at their home town of Newington Butts. It would be difficult to live down.

Even today families do not always view mixed marriages with equanimity. In 1873, the disgrace involved was serious to a respectable middle-class Victorian household. That the Shereef of Wazan was a man of considerable importance who commanded more power over the people of Northern Morocco than the Sultan himself, mattered little to John Keene. His future son-in-law was a Prince with a lineal descent that could be traced back without a break to the Prophet Mohammed. That this ancestry caused the Shereef to be regarded as a Saint by his people was not only by the way, it was ridiculous and embarrassing.

The Shereef was admittedly good-looking and dignified. He had a fine face with bright dark eyes, boldly carved features, but he was not quite white. And not British. The situation confronting John Keene, who was an authoritative man of property, well-respected in London, was an unhappy one. The world conquerers and colonisers of Victorian England were not accustomed to the idea of their women marrying Non-Christians who were to be pitied for their misfortunes in being neither white nor Christian.

Supremely confident of their superiority, it was unthinkable that an Englishwoman of good family should even contemplate marriage with a man of a different colour and faith.

The Keene family were middle-class and progressive for the age. They were greatly in favour of education and had paid as much attention to their daughter's schooling as they had to their sons'. John Keene himself was a widely read and intelligent man, and he had tried to argue with his daughter intellectually, leaving emotions aside. He stressed the view-point of the Moslem: the equal disgrace that the marriage would bring to the Shereef. He emphasised the fact that Moslems were allowed four wives and that divorce was absurdly simple. He said he not only feared for her happiness but for her safety, should the marriage take place. He painted a gloomy picture of Purdah, desertion, of the Arab's different attitudes to women, marriage and their supposed predilection for young girls. What, he asked, would happen when a few years had gone by and the Shereef's dark eyes alighted on someone younger, fresher and perhaps more submissive than it was possible for any European, educated girl to be?

'Have you not thought that I have considered all these things?' Emily had said. 'Remember, papa, by Moroccan standards I am already quite old. Girls here are married before they are fifteen. Besides, Sidi is different, which makes the situation different.'

'It always seems different in the beginning,' he told her.

The bare thought of the marriage had come as a bombshell to the Keene family, secure in their large house in the New Kent Road on the outskirts of London. Life had gone on its orderly and predictable way there until a letter had arrived from Emily telling them in her usual direct fashion that the Grand Shereef of Wazan had proposed to her on three occasions. She wrote that she had rejected him twice, but that on making considerable enquiries of those who knew him, she had decided to accept his offer. She was on her way home with two notaries, especially appointed by the Shereef himself who were to ask formally for her father's permission for the wedding.

Knowing his daughter, John Keene understood that the 'formal permission' was no more than a sop to his dignity. If Emily had made up her mind, nothing would stop her. At twenty-two she was legally of age to make the decision for herself, regardless of the family's feelings in the matter.

After long discussion, he and Emma Keene decided that the rest of the family must be told. With Emily arriving, plus two Moroccans, Newington would be buzzing with gossip. Their biggest problem must have been concern that the notaries would not be too conspicuous, and what was to be done with them? Should they stay in the house? Indeed would a hotel even accept them?

Emily's letter was the end of Emma Keene's plans for her eldest daughter. She herself had been married at St. John the Evangelist, Westminster in 1847 and had saved her veil and dress for her daughters to wear when they married at their own Parish Church of St. Mary's Newington with all the family and friends present. This could not happen if Emily were to marry a Moor. Distressing recollections of Othello filled their mind. *Were* Moors black?

The Keenes were to be disappointed as to the discreetness of the notaries. One gentleman, decidedly foreign looking though not negro, was robed from head to foot and brazenly dignified. The other was Portuguese and less conspicuous. Their arrival with Emily put all of Newington in a state of extreme curiosity. The visitors appeared barbaric in the bustle and modernity of the fast growing borough on London's outskirts, but they seemed to regard all of the town's advancement with a certain amount of superiority.

The time they stayed must have been a time of embarrassed misery for the Keene's, particularly when the local paper The *South London Press* went so far as to report upon the notaries' presence and speculate on their reasons for being in London.

One, a M. Felus, who was also a Khalifa and an important man according to Emily, had as the Shereef's representative, asked for Emily's hand in marriage to the Prince he served. He spoke good French, and John Keene, a linguist himself, reluctantly acquiesced, using the same language. Only the younger sisters had thought the story romantic, and much whispering went on behind the nursery door as well as direct questions as to whether their big sister was to become a princess, and if so, could they visit her?

John and Emma Keene agreed to return to Tangier with Emily to attend the wedding, and they left just after Christmas 1872. The five day journey overland to Cadiz had gone too quickly. As the weather grew kinder, John Keene's persuasions had grown more desperate as he tried to convince his daughter of the folly of her actions. And now, on January 17th, 1873, John Keene, a thousand miles away from the stability of Newington and his assured position in the community put one last appeal to his daughter. Even here, while there were British authorities, he had some influence. There was a man 'o war in the bay. He had arranged that Emily could be taken aboard her to Gibraltar. There was still time for her to leave.

'Papa,' she said, 'I have told you. According to Moroccan law, I am already married.'

'And I refuse to accept that the ceremony has any authority,' John Keene had said testily.

It would have been impossible for a staunch member of the Church of England faith to believe in the legality of the Mohammedan marriage ceremony that had taken place two days before. Most disconcerting, the bride-groom had not even been present. But a kind of ceremony had been performed. Two formal contracts of marriage, one a normal Moroccan document, the other drawn up by Emily herself with help from one of Tangier's British residents, William Kirby-Green and written with Victorian attention to detail had been produced by M. Felus and his fellow notary. Emily had signed both, and laughed because she had made a mistake in spelling her new name. She had confused French and English, signing herself La Cherifa d'Wazzan. It should have read La Cherifa d'Ouezzane.

She never signed her name any other way afterwards believing the mistake to be a lucky one.

The notaries had been amused by her error, but to John Keene it was no laughing matter. Nor were the contracts; complicated documents which safeguarded his daughter as much as possible, but appalling in the practicality and lack of emotion which the clauses revealed. Reading the promises the Shereef had made, John Keene (who held to the British view that to anyone other than an Englishman, promises were piecrust) could not help but think how unnecessary the whole thing would have been if Emily were marrying a man from her own country. The knowledge that a Moslem was allowed four wives plus as many harem women as could be supported was always foremost in his mind. The contract contained a clause that the Shereef would take no other wife, but John Keene had no faith in the legality of such a document in a country where women were considered as property. His only consolation was that the Shereef planned to settle in Europe with Emily a short time after the wedding, though he must have quietly hoped they would not decide to make Newington Butts their future home.

The notaries had been extremely businesslike. Once the contract had been signed they enquired of the bride if indeed her father was her representative in the matter.

'He is,' said Emily serenely. Already she had acquired the dignity which together with her strong-will was to stand her in good stead in her new life. She had always had more than her fair share of downright unfeminine confidence, but now she suddenly seemed totally adult and sure of herself in a way her parents deplored.

Because the marriage pained them so greatly they missed the most important point. Emily was in love. A sensible girl, she was pleased that financially her future appeared to be assured. The Shereef was a very rich man. But more important was that she cared for him very deeply. She was genuinely passionately in love, so much so that her meeting with her husband that night needed great restraint.

She returned to the hotel glowing with happiness.

'He said,' she told her parents, 'that we are already man and wife by Mohammedan law. But I told him—not by Christian principles.'

Her words made the fact of the marriage unpleasantly clear to Emma and John Keene. The wedding night would indeed come later, after the brief legation ceremony had been performed in two days time, and with the wedding night the inevitable physical contact between their daughter and her dark and foreign prince. Grave, courteous and pleasant-looking as he was, the prospect to them was distasteful.

But not to Emily. She said:

'I told him that he might have a wife, but I do not yet have a husband.'

'Emily,' her mother said sharply, hiding other emotions in anger. 'Please do not be indelicate.'

'Indelicate?' Emily raised her strong eyebrows. 'Sidi did not think me indelicate. *He* laughed.'

John Keene was forced to realise that there were depths of sensuality in his daughter, which might well be the cause of the situation. Yet she did not look like a sensual woman. Her best feature was the thick, floor length chestnut brown hair which was hanging loose for the wedding. Her face was intelligent and strong, rather than pretty, the eyes direct, the chin firm. Only her incredible hair and full bosom beneath the dark-blue, looped-up riding habit in which she was to be married gave a clue to any hidden sexuality.

Today, for the marriage ceremony the marvellously luxuriant hair, flowing down her back, was tied with a bow of ribbon in red, the Moorish national colour. The Shereef had sent her the ribbon with a special request to let her hair fall free. Like all women of the period she was not accustomed to appearing in public with her hair loose and John Keene felt disapprovingly that it was a style for the bedchamber and not the street. He could not help but remonstrate.

Emily said: 'Never mind. It will please Sidi,' and placing a semi-brigand shaped hat with a long white ostrich feather on her head was ready to go.

She left the hotel ahead of her parents into a typical North African winter's day with a warming sun glinting on the tumbling progress of the sugar-cube houses down to the sea. The air was sharp. Domes and the mosques curved delicately against the blue-white light, the minarets pointing. A brisk wind tugged at the ribbon in her hair, ruffled the blue waters of the broad bay, and stirred the *haiks* and *djelabah*s of the noisy, hostile crowd who waited outside the hotel to see her leave.

A low buzzing murmur went up as she hesitated in the doorway. Hearing it, Emily drew herself up taller and straighter, waiting while a slave came towards her, leading a chestnut horse with three white stockings and a white face. He was pure Arab, untouched by the heavy carthorse strain that appeared in so many Moroccan horses after British royalty misguidedly presented the Sultan with a shire horse that sired considerable progeny.

Emily's glossy chestnut, chosen to match her hair, wore a brand new saddle, an English bridle and a red saddle cloth edged with thick gold lace. There was a riding whip in silver and silver spurs. All were wedding gifts from her husband. Two dark-skinned slaves, their faces impassive, waited to attend her.

Emily Keene rode to her wedding, which pleased both her and her husband. She was a fine horsewoman, and their romance had begun because of a horseback meeting. Besides, it was either that or walk. In 1873 Morocco had known and forgotten the wheel. It had rolled out of existence in the land of the far West when the Romans left about 400 A.D. The country possessed no roads, no railways, barely a cart-track since there were no carts either. Horse, mule, donkey—or foot—were the only methods of transportation.

Her parents walked the short distance to the legation on Tangier's one square. They picked their way over the rough streets hurrying through the hostile and curious crowds, feeling the explosive quality of the mob who had gathered to watch the small procession. In the bay, the man 'o war, *Lively*, in which John Keene had hoped to take his daughter to Gibraltar, fired a salute.

Both John Keene and his wife had been glad of the presence of the ship and the sound of her guns. It seemed like a protective gesture from the British Raj, surrounded as they were by dark and threatening faces. Emma Keene held on to her husband's arm, lifted her skirts from the refuse in the streets, and looked straight ahead, ignoring the crowd of staring black, yellow and brown faces that swarmed around them. Some of the heads were shaven, apart from a long tassel of hair, left for the Prophet to take hold of and raise them to heaven when their time came, others wore their hair Biblically long. Old women were cloaked and hooded like a congregation of sinister monks. Half-naked children darted between the feet of the crowds, women and slaves balanced stone jars of water on their heads, and young girls in white *haiks* turned their veiled faces away at the sight of the Nazarene passing by, and raised their hands in a gesture to avert the evil eye. Over everything hung a quite indescribable smell of decay, of spices, of rotting animal carcases and of flowers. Emma Keene, a little fearful, took her husband's arm.

Their daughter, however, was quite disinterested in the hostility of the crowd as she rode sidesaddle to the Legation, two slaves running at her side. She was certain that complete contentment lay ahead. Always a little exhibitionistic, she was acutely aware of every clip-clop of her horse's hooves, the gleaming sweat on the black faces bobbing at her side, enjoying the feeling of solitariness. She did not see or fear the people because she did not choose to, but she was aware of being the centre point of the day and the disapproval surrounding her merely made her actions all the more sweet. She rode with a straight carriage, enjoying a feel of power.

She was extremely happy.

There was no doubt of Emily Keene's feelings for Hadj Abdeslam Wuld Sidi Hadj el Arbi, Prince and Chief Shereef of Wazan, though he was nearly forty at the time of the marriage: a big, aggressively masculine man, strongly built with wide shoulders, capable of taming a violent horse and controlling the wild hill-men. He was haughty in temperament and yet, like most manly men, capable of tenderness and sentimentality. He had been married four times, was the father of two grown-up sons as well as a small boy and a girl, and yet Emily Keene, the conventionally reared girl was able to put all this from her mind and marry him.

It was an incredible thing for a young Victorian woman to have done. Although wilful, she was entirely respectable, yet not a delicate plant to be afflicted with the vapours. And fortunately her character was tough enough to stand up to disapproval. Her father had already discovered the positive quality in her nature; her husband was to find it, too. But she was not in the least hard, basically a true child of the times, full of a sense of duty towards others less fortunate. Like most Victorians who survived the ordeal of being born at that period, physically she was strong. The climate and the dirt of Tangier never bothered her. She was the ideal pioneer, and it was sad that some of her family never completely forgave her for the scandal she caused, not appreciating that her temperament needed a challenging and exciting life.

Her action caused all round embarrassment. In Tangier itself, Emily had done the unforgivable thing when she broke the rules and stepped over the line which separated the foreign and native communities. For her family in England there was no chance of the wedding remaining a family skeleton to be buried in some musty cupboard. The newspapers of the period fully reported her story.

But no guilt or second thoughts lingered in her mind as she left her horse to be held by a patient slave, and, riding crop still in hand, swept into the British Legation, passed the stuffed hyena which stood in the hallway and always terrified the servants. Walking alone she went on into the room where her marriage was to take place and where the Shereef waited, magnificent in his soft, white robes. He moved towards her, a smile softening his usually reserved face and took her hand. Sir John Hay Drummond Hay, equally splendid in his orders waited to conduct the brief ceremony, surrounded by as many dignitaries of the British community who had been persuaded to be present. They were mostly men.

It was fortunate for Emily Keene that the wedding was conducted by Sir John. A remarkable man of great intelligence, Sir John Hay Drummond Hay, KCB, was Her Majesty's Minister Plenipotentiary to the Court of the Sherifian Empire and Consul General in Tangier. His father had held the consular post before him, and he had spent many years in Morocco. He had genuine affection and respect for the Moroccan people plus a real interest in their welfare in spite of being afflicted with the prevailing British habit of treating all native people as children. His influence was considerable in the Maghreb, and the Moroccans returned the affection he showed them which may have even helped for a short time to hold back the Moslem resentment at Emily's marriage.

It was due to the work and efforts of men like John Hay Drummond Hay that the Moroccan people found it easier to accept the British than any other Christian power. Though the current attitude towards any Christian was one of hatred, and Tangier itself was known by the Moors as 'the city of dogs and the spawn of dogs' (Christians) because of the size of the European community, there was a slight affection for the British. They were referred to as 'the mad Christians'—a dubious compliment but a genuine one, as Mohammedans believe that the insane are holy and therefore blessed.

Sir John, disapproving at heart, married Emily to her Shereef perhaps reflecting that the Moors had a point when they thought of the British as insane, kindly turning a wise and blind eye to the quite false statement of the Shereef that he was a widower, and entering the fact on the British Government's legally binding marriage certificate without turning a hair. He knew this was a face-saver more for John and Emma Keene's benefit than for the bride's. She knew perfectly well that her husband had divorced three wives in order to marry her. Emily, though scrupulously honest in most ways, could be a great dissimulator if the occasion warranted it.

It was not customary for Moroccan women to wear wedding rings, but the Shereef had one for Emily. A broad band of bright yellow gold, especially mined at Talifit in the South, it was engraved on the *outside* with the Shereef's own name in Arabic letters.

'That is because I want everyone to see you are my wife,' he told her, interrupting the ceremony, as he slipped it on her finger.

The guests, at least, were reassuring to the elder Keenes. Witnesses to the wedding were Horace P. White, the vice-consul, a man caught up with that curious affinity which seemed to appear so often between British Victorians and Arab people. The other witness was Rear Admiral R. J. McDonald, from the *Lively* in the bay, now reconciled to the fact that his ship would not be needed to rescue a British maiden from her fate.

It was all over in five minutes. Emily Keene from Newington Butts was now Her Royal Highness the Grand Shereefa of Wazan with the English way of life left behind her for ever. The new Shereefa was congratulated by those present. Emily's mother and father managed a kiss and a loving word for her, although it must have been an effort to find the right phrases.

Pink and flushed, the bride took her husband's arm and prepared to leave the legation, and the witnesses, encouraged by her pleasure and excitement, crowded behind them, through the reception rooms and out into the paved courtyard outside.

The Legation, surrounded by those of other European countries, was only a minute's walk from the sea and stood on a narrow street near the town's principal mosque, the Moulay Taieb, named after one of the Shereef's most illustrious ancestors, and where his mother was buried. Once on the street, the Shereef bowed goodbye to his bride and the other guests, and attended by his servants, mounted his horse and rode away.

John Keene looked after his son-in-law in amazement. 'Where on earth is he going?' he asked.

Emily calmly pulling on her riding gloves, explained that her husband was going to the Mosque. It was Friday, his holy day. It was necessary to pay his devotions.

Emma Keene was horrified.

'He is leaving you to ride back alone? On your wedding day?'

Emily ignored the question and explained that people were not normally married on a Friday in Morocco. Tuesdays and Thursdays were considered the lucky days, but the Shereef was not in the least superstitious. Something very unusual in Morocco.

'The people are riddled with superstition and very complicated it makes their lives, too,' she said. 'Shall we go?'

She smiled at her parents, remounted her horse and set off down the narrow road, the negro slaves trotting at her side.

Emma Keene was angry but Sir John stepped in to smooth over the situation with an offer to escort her and her husband back to the hotel where the guests were waiting.

First to arrive at the Victoria, Emily slipped upstairs to her room where she changed from her riding habit into an elegant white silk frock embroidered all over with little green sprigs. It had a bustle and the skirt swished in a most satisfactory way. The bodice was liberally frilled, but still showed off her fine shoulders and she debated whether to leave her hair free or whether to coil it up on her head. Reluctantly she decided it would be more discreet to put it up as the sixty invited guests were European and might well think her unladylike if it were left the way her husband preferred. She decided to wait until he reappeared before returning downstairs. If possible she wanted no more clashes with her parents that day.

About half-an-hour later she heard a disturbance in the street below and, looking from her window, saw that the Shereef had returned. It was a fine sight. Flanked by a guard of Moorish soldiers his progress was impressive. The soldiers were turbaned, robed in white with splashes of red. All were fierce bearded men from the Riff Mountains, who carried long, heavy flintlock rifles. By now some of the male spectators who lined the streets had put on their gala dress for the Shereef's benefit—large muslin Kaftans, wound about by white robes. The crowd pressed forward to touch the hem of the Shereef's robe and to kiss his foot as he sat above them on a white horse. Emily thought he looked very splendid.

Her parents, watching from the ground floor windows were less impressed.

Emma Keene wanted to know why all the ragged men

were kissing his feet. She thought it rather insanitary.

'He possesses the *baraka*,' Sir John explained. 'It means he is holy, and it is good luck to see him—better to touch him. It is the custom here.'

As soon as the Shereef was inside the hotel, the crowds dispersed, the guards were left to lounge outside the hotel entrance, and the wedding breakfast began. It was typically European, prepared by M. Martin, the French manager of the hotel. There was a huge white wedding cake which had been brought from England, a present from the bride's godfather, and plenty of champagne.

A little later Sir John, a small, heavily bearded man with twinkling eyes, proposed the toast and John Keene responded with good grace. Perhaps the normality of the occasion; the knowledge that nothing could be changed, and the Shereef's ease with Europeans had given him fresh heart. He may even have been reassured by the way in which his holy son-in-law was enjoying the champagne. A comfort not normally permitted to followers of the Prophet.

Perhaps because of the champagne, the party was a success and eventually Emily returned to her room to change back into the dark blue riding habit for the ride to the house where she was to spend her wedding night. With the Shereef at her side as she left the hotel, she found Guards from the different legations, bright and smart in their colourful dress uniforms were lined up to salute as the newly married couple passed. The crew of the *Lively* were also at hand, waiting outside the hotel to cheer lustily as she came by.

The guests threw slippers and rice as the couple mounted their horses and there was a great deal of noise and laughter. This completely baffled the watching Moroccans and somewhat baffled the Shereef himself.

'I have enough rice in the hood of my Ljelabah to make a meal,' he said as they rode away. 'What was the reason for that?'

'Just for luck,' said Emily. 'It's a custom. Now, lead on McDuff before they catch us up.'

The Shereef was puzzled. 'What is McDuff?'

Emily said: 'He was a great chieftain like yourself. A

character in a famous play. He was a brave, fierce man and "Lead on, McDuff," has become a saying, so I shall call you McDuff.'

'Brave and fierce, eh?' he said. 'I like that.'

They were alone together for the first time that day. The crowds, clamouring for blessing, had been left behind and they slowed down their horses letting them pick their own way up the hilly path to the Shereef's house out of town. It was early evening and the sun was setting in a firey blaze that turned hills and ocean crimson and touched the white of the houses behind them with glowing pink.

'I know why your ancestors christened this the sun-set land,' Emily said.

'It was because it was as far west as they could go,' he said, 'but it was a pretty choice of phrase. *Aska el Maghreb*. Your first lesson in Arabic.'

'Yes,' she said, her eyes on the beauty of the sun-set. 'I shall have to learn now.'

She found she had much to learn, even on her wedding night. The Shereef's house was swarming with relatives, servants, and dependants. Marriage was a very public affair in Moslem lands, and as yet another face peered at them from behind a pillar or arch she wished for more privacy than the house could afford. She complained a little, but he was not sympathetic, explaining that had she been a Moroccan girl for the first seven days of their marriage he would only have visited her at night and she would have spent her days with young women while waiting for his return.

'And,' he added warming to his theme, 'the marriage would have been very different. As you are not a Shereefa, you would have been obliged to come to me on foot, as near to dawn as possible. The seven days before you would have been in seclusion except for visits to the *hammamm*—'

She interrupted to ask what was the *hammamm*?

'The bath. Brides must bath every day for seven days before a wedding.'

Emily said rather crossly that she bathed every day as it was.

The seventh day after the wedding she would have to visit the *hammamm* again, and be girdled and dressed by her women as befitted a married lady. And, he pointed out, she would have been painted with henna in a variety of designs all over her legs, hands and arms. And her face would have been decorated with circles and triangles.

'Shall I go on?' he asked.

'No,' said Emily. 'I think we make better arrangements in Europe.'

The following day there was another ordeal—a party for the local Moroccan dignitaries. Lunch was served at the Marshan house, and the Sultan's representatives the Pasha of the town, the Caid (judge), the custom's officials, all the men in authority were invited. Though none truly approved of the marriage, respect for the Shereef and perhaps some curiosity about the bride, brought them there. But it was a difficult afternoon for Emily. She and the Shereef conversed in Spanish and she spoke no Arabic at all. None of her guests spoke any language other than their own, and even if they did, they stuck determinedly to their mother tongue. Added to her problems was the fact that in the normal way no Moslem would have dreamed of presenting his wife to another man—certainly not to a gathering of men, and the guests, though polite, were disapproving. In the normal way had they so much as laid eyes on a Shereef's Mohammedan wife, even by mistake, the penalty for seeing her face could have been death. It was a confusing situation for them, to see this Nazarene girl smiling, offering food, even trying to make conversation in what was to them an incredibly immodest manner. No harem woman, let alone a wife, would have dreamed of behaving with such familiarity.

The new Shereefa was rescued by a French friend of her husband who spoke enough Arabic to translate a little and, with his help the party staggered on to the end. She had made her first contact with her husband's people, and it had not been too much of a failure. In fact, her personality and smile had made some inroads into the prejudice they felt for the Christian woman their Shereef had been insane enough to marry.

It had been decided that Emma Keene would stay on in Tangier with her daughter for a period of time to help over any problems that might lie ahead and to help pack and prepare to return to Europe when the time came for the Shereef and Shereefa to find a permanent home there.

They had almost decided on France as their future home, but the Shereef had his affairs to wind up, which he said might take some time. Nothing was done in haste in the Maghreb.

John Keene decided to return to England immediately. His wife seemed to have accepted the fact of his daughter's marriage, but he could not, and in any case, he could not stay away from his work indefinitely. A worried and unhappy man, he set out for Gibraltar on the little paddle boat *Hercules* a few days after the wedding and on arrival there was aghast to find that the *Gibraltar Chronicle* had printed the story of his daughter's marriage in full mocking detail, adding:

'For the benefit of any of the fair countrywomen of the bride who may be disposed to follow her example it may be as well to add that the Shereef now has four wives, that a Christian marrying a Mohammedan forfeits the protection of English law, and that Mohammedan husbands are by the Alcoran (Koran) (Chapter 4, verse 3) strictly enjoined to beat their wives in case the latter are disposed to be refractory.'

The story had also been picked up by the *London Times* which thundered in its usual way that her action should be taken as an awful warning to others, saying: 'This unfortunate Christian girl who makes four wives (for the Shereef) and has no protection from the law.'

The Times, too, added chapter 4, verse 3 of the Koran to their report. John Keene did not know at this time that his own local paper, the *South London Press,* had also run the story, and that London was buzzing with gossip about Emily's rash and un-British action.

He did know that he was monumentally angry at the intrusion into family matters, the cheapness of the comment and the insult to his daughter. Whatever he felt about the situation, family honour came above all else. Apologies must be made, at once.

His top hat rammed firmly on his head, his usually pleasant round face grim, he had set off up Gibraltar's main street looking for the newspaper offices. He found them in a small back street, and pounded up the wooden staircase and demanded to see the Editor.

The Editor, startled by this very English gentleman who had arrived unannounced, demanding to make a statement, hurriedly sat him down, and John Keene, in forceful terms, dictated what he felt must be said. The Editor was an astute man. He had done very well on lineage from London with the original story. It could do no harm to keep the interest going.

Duly, the *Chronicle* the next morning reported under the heading: 'The Anglo-Moorish Marriage'—that—'Mr. John Keene, the father of the lady whose marriage with Prince Hadj Adbeslam, Grand Shereef of Morocco which was described by a correspondent in the *Gibraltar Chronicle* of the 20th requests us, in justice to his daughter, to correct certain errors which several English journalists have adopted from statements in Gibraltar papers.

'He says: "The facts are that the Prince was not at the time the husband of three wives, but a widower, as proved by his declaration made before two notaries public, and now filed in the office of the British Consul General in Tangier. By the marriage contract he binds himself to take no other wife: my daughter retains her religion and all the freedom usually granted by Englishmen to their wives, and any children of the marriage to be educated in Europe. Although it is true that by this marriage the lady had lost her nationality, a like result would follow her marriage with any other than a British subject.'

John Keene believed that was the end of that.

But it was not.

By February 20th, 1873, *The Times* in London had also published John Keene's statement, without any comment, which must have lightened his heart back in the big house at Newington Butts, empty without his wife. Two days later, so did the *South London Press*. But the story was too good to let go with a simple correction. And the *South London Press* had a vested interest. The Keene's were local gentry. They headed their story: 'A South London Princess' and tongue in cheek, reported:

'The days of romance are not over, nor has this sober metropolis ceased to be identified with incidents which would have well befitted a tale of the middle ages. From our very midst, in the New Kent Road, a young lady of prepossessing appearance, of tall and commanding figure, has been wooed and won by a Moorish prince.

'The heroine in this romance is Miss Keene, who left England some time ago as companion to a lady, and while in Barbary (Tangier) created a great impression on a prince with love darts and received a proposal in due form. It is stated that the lady wrote to her parents in the New Kent Road reporting the fact that she had refused the offer on the ground that her would-be suitor had already three wives. This her father now contradicts. Miss Keene, however, afterwards altered her mind, and decided to alter her name, prior to the latter of which she visited London escorted by two real Barbary attendants sent by the prince. There was some amusement created at the residence of the parents and in the neighbourhood by the visit of her attendants in Oriental garb, and also at the residence of the fair one's grandfather (the keeper of Horsemonger Lane prison).

'The young lady, who has returned to her adopted country, was married at the British Consulate in Tangier, in the presence of her father and mother, the latter of whom remains in that city, and the former has returned to London. We wish the illustrious Shereefa—as she will be styled—our young and courageous friend and late neighbour who is stated to be likely to visit this and other countries of Europe next summer, all the joys which can attend her in her new career.'

The report went on to describe yet again the marriage itself adding: 'Soon after the conclusion of the breakfast, the happy couple rode away on horseback, and the old

English custom of throwing the slipper was not forgotten, which appeared much to surprise the natives.'

And then repeated again was John Keene's statement to the Editor of the *Gibraltar Chronicle*. He rued the day he had ever opened his mouth. And no doubt rued even more the day he had permitted himself to agree to letting his daughter go abroad at all.

Chapter Two

A ROMANTIC ENCOUNTER

The new Shereefa of Wazan had always been independent and strong-minded—perhaps fortunately, as these were the two qualities which would help her the most in her new life. She had been difficult to control, even as a schoolgirl. Once grown-up, her singing had been the bone of contention. She had given recitals on the stage, brazenly, by her family's standards, showing herself off to an audience and being paid for it.

John Keene had stopped this, though he might never have known of her activities—she having the wit to keep them secret—if a friend had not attended one of her concerts and complimented him on his daughter's voice and looks. He had been very angry with her, but she was merely indignant that he 'chose to suppress her talent'.

Eventually he won that battle, only to lose the next which began when Emily began to beg and plead to go abroad as a companion to Mrs. Ellen Varley, an acquaintance of the Keene family. There had been good reasons why she should not go, but the house had been in an uproar when he refused. There was no peace for anyone until he agreed to recommend her for a passport. And on December 11th, 1871, aged twenty-two, she won the battle and received her first passport from the Foreign Office. Ultimately, John Keene could not prevent her from going abroad; she was old enough to make her own decisions.

Perhaps the oddest aspect of Emily's extraordinary story is that she ever found herself in Tangier at all. It seems incredible that she was able to persuade her family into travelling abroad with Ellen Varley—who by the time of their arrival in Tangiers was calling herself Madame Perdicaris with no legal reason to do so.

Mrs. Varley's husband was a brilliant electrical engineer and inventor. He was little more than a year older than Emily's father, and both had been educated at St. Saviour's, Southwark.

Cromwell Fleetwood Varley had been responsible for the laying of the first cable between Britain and America, and was a member of the Institute of Engineers. He had also been elected to the great honour of being made a Fellow of the Royal Society and a Member of the Council in London.

The Varleys generally were a talented but eccentric family. John Varley, Cromwell Fleetwood's uncle, was one of the great painters and art teachers of the day. Turner had been his pupil, and there were stories of wild dinner parties where Mrs. John Varley was thrown across the table from guest to guest. As a family they were caught up in the current obsession with spiritualism and astrology.

Ellen Varley was different from the family she had married into. A Miss Rouse, her father was a gentleman from Hampstead. She was remarkably good-looking with red hair and a naturally aristocratic manner. In later years her family referred to her as Queen Elizabeth behind her back and there was a distinct resemblance. She married Cromwell Fleetwood (named after two of his ancestors, Oliver Cromwell, and Admiral Fleetwood) in October 1855, when she was just eighteen and he was twenty-seven. She bore him four children. The young Ellen Varley was gay and luxury loving. Perhaps her husband had inherited a Puritan streak, for as the years went by he became more and more engrossed in his work, while she became increasingly bored.

Then, early in 1871, Mrs. Varley went to Malvern to take the waters for her health. There she met the gentleman from Trenton, New Jersey, named Ion Perdicaris. The Perdicaris family had contributed considerable money to the Southern cause in the American Civil War. Ion's father, George A. Perdicaris, had been a Greek refugee and arrived in America under sentence of death from the Greek Government. For some time he had taught his own language at Harvard, before resigning to interest himself in the formation of gas companies in cities all over the United States.

Gas was the coming thing, and the Perdicaris family became extremely rich. When Ion was twenty-five, with plenty of money in his pocket, he left Trenton, N.J. to wander around Europe, where, eventually he encountered Ellen Varley and discovered that one of the things they had in common was a love of music.

Their meeting at Malvern was to completely alter a whole string of lives—including Emily Keene's.

Mrs. Varley and the young American were immediately attracted to each other. Ion Perdicaris, apart from being charming—a short, stocky, heavily-bearded man with twinkling eyes—was also extremely rich. Not that this would have influenced Ellen Varley—her husband was also well-cushioned against any hardship.

They ran away together and one night Cromwell Varley came back to his home in Beckenham, Kent to find his wife and all her belongings gone.

Almost certainly the Keene family knew nothing of Ellen Varley's relationship with Ion Perdicaris. They were not close friends—more acquaintances—and the full truth of the scandal was not entirely known until February 1873, a month after Emily's marriage, when the London *Times* announced primly that 'She (Mrs. Varley) formed an improper intimacy with him (Ion Perdicaris) and the result was that during her husband's absence abroad on business, she left her home in Beckenham and went to live with the co-respondent. They have since left England together.'

Emily left with them, and two of Mrs. Varley's four children, Cromwell and Hebe. She had been offered the job, and she took it, perhaps concealing the fact that Mrs. Varley was not travelling alone. It is hard to understand why the Keenes let her go with someone who would no longer be accepted by Victorian society, unless their knowledge of the situation was not complete. Divorce in the early 1870's was such a disgrace that Cromwell Varley himself may have covered up the situation. But more likely

Emily's strength of character, plus her determination to take the opportunity to travel, left them with little choice. She was over 21. She was also an exceptionally tolerant person, never interfering in what she considered other people's business. Completely moral herself, she nevertheless would never judge others.

It might also have been that Ellen Varley, who was only twelve years older than Emily, was using her as a chaperone to help conceal that the man she was travelling with was not her husband. But whatever the truth of the matter, the background to the Perdicaris affair was never discussed in front of the children of the Keene household.

Emily's younger sister, Helena Winifred, who, many years later was to live for seven years in Tangier, wrote, not long before her death, a short history of her sister. She describes very briefly and in the circumstances, inconclusively, the events which lead up to Emily's arrival in Tangier.

'She (Emily) was the eldest of eleven (eight of whom lived) children and our parents were very Victorian. My mother had a lovely voice and a favourite song was called The Moorish Bride. I still have it copied out in her hand, and I wonder if this in any way influenced my sister's choice of husband. She was a high-spirited girl, clever and rather difficult to manage. She hated the perpetual nursery atmosphere of the home, and begged to be allowed to go to boarding school in London. Here she did well and was very popular with teachers and pupils.

'One day a new girl arrived, a very homesick little person, and my sister took her under her wing. This led to a lifelong friendship, and was really the foundation of Emily's romantic adventures. The grateful child begged her mother to invite Emily to their home for the holidays and she became a constant and very welcome guest.

'The years passed by and on one of these visits her hostess was dangerously ill. My sister nursed her devotedly, and by her prompt action saved her life. Her patient was grateful and being ordered abroad, invited Emily to accompany her. This she gladly did, it being the great desire of her life to see the world.'

Emily's hostess was Mrs. Ellen Varley; the life-long friend, Mrs. Varley's eldest daughter, Ada, and the illness through which Emily nursed her hostess the one which eventually led her to Malvern, the meeting with Ion Perdicaris and the flight abroad.

Helena Keene continued: 'The travellers roamed over Spain and Emily's letters home were eagerly awaited. Her letters were always most interesting, describing the country and the people she met, and mother would read out extracts to us small children. I was eight. There was no hurry and my sister enjoyed herself with her kind friends. One day we heard they were in Tangier. Morocco was very much a land of mystery and adventure. Christians were not welcome, especially in the interior ... my sister wrote glowing pictures of the country as she saw it. "Just like living in Bible times," she said.

'We eagerly awaited her letters, a sort of continuation of a fairy story. Nothing like this had ever happened in our prosaic family.'

Actually the Perdicaris' left first for the South of France, but they were restless, and wandered through Spain down to Gibraltar where they arrived on the 16th of April, 1872. The following morning they decided to take the paddle steamship *Hercules* from Gibraltar Harbour to look at exotic Tangier.

The little ship, first of its kind to cross the Straits, chugged on, while Africa ahead became clearer on the skyline. Taking nearly three hours the ship paddled desperately past Cape Malabatta before turning into Tangier Bay. And it was then Emily caught her first glimpse of the town that was to be her home for the rest of her life.

An uncomfortable experience lay ahead of her and her companions. Landing. Tangier possessed no harbour, only the remains of a mole built by the British in the seventeenth century when Tangier was a British colony, and blown-up when the English troops were driven out by the Moors.

An eye-witness account of the problems of landing at

Tangier was left by the special correspondent of the *Gibraltar Chronicle and Commercial Intelligence.* He wrote floweriy for his paper on May 1st, 1873:

'The sultana of Moorish cities, Tangier is sometimes called, and truly she does wear a regal, sultana like air as seen from the distance, cushioned in state on the hillside, her white flat roofs rising one above another like the marble steps of a stately staircase, the tall towers of the mosques piercing the air, and the multitudinous many-coloured flags of all nations fluttering above the various consulates.

'But in this, as in many other cases, it is distance lends enchantment to the view. A flotilla of tubs puts out to meet us; we descend into one manned by a brawny negro and a Moor, and put off for shore—that is, for as near the shore as our landing will allow. The instant the boat grounds, while we are yet some fifteen yards from the beach, a lot of wild fellows in skull-cap, and shirt tied at the waist, and short cotton drawers, plunge into the water and advance to meet us. On they come till they are waist-deep, and before I well know what he is about, the foremost seizes me by the legs, slings me athwart his shoulder, and wades to the land.

'This is the undisguised mode in which the Frank makes his appearance among the Moslems and Barbary.'

The London *Times* was a little more laconic.

'Every passenger arriving has to be carried on shoulders through the shallow water. The Moors will not carry the Christians, so this has to be done by the Jews, and on Saturday when an arrival of passengers takes place, the Christian has to be carried on shore by the Spaniard and Portuguese.

'Ladies are occasionally privileged by being carried in on chairs, but always amid the screaming and quarrelling of a crowd of Jews.

'Each Jew gets hold of a small parcel—all scramble for payment and many times the wrong one is paid and the money has to be paid over again to the right person.'

Emily arrived in Tangier, carried on a chair from the boat in the shallows, her feet wet and her hair tumbled. She was lucky not to have been dropped into the sea. This was not an uncommon occurrence when passengers were landed from the *Hercules*.

On the morning of arrival, once off the fine sand of the beach where people had been riding there was a confusion of new sights, sounds and sensations to drink in. It was the most romantic place that Ion Perdicaris and Ellen Varley had found since they ran away together, and the town fitted in with their mood of throwing convention to the winds.

First impressions of Tangier were always exciting. It seemed impossible that such an incredible collection of people of every shade of skin and wild variation of dress should exist so near to Europe.

The streets going off to the side of the main road were narrow—so narrow that the inhabitants could pass things across to each other, and a hole with a grating seemed to do duty as a window. The lanes zig-zagged up and down over hard cobbles in a drunken stagger. Buildings which Ion Perdicaris pointed out as mosques and shops were entered by horse-shoe arches and in the Soke—the main market place—squatting women sold hot cakes, men guarded cylinders of matting with nets caging the apertures which held live cocks, hens, rabbits and pigeons. There were people selling sweetmeats, charms, snuff boxes made from beads and coconuts, jars of milk, honey and baskets of dates. At the fountain negro slaves, males and females with brass curtain rings from Birmingham in their ears came and went, chatting and arguing with the Moors. It was all novelty, noise and change, and the smells, though certainly not sweet, were bearable as part of the colour and foreignness.

Tangier itself enchanted Emily and the Perdicaris' from the first. Emily was delighted when her employers decided to settle there without any more ado and took rooms at the Hotel de France while they looked for a house. The

Hotel was high in the town, a charming, white painted building set in a pretty garden above the Soke. Once settled, Emily's duties were not arduous. She had plenty of time to explore the town thoroughly and soon the sights and smells of the place became familiar. She did not mind that there were no roads, no carriages and that it was four legs or shank's pony to get about. There was no theatre, no cab stands, no daily paper, no sewage, no drainage and very little to do. But plenty to watch.

Her room at the back of the Hotel overlooked the Mosque of Moulay Taieb, and she watched the cloaked and muffled crowds arriving for their devotions on Friday mornings while the trembling cry of the Muezzin woke her at dawn. 'Prayer is better than sleep. Prayer is better than sleep,' he said. But she did not know that was her future husband among the Friday worshippers.

Even in the earliest days of her life in Tangier Emily was content in the fascinating, enchanting and unpleasantly smelly and dirty town. She felt a great rapport with the women who watched her from behind their veils, elongated dark eyes regarding her with the same curiosity that she felt for them. She was anxious to get to know some of the real people of the country. But this was difficult.

The British community was small. Only 54 subjects of her Brittanic Majesty clung together in isolation in this corner of Africa, so near to Europe and yet so far removed in thinking and custom. They mixed with the French residents, tolerated the Italians and despised the Spanish, most of whom were professional hunters and nearly always drunk. The 54 British did their determined best to live an English life and to keep up the standards that applied at home. They certainly did not mix socially with the Moroccan people.

This was frustrating for anyone as curious as Emily, but there was little she could do to widen her knowledge of the country.

Eventually the Perdicaris rented the most beautiful house in Tangier, the El Minzah Palace.*

The couple moved in and very quickly became the

* Where the hotel of the same name still stands.

centre of the town's social life. Only very few of the most respectable and hidebound European inhabitants refused to call upon them when the scandal leaked out—as it inevitably did. Then, (as now) in Tangier, money talked. And besides, married or not, company was short, a new face welcome, and the Perdicaris were both charming and hospitable.

When Emily first saw the El Minzah Palace she was startled by its grandiose splendours. She did not come from a poor family; the Keene family house in the New Kent Road was roomy and comfortable, but the El Minzah Palace was something quite different: a vast, superbly decorated and furnished Moorish home. There was an enormous ballroom with coloured parquet floors and matching ceiling; arches, gardens, fine courtyards and big airy rooms. A regiment of servants had been employed to run the place and no expense was spared to make it a showpiece. Ion Perdicaris had the same ability as his father to make money, and even in the short time he had been in Morocco land and property speculations were increasing his income.

Emily moved into the El Minzah Palace and found she had little to do. She wrote a few letters, attended the musical soirées where she accompanied on the piano, and was gradually drawn into the normal social life of Tangier. And then in June came the hot weather. The sun blazed down on Tangier, and more and more water was needed to stop the Moorish garden surrounding the house from turning seer and brown. The pretty fountains were reduced to a sad trickle, and Mr. Perdicaris said he thought it was time they moved.

Everyone of substance had two homes—one in Tangier for winter; one on the mountain outside the town for the blazing summer months. The Perdicaris were no exception.

Great packings and preparations were carried out for the half-an-hour uphill ride out of town. Mrs. Varley rode in a litter between two mules, Emily and Ion Perdicaris were on horseback, while the crowd of servants followed on mule, donkey or foot, coping with the overflowing baggage.

They crossed the Marshan, a large, flat open space of

ground where many of the European community lived, and then down again from the plateau to cross the '*ad-al-Ihoudi*'—'The Jew's River,' a pretty little stream, now nearly dry, which in the winter became a roaring torrent, cutting the Tangerines off from their homes on the Mountain.

Once across the stream, the road climbed again, on a path which could have been part of a garden. Myrtles, jasmine, palms, fig trees, lemon, olive, pomegranate and orange trees, some just losing their blossom, grew wildly, and sweet scented roses clung to their trunks. They passed some fine houses, one of which belonged to Sir John Hay Drummond Hay, her Majesty's Consul and the leader of the British community.

The horses picked their way delicately over the rough mountain paths, while behind lay a superb view.

Below to the right was Tangier and beyond plains and mountains until in the far distance there was the snow-capped mountain range of Tetuan, fifty miles away. To the south at a much greater distance was an enormous crag, the Shesouan mountain, over 7,000 feet in height.

In front, across the misty blue Straits lay Gibraltar, and clearly visible behind it the snow peaks of the Spanish Sierra Nevada above the tranquil bay of Trafalgar where Lord Nelson fought and died, and even further in the distance the Bay of Cadiz could be seen.

This was the view from the Perdicaris' summer home, and when they were all settled in the pretty house, surrounded by scented gardens there was even less work for Emily to do. She spent most of her time out of doors and the long enchanted summer that was to culminate in her falling in love began.

The story of her meeting with the Grand Shereef is family history to her present-day descendants in Morocco; a family reminiscence which they tell with pleasure. And it is a charmingly romantic tale.

It happened that every day Emily would ride down the mountain and the cliffs which tumbled to the sea below to bathe in the clear, blue waters of the Atlantic. She wore the unflattering bathing suits of the period, but knowing herself to be unobserved on the lonely stretch of African coast, daringly changed without the benefit of a bathing hut. After her swim she would sit on the rocks, combing her incredibly long hair, dreamily watching the hazy coast of Spain and the great headland of Trafalgar shimmering opposite in the heat haze. Then dressed, she would leisurely make the climb back up the steep cliff to the rough track where her horse, patiently snuffling at the brown grass, waited.

One morning she was coming down the moutain, rather earlier than usual. The night had been so hot that sleep had been difficult. Perhaps the groom had been suffering from the heat too, for as her horse trotted confidently down the rocky mountain path, the saddle began to slip slowly downwards on the side where she sat.

Emily had never been known to panic in her life, but she was frightened then. The path was about to bend sharply and the ground below was hard and steep. She realised that when she fell, she would probably fall quite a long way.

Carefully she tried to ease the horse to a slower speed, but he too had felt the slipping saddle and unlike his rider panicked. He reared.

A small scream escaped. She shut her eyes and hung on to the reins. At that moment a firm hand took the reins. A voice, in Spanish, said: 'It is all right.'

The horse, shivering, stopped, and as she and the saddle slithered ground-wards, an arm caught her around the waist and set her firmly on her feet.

Without looking at her rescuer she said faintly: 'Thank you.'

There was no reply.

She looked up and saw a tall, black bearded Moroccan with a dark complexion and beautifully elongated dark eyes. He wore soft white robes, yellow slippers and a bright green turban twisted on his head. Behind him a white horse cropped the grass, a long rifle fastened to the saddle.

'Do you speak English?' she said. Her hair was tumbling down from its fastenings and her hat, the plumes dusty, lay on the ground.

He bowed and said: 'Espanole. I am the Grand Shereef

of Wazan, Hadj Abdeslam.'

'I am Miss Keene, Emily Keene,' she said. 'And thank you.'

'A pleasure,' he said. 'A very great pleasure.'

She was having difficulty in keeping her composure. The relief to be safe on the ground, unhurt, had made her legs tremble a little, and she was affected by the fine, dark eyes watching her. She found herself blushing and feeling absurdly shy.

Without speaking, he busied himself with the saddle while she watched. Then he bent, picked up her hat, and banged the dust from it with his hand before handing it to her.

'There,' he said. 'You can now go for your bathe.'

She looked at him sharply, the awful thought occurring to her that perhaps the beach was not so secluded as she had believed, but his face was expressionless as he put his hands at her waist to help her remount. She let him lift her and settled herself in the saddle again. He swung himself on to his big white horse and with polite farewells they both went their own ways. She down the mountain to the beach and he up towards his home.

The encounter had also proved somewhat disturbing to His Highness Hadj Abdeslam Wuld Sidi Hadj el Arbi, Prince and Chief Shereef of Wazan. This was not the only time he had seen Emily Keene. His first glimpse of her had been as he rode past the Perdicaris' mountain home early one morning. It was his habit to hunt for rabbits or game just after dawn and on his return this particular morning he had heard singing and looked up to see a young girl brushing her hair. But what hair! It was a length that he had never seen before, and shone a natural chestnut brown—nothing like the dull hennaed purplish shade that Moroccan women used for a dye. This hair was quite extraordinary, and the girl had lifted the mass of it out of the window. It hung like a length of fine silk, drying in the sun.

From that time he was determined to somehow get to know her, but he was sufficiently aware of European custom to know that formal introduction was necessary. More than that, Hadj Abdeslam was a shy man who thought a great deal and said very little. He began to look out for her, which was not very difficult as they were almost neighbours. His mountain house was set just below that of the Perdicaris and he found that he could watch her in the garden of her home from the garden of his house. She spent a great deal of time in the olive groves, riding on the mountain and swimming on the beach. He watched her constantly and fretted over the problems of meeting. Had she been a Moroccan girl it would have been so simple, but Europeans were not so impressed with his titles, his position and his wealth.

His situation was a strange one. He was the second most important man in Morocco after the Sultan Sidi Muhammed, though in fact, he possessed considerably more power than the King. The Wazan family could claim a purer descent from the Prophet Mohammed and were therefore Holy. Morocco abounded in Shereefs and Shereefas all of whom could claim the Prophet as an ancestor, but there was only one Grand Shereef of Wazan. The line was so perfect that their holiness exceeded even that of the Sultan. Their sanctity had made the family rich; for those descended from the Prophet were believed to have the *baraka*—the power to bless and the faithful pressed gifts upon them in return for their blessings.

Hadj Abdeslam also controlled a religious brotherhood, in many way not dissimilar from the Masons of the West. It had been founded by an ancestor, Moulay Taieb, and many of the customs and beliefs they followed were founded on a more ancient Indian cult of Mohammedism which had its roots in Bombay. The Society of the Moulay Taieb admitted members of both sexes, unusual in Islam, and though believers were scattered throughout the Mohammedan world, most of the members were centred in North West Algeria and the North of Morocco.

To Europeans, the Brotherhood had sinister undertones. It was virtually a secret society within a religion and as the organisation's spiritual head, the Shereef had almost complete control of the interminably turbulent tribes of

Algeria and Northern Morocco. He was the one man who could halt tribal wars and uprisings against the State.

His position was that of the man permanently in the middle. The French Government wooed him on one side with the intention of advancing their interests in Morocco and to enlist his aid to keep peaceful the tribes in Algeria which they had already colonised. The Sultan needed his assistance and goodwill for the same reasons, but resentfully for it was well known that the Grand Shereef had European leanings. Should he throw in his lot completely with the French it could bode little good for Morocco's independence in the future.

History—European history—has categorised Sidi Hadj Abdeslam as a collaborator. This he was, but he was also a patriot who thought. He believed in the European methods of progression, and wanted the more advanced countries of the world to be permitted to trade, open businesses and put money into Morocco. He wanted his country to step into the nineteenth century and was intelligent and politically minded enough to know that if Morocco was ruled and run in the way it was at present the eventual end must be annexation by a foreign power. He did not think that this in itself was a bad thing. But it was not possible to explain these views to a feudal ruler whose one intention was to keep out the Christians. Mention of the subject would be enough to cast suspicion on himself as preparing the country for the Christians to take over.

And how much more suspicion would he incur when he married that girl with the magnificent hair he wondered? For he was determined to do so.

At the time he met Emily Keene he was out of favour with the court. He preferred life in Europeanised Tangier than in feudal Morocco City (Marrakesh) or Fez where the Sultan resided. He was tired of being an object of suspicion to his own people and a pawn in the power game the French were playing. He had made up his mind to live somewhere out of Morocco, probably France, and settle down with a European wife.

The Sultan, Sidi Muhammed was well aware of these

plans. A year previously the Shereef had become engaged to a young French girl whom he had met in Tangier. Her mother, an ambitious woman, approved the match and chaperoned the daughter assiduously throughout the courtship. But the Shereef, unable to stand the mother and finding the girl lacking in intelligence, had broken it off. Their insistence on marriage under the rites of the Catholic Church would have been too much for his subjects, and indeed for him, to stomach. That insistence had ended the engagement. Relieved at the turn of events, the Sultan demanded that the Shereef attach himself permanently to the Court. Hadj Abdeslam knew exactly why—the King could keep an eye on him there and he would always be at hand to use his influence with the tribes to ensure peaceful journeys when the time came for the Sultan to travel the country to collect the taxes from the citizens. His father, the Grand Shereef El Arbi had always been available at the Sultan's beck and call. The son was less pliable.

Just a few months previously, Sultan Sidi Muhammed had detained the Grand Shereef at the court for several months. Used to Court intrigue he scented a plot to keep him there as a permanent State prisoner and under those circumstances his life would have not been worth a *flus* —the useless copper coin that circulated in Tangier.

Sidi Hadj Abdeslam left Morocco City abruptly without taking leave of the Sultan and returned to his estates in the mountain town of Wazan. He reflected with a certain pleasure on the uproar that his departure had caused at the Court. Officials followed him with offers of money and grants of land in an effort to persuade him to return, but Sidi Hadj Abdeslam pleaded ill-health and stayed in his Wazan stronghold, surrounded by his fanatically loyal tribesmen. He sent his eldest son Mulauy Alarbi, to take his place at the court and when all the fuss had died down, the Grand Shereef had returned to his home in Tangier where he had every intention of remaining.

However, he decided as he led his horse to the stables after meeting Emily Keene, a rabble of servants and slaves at his heels, the political problems could all be thought out later. For the time being, he had to find some way of officially meeting the long-haired girl. And perhaps he had better divorce his three present wives in the meantime. A European lady would never accept that situation.

* * *

The Shereef could not fail in his wish to meet Emily. His position and title as the head of the Moorish community made him a social catch even to the clannish Europeans and he was eventually invited to El Minzah where the Perdicaris were delighted to find that he, too, was musical. He had a fine tenor voice (Emily believed he could have made a fortune on the halls) and he played the violin very well. The only offputting aspect of his performance to the Europeans was that he held the instrument like a cello. They did not understand that this was the customary way to play a violin in Morocco.

He became a frequent visitor to the house in the mountain as well as El Minzah. A little too frequent for Mrs. Perdicaris' taste. He was not a European, even if he was a Prince. But the more often he appeared, the more pleased Emily was. She would catch him watching her as she sat at the piano and would modestly drop her eyes. She knew that being the Grand Shereef was something rather important, but it meant very little to her. The European community on the whole had little curiosity about their Moroccan neighbours and with the exception of men like Sir John Hay Drummond Hay and William Kirby Green probably were unaware of his extreme power.

It was obvious that he found Emily Keene attractive. It was unmistakable; the way he would mysteriously appear when she went riding, and the way he haunted the Perdicaris' home. She was flattered. The Shereef was darkly handsome, and she had a poor opinion of her own looks. Her only good point she felt was her hair. The face in the mirror each morning disappointed her. She did not understand that the warmth and strength of her personality, her interest in life, gave her an attraction of a more lasting type.

Curiously Mrs. Perdicaris never noticed the Shereef's interest in Emily. Like many rich Victorians, though not in the least unkind to those she employed, she was genuinely unaware of them. It never occurred to her that a guest in her home might be attracted by Emily.

As Emily had no friends of her own age, and no one whom she felt would be interested in her affairs, the romance was unintentionally conducted in secret, with meetings on mountain walks, horse rides and in scented gardens.

She liked the Shereef very much. She enjoyed his company though he was still rather silent and shy and she had to carry most of the conversation. She did not mind. It was good for her Spanish. But even though she knew he was permitted one more wife to add to the three he had living in Wazan, it never occurred to her that he would propose. When he did ask her to marry him, rather abruptly on the mountain one day, she was quite astonished and said 'no', pleading for politeness' sake that they hardly knew one another.

'Then we shall have to get to know each other better,' he said, and on their very next meeting got to work on the problem, questioning her about her life in London.

It was fortunate for the Shereef that Emily Keene was a good conversationalist with a lively turn of phrase—and more important, a linguist. Explaining her background; describing even the most simple details of her life in England conjured up a world so far removed from his comprehension—as his life was removed from hers—that it seems incredible that they were able to live together happily. It is not difficult for people of totally dissimilar backgrounds to fall in love—the problems come with attempting to adjust after the marriage.

Emily Keene never lost her Victorian principles and her most deeply engrained behaviour patterns, but she was able to settle and accept life in Morocco. Most of the necessary adjustments were made by her.

Yet there was nothing in her childhood that could have given a clue to the extraordinary course that her life was to take after the age of twenty. She was a typically well-brought-up, comfortably-off, middle-class child of the mid-nineteenth century.

Her grandfather was the Governor of the Surrey County Gaol, or, as it was known locally, The Horsemonger Lane

Gaol. The Keene family had held the post for four generations, and it was a matter of course that when John Keene senior retired, his son, Emily's father, John Keene junior would take over.

All of her childhood was dominated by the gaol. It was a grim place, described by Charles Dickens in Little Dorrit as 'an oblong pile of barrack buildings partitioned into squalid rooms standing back to back, so that there were no back rooms, environed by a narrow paved yard, hemmed in by high walls, duly spiked on top....'

It had been built in 1789 when it was the last word in modernity, designed by John Howard, the prison philanthropist.

The Governor's house, where her grandparents lived, had a certain style. It was a three storied Georgian building with a basement, double-fronted and with an elegant flight of stairs up to the big, curved front door. Unfortunately it was crowded in on both sides by the brick built wings of the Debtor's prison. The view from the front windows was on to the grim gateway, on the roof of which public hangings took place.

The prison stood at the back of the Surrey County Sessions buildings (which still exist), and was eventually demolished in 1878.*

Emily's father, John Keene, worked at the prison from the time his education ceased. He began as his father's clerk, and was employed in the same post when he married Emma Wharram, the dark-eyed daughter of the Coachmaster at Newington Butts. The Wharrams owned a livery stable, fine funeral horses and a considerable amount of property in their area.

The marriage was a happy one. John and Emma Keene moved into their own house at No. 6 Church Road, Newington—a short street of undistinguished early Victorian houses owned by the Trinity House. Church Road ran from smart Trinity Square and down to the prison.

The house was poky by Victorian standards. Naturally, there was no bathroom, the lavatory was at the bottom of

* The prison area is now a charming garden and children's playground.

the fairly long back garden, and the kitchen in the basement was small and inconvenient. But there was running water and a tweeny to do the work.

Emily was born in the front, upstairs bedroom on the 17th of September, 1849. Outside the long windows loomed the ugly bulk of the prison, and it was in the year of her birth that the Mannings were hung publicly (on November 13th) from a scaffold erected on the great gateway of the prison.

Frederick George Manning, a small-time criminal, had married a Swiss girl, Maria le Roux, who was by far the stronger character. Maria had been involved with an Irishman, Patrick O'Connor, whom she could beguile into parting with large sums of money. But sometimes not quickly enough to satisfy her husband's needs.

Mrs. Mannings planned Patrick O'Connor's death at her house in Bermondsey. She and her husband bought a spade and lime, and one night when O'Connor came to dinner, they shot him dead.

The Mannings buried him in the kitchen, and the next morning Mrs. Mannings went to his lodgings, ransacked his room and came home with a number of securities as well as ready money. So cool was she that for four days she sat knitting in her kitchen over her victim's grave. Her husband, made of weaker stuff, found forgetfulness in a nearby public house.

Eventually they separated—she fled to Edinburgh and her husband to Jersey. The police exhumed the body, and both were caught and brought back for trial.

Emma Keene's husband and father-in-law officiated at the hanging. Left alone at home, with her two month old baby, Emma would have heard outside her window the howling mobs who had gathered from all over London to watch the spectacle of two people dying. The scaffold had been mounted on the top of the gate the night before the death penalty was to be enforced, and from the early evening through until dawn the crowds increased.

Charles Dickens, a resident of the area, went to watch not the hanging but the crowd and was sickened by the bestial behaviour. He wrote an impassioned letter to *The*

Times, condemning the whole practice of public execution and its brutalising effect on those who watched.

But many more public hangings were to take place on the gateway at Horsemonger Lane and other prisons until the last was performed at Newgate Prison in May 1868.

Newington Butts (now better known as Elephant and Castle) had already lost the country-village-by-the-Thames atmosphere which had been its chief charm only twenty years or so before. Overtaken by London, the borough teemed with people, was beleaguered by small-pox, cholera, murders and even the plague itself, and having been brought up in that area, perhaps it is not surprising that Emily was able to accept many of the barbaric practices of nineteenth century Morocco with such aplomb.

Accustomed to the idea of public executions literally on her doorstep, the sight of the salted heads of rebels mouldering on the gates of Moroccan towns would not have seemed particularly horrific. Morocco had a small-pox problem—so had Newington. The lash was commonly used in the Maghreb, but then prisoners in London gaols were flogged, too. The murder rate in Morocco was probably lower.

Though civilised on the surface, London in the mid-nineteenth century was in many ways a barbaric place. The Moroccan slave system was frequently preferable to the life of a tweeny. Slaves were property and therefore treated well—as members of the family. Tweenys worked harder—lived harder. And if Emily found the religious fanaticism of the Moors strange, she had the example of the same excess of emotion in the success of Mr. C. H. Spurgeon, the evangelist, then building his Tabernacle a three minute walk from her home. Mr. Spurgeon was able to pull in an enthusiastic congregation of over 10,000 people on every occasion that he spoke.

And nearby her home were the headquarters of a sect of Holy Rollers—not dissimilar from the Assoiwa Sect in Morocco—both of whom were off-springs of the whirling dervishes. All three religiously fanatical groups—British, Moroccan and Turkish—fell into trance-like states, suffering a kind of epilepsy for religion's sake.

A book of the period written by an Englishman says:

'At present Fez and the other great cities of Morocco are in a far higher state of civilisation, and less given up to crime, than any of the poorer quarters of our metropolis. It is safe to walk the streets—for a Christian as well as a Moor—by day or night—yet there are no police, nor does one see the flagrant immorality that exists in even our most fashionable quarters at night.

'Far be it for me to preach, but comparing the two capitals, London and Fez, together, and seeing the advantages and disadvantages of both, I say, without hesitation, and after careful thought, that it will be an evil day for the Arabs and the Moors if ever they become Christians. It will be but the kicking away of the few steps of the ladder that exist between them and destruction.'*

Her childhood background was good schooling for the unknown life ahead. The family grew. Emma Keene went through twenty pregnancies, losing twelve of the babies. Emily, the eldest, enjoyed the company of her sisters Alice, Kate, Helena and the baby Gertrude, brothers John, Walter, and Horace. Not surprisingly she picked up considerable knowledge of coping with small children, even though the Keene's ran a nursery and employed a nanny once they moved into a house big enough to contain one. Immediately the second baby, Alice, was born and survived, No. 6 Church Street became too small so John Keene moved his family to a bigger house—in Harper Street, still just outside the prison walls.

Eventually, Harper Street was outgrown, too, and the family moved to the New Kent Road where they settled until it was John Keene's turn to take over the Governor's house at the gaol—just a short time after his eldest daughter was married to the Shereef.

Emily was a bright child. She went to private school as the nearest school to the Keene's was St. Mary's Infants, run on voluntary subscription for the poorer children of the neighbourhood, and costing its pupils twopence a week for their schooling. One master and a mistress taught a

* Walter Harris, *Land of an African Sultan.*

hundred children and paid for the coals to warm the classroom from their salaries.

John Keene would not have contemplated St. Mary's for his children's education. Emily, as her sister recorded went to boarding school when she was older, and it was there that she learned the rudiments of French, Latin and German, and also how to ride a horse. This was fortuitous; she needed to be able to ride well in Morocco. She also needed French—it was the language spoken by the European residents. Tangier's second language, Spanish, was made easier for her by the Latin Grammar she had learnt at school. She had the Keene family's gift for picking up foreign tongues even though she never spoke them particularly grammatically. By the end of her life, she had mastered seven, including Arabic. Her great grandfather had been a scholar of Hebrew, Greek and Latin. She had inherited his gift, and it could not have been more fortunate.

The Keenes were entirely typical of their class and period. They were religious. Emily was christened at Trinity Church—the same at which some unfortunate met his doom in the music hall song of the period—and worshipped there until the family moved to the New Kent Road, when they used the Parish Church of St. Mary's Newington.

They were musical. Emily had the fine contralto singing voice which was to lead her into temporary disgrace with her father, and shone at musical evenings, though living descendants remember with pain her visits home after the turn of the century when she played at the piano and sang interminable Moorish laments.

The house was run Victorian fashion, with nursery, drawing room, dining room and the study cum smoking room where John Keene played chess with his sons and where daughters were not permitted.

Emily described this life vividly to the Shereef on their quiet ambles over the Mountain. He would listen and from her stories of the wonders of life in a great Metropolis, pick the flaws. He probed beyond Emily's own education and asked about the education of the poor—how thorough was it, how long before they left school? To her chagrin, Emily found that if she answered truthfully, the system did not sound very satisfactory and he was able to point out that things were not so different in Morocco. The children of the rich were properly educated; even sent to University at Fez, while the children of the poor were simply taught to read and write using the Koran as their textbook. The Shereef inquired into the wages of a Victorian tweeny and how they lived and announced calmly that he felt a Moroccan slave had a better life.

Emily listened to his viewpoints, but privately thought that there were too many other things wrong with his country. The way it was ruled and governed; the lack of roads, railways and police. The pernicious system of taxation.

His views were, of course, an oversimplification of the problems. There was a great deal to be done in Morocco. She would have listened to the dinner table conversation of people in authority and learnt from them the corruptness of the Government and the misery of the poorer people. Pointing out the evils of London, did not decrease the evils of Morocco.

Her memoirs show that even so early in her life in Morocco, she realised improvement would have to come from the top. She felt it was possible that the Shereef with his thoughtfulness, intelligence and love of the country, combined with his interest in the European way of living, would be the man to do something about it all.

Eventually the Shereef said to Emily: 'Have I convinced you that my country is not so terrible as most people think?'

'I, Sir,' said Emily, 'never thought your country terrible. You assumed.'

'In that case,' he said calmly, 'why will you not marry me?'

It was difficult to reply to this. Emily was not insensitive, and knew that despite the lightness of his approach there was an undercurrent of purpose. It would have been insulting to his intelligence to pass off the question with a light answer. It was a time for honesty.

At that point she did not know the answer herself. She had relived time and time again the first, abrupt, surprising proposal, and for all her good commonsense and determination to behave sensibly had to admit that she was very much attracted by the Shereef of Wazan. That same commonsense made the problems of marriage to him seem an impossibility. After several months of Tangier life she knew the reaction of the European community towards the Moroccans—the 'they are charming people, but not like us, one must not become too friendly' attitude. She had heard the comments when the young Spanish and Portuguese girls in the town had 'taken up' with a Moor. Her own feelings were that such postures by the Europeans as foreigners in the land were an impertinence, but nevertheless, such a marriage would need more courage than she was certain she possessed at that time.

She told him that though her feelings were deep and strong, marriage was not possible. She pointed out that they came from two entirely different worlds, and perhaps more important, two different religions. A marriage between them could harm him and probably divide her from her own people. She did not have the courage.

The Shereef said simply: 'I have the courage.'

At that moment he must have appeared totally alien. The robes he wore were white and soft. He wore a green turban, denoting his rank. His long boots, buttoned up the back, were of the most supple leather. His beard was thick and strong; eyes black, the mouth full; skin dark. He was romantically attractive, but his life and hers had no meeting other than their affection for each other.

It was then that Emily Keene pressed all the doubts she felt regarding her relationship with the Shereef—his three wives who lived in Wazan; the fact that his religion would permit him to divorce her with ease and even to take more wives.

What she did not know until she raised the subject was that the Shereef had already divorced all three of his wives. He had foreseen the time when she would question their existence and taken steps accordingly. Emily found herself both shocked and disconcerted by the casual way these three unknown women had been put aside, and protested he might dispose of her with the same ease, should he tire of her, and added that he might feel inclined to take more wives—a situation that she would not tolerate.

The Shereef never spoke a great deal, but what he said was always succinct. He said:

'If I were married to you I would never want another wife.'

'It would be impossible,' she told him, but indecisively.

He told her that they would speak of it again—when he returned to Tangier. He was going away for a while. Both of his sons were marrying for the first time, and there were to be month long celebrations at Wazan at which he would have to officiate. His second son, Moulay Abdullah was to marry the daughter of the Pasha of Larache. The girl had been offered as a present to the Shereef himself—with only three wives living he was permitted another—but he had already made up his mind to marry Emily, and he had declined the offer. However, as it would have been a great insult to have returned the girl to Larache, the Shereef had decided to present her to his son. That way no one would be offended. Neither the Pasha's daughter—who was five year's older than her husband-to-be, or Moulay Abdullah had any say in the matter.

He explained this to Emily as they rode back up the mountain and she found the conversation exceedingly distasteful. She was not certain whether or not the Shereef was quite deliberately shocking her European susceptibilities, or whether it had not occurred to him that she would find the conversation strange. She said goodbye to him almost with a sense of relief.

She did not see the Shereef again before he left for Wazan. In Morocco at that time the preparations for a journey, even as short as that to Wazan, were complicated. A Shereef could not travel without a considerable retinue to show visible signs of his importance and power. Camping for the night on route was no simple matter; a small regiment of servants, tents, baggage mules, carpets, bedding, cooking utensils all had to be taken. It required considerable supervision.

Left rather to her own devices Emily found she missed him very much. Even after she knew he must have left Tangier, she kept looking for him on the mountain, though she knew perfectly well that he was many miles away. She found sleep hard to find for thinking of him, and the thought of a marriage began to seem less and less of an impossibility. The obstacles became more negotiable with every day that passed.

Then she received a letter from him. It proposed marriage yet again and explained that he felt she should know that he had divorced his former wives in the hope that she might become his wife. He also explained that his previous marriages had been ones of convenience—arranged in order to strengthen family ties and please other powerful shereefs. This was the custom in his country, he said, but now he was very much in love with her, and he begged that she would reconsider her decision.

Without their meetings in the countryside; without him to point out the many wild flowers, the birds, the small animals—to show where lions had been seen, reduced the charm of Morocco. Still beautiful, the mountain and the bare brown hills stretching away into the distance were lonely.

Emily did reconsider. But she decided that enquiries must be made. She was sensible even though in love, and she was determined not to leap into any decision that she might regret. While every day she missed him more, those same days made her more aware of the divisions of race and creed that separated them as she grew more familiar with the people and the customs of the land. She needed to know if those divisions could be overcome. She made her enquiries secretly, without telling anyone what was in her mind.

William Kirby Green one of the senior residents of the town and Horace White were the most fruitful sources of information. Both men had a genuine interest in the country where they lived, they were pleased to expand upon the system which produced the people and their thinking.

Horace White in fact, delivered quite a lecture. Her

opportunity to question him came when he was bemoaning the Consulate's latest problem. They were struggling with a situation that was hard to control as they had no true grounds for attempting to control it. Back in London, Sir Moses Montiefore, head of a powerful Jewish family had been lobbying the foreign secretary, the Earl of Granville, to bring pressure to bear on the Sultan of Morocco to stop persecution of the Jews in Morocco. The Earl of Granville had merely passed on the problem.

'It is a little complicated,' Horace White said, at a gathering at which Emily was present, 'because the complaint is not persecution in the normal sense.'

It seemed that when the Sultan rode out to put down rebels from the dissident tribes, the heads of the slaughtered tribesmen were brought back to their home towns and there the task of the Jews was to salt these heads, prior to them being placed on the town gates *pour de courager les autres.*

It was not that the Jews had any objections to salting the heads in the normal way. What upset them was when the Sultan insisted that they performed the work on Saturday, their Sabbath. It seemed that there were an abundance of heads for treatment on Saturdays, puzzling as Friday when the killing was presumably done was the Mohammedan's Holy Day. The correspondence on the matter between Lord Granville, Sir Moses Montiefore, and the Consulate was interminable. 'But,' said Horace White, 'I fear the Sultan largely disregards our correspondence on the matter.'

'I have heard, Sir,' said Emily, 'that the Grand Shereef of Wazan who frequently visits the home of Mr. Perdicaris has certain influence. Could he not help in the matter?'

'Relations between the Grand Shereef and the Sultan are not as friendly as they might be, Miss Keene,' Horace White said. 'The Shereef is too Europeanised for the Sultan's taste, but you are right. If the problem were here in the North, the Shereef could settle it all in a moment. But his power wanes in the far South.'

'And why is that, sir?' Emily asked

'If you do not mind a history lessson—' said Horace

White and promptly gave one.

Riding back to the Perdicaris' house Emily had much to think about. She had not realised just how important the Shereef of Wazan was to his country, and just how far his ancestry stretched back. She had been brought up to be proud of her own family tree; the fact that on her father's side of the family, his father and his father's before him had held the same responsible post, and on her mother's side, an ancestor, Archbishop Wharram, had preached the sermon in Canterbury Cathedral at the time of the Reformation. She had been taken as a small girl to see his portrait in Lambeth Palace.

But this paled into insignificance against the long, long line that stretched back to 700 A.D. and which was now represented on earth by the Shereef.

Horace White explained how when the Arabs first came to Morocco from the East, the tribe who had become the ruling family in the land of the furthest West, as the invaders called Morocco, had split. One branch had settled in the Southern interior in the Sus and Dra countries, while the others came to the North and settled along the Mediterranean Coast and in the bordering Riff Mountains.

It was the branch from the Sus who eventually took the throne of Morocco, while the richest and most powerful of the Edrisi branch in the North made their home at the small town of Wazan and amassed considerable wealth by reason of the strength of the *baraka* they possessed.

Eventually the reigning Grand Shereef, Abdullah, was so powerful that he was able to build a magnificent mosque in the town of Wazan. He called it Dar Demana, meaning 'the house of refuge'.

It was Moulay Taieb, the grandson of Abdullah, who extended the authority of the Wazani family far beyond the town when he founded the brotherhood of the Moulay Taieb, at the end of the seventeenth century. The Sultan of the period, Mulay Ismail, was possibly the most barbaric, cruel ruler that Morocco had ever known. He was a murderer, a sadist and a bestialist, but at the same time, a brilliant Sultan. Morocco's great days were under his rule. Mulay Ismail was well able to control the ambitions of Moulay Taieb but there came a point when the Sultan determined to rid himself of so dangerous a rival.

Shereef Moulay Taieb was not lacking in diplomacy. He saved his head and his brotherhood, reassuring the Sultan by saying: 'Yee (being the Saaidian dynasty of kings) to rule and we (the Edrisite Shereefs) to consecrate your authority.'

He had been reminding Mulay Ismail of the situation where no Sultan could be proclaimed without the approval of the Grand Shereef of Wazan. The kings of Morocco were elected to some extent. No divine right of succession for the eldest son existed. The King put forward his wishes as to whom his successor should be, and on his death, those in power at the Court generally followed his decision. But the choice had to be sanctioned by the high religious authority of the Grand Shereef of Wazan, whose descendence from the Prophet Mohammed was so much purer than that of the Royal Family.

Without the Shereef's approval, the northern tribes would rise in rebellion, but once their religious leader had confirmed the new Sultan, they would then bow to this high religious confirmation, and regard the Sultan as Prince of Believers. His authority had been approved by another and even more powerful authority—the Shereef—a man so saintly as to surpass the holiness of any other living being.

Emily tried to see the Shereef as a saint; a holy man whose touch meant healing and the fulfilment of desires for thousands of people, but she could not. He was a man; a thoughtful, thinking, intelligent man. Her mind could not encompass that to the Moslems he was considered God's representative on earth.

Horace White had told her that the family had a reputation as miracle workers. Hadj el Arbi, the Shereef's father, had been known as the miracle working Shereef. He was said to be able to cure blindness and produce water in a dry season. He had once struck a rock near Wazan from which water had gushed in a stream, and, according to legend, the stream ran to that day.

But all the sanctity and worship apparently did not make for friendly relations with the Sultan. The Shereefs of Wazan had the right to protect any man, whether he be criminal, transgressor or tax-evader. It was their duty to give protection to all their followers. Their homes, like middle-age churches, were sanctuaries, and they themselves paid none of the ruinous taxes demanded from the ordinary people for the royal coffers, and they received their income, food and indirectly housing, as gifts from the faithful.

It seemed the Shereef of Wazan was the most influential and powerful man in Morocco at the time, but the Sultan would not have been unhappy to find a method of undermining his authority, mainly because the Grand Shereef was strongly pro-European. From the Government's and the Sultan's view-point, this predilection was a serious matter. With the French so firmly entrenched in Algeria and sniping away at Morocco's Eastern frontier, it was easy to see that a man with so much influence over the tribes of the North could be a considerable ally to France. The Court was afraid of him.

It was history of another kind that she learned in her quiet investigations when she found an excuse to talk about the Shereef to the people of the town. All were charmed by his good manners, but whispered stories about the manner in which he had become Grand Shereef. And it was a story which can have done little to ease Emily's decison as to whether she should marry him or not.

Several contemporary writers tell the tale of the Shereef's elevation to the head of the family. One, Philip Durham Trotter sums it up briefly in his book 'Our Mission to the Court of Morocco'* in the following way:

'He (the Shereef's father) had amongst other wives, a dusky consort from the interior who was gifted with all the cunning of her race, who was the mother of the present Shereef. When the old man on his death-bed, as is the custom, was asked to nominate his successor, he replied: That son of mine, who, at my death which is close at hand,

* Published by David Douglas, Edinburgh.

shall be found in possession of my stick. This remark being overheard by the above mentioned lady, she secreted the stick among her son's things, where it was found on his father's demise the following morning.'

According to other sources, the mother was a negress from the Sudan; a fact that must have caused Emily to consider even more whether or not she should accept the Shereef's proposal. No doubt she reasoned out her emotions—as she was always to reason problems—and came to the conclusion that his black blood, and his coming by the title dishonestly—(should the story have been true)—had nothing to do with him and the man he was. If she admired him and was attracted by him before she had learnt more about his background, it should make no difference now. This particular piece of gossip must not only be disregarded, but forgotten. It did not affect the issue.

A summing up of the rest of her knowledge gave a picture of a man who was well-educated, rich, socially acceptable to Europeans and whose leanings and interests were all entirely Western. All of that she had judged for herself. She had also found that though he was a Holy Man in the eyes of the Moors, he was not in the least fanatical and enlightened enough to be disinterested in religious differences. No one had a bad word to say of him, and a conviction that the marriage might be possible began to grow in Emily. The one thing certain was that emotionally, she wanted to marry him very much.

About a fortnight after his departure she sat down and wrote him a letter saying that she would accept his offer—on certain conditions. These she would like to discuss with him when he returned home from Wazan. She then pondered on whom she should ask for advice in framing the conditions.

She hesitated to approach Horace White. He was such a busy man and as a British subject in Morocco she was to some extent under his protection and he would be shocked and distressed at her decision. He might even feel responsible for the situation, and it would be unfair to add to his concern by expecting him to give her advice on a matter of which he could not possibly approve.

She thought of William Kirby-Green. He was a kind man who appreciated and understood Morocco and its people. He was also wise with a deep sympathy for his surroundings. She chose to see him to ask his opinion on what conditions she should make.

Like every other European who was to hear her news, Kirby-Green was horrified and tried to talk Emily out of any idea of marriage to the Shereef. But she had made a decision. There was no shifting her, and in the end he gave in and helped her to prepare a rough document to present to the Shereef, trying to make it as much of a safeguard as possible against all the eventualities which marriage to a Moslem could entail.

Emily was a little unhappy about the lack of romance that the conditions in the contract suggested, but Kirby-Green was firmer than her on this point and persuaded her that the document would not seem in the least unromantic to the Shereef. He explained that this was the way things were done by the Moroccans. There was always a marriage contract drawn up by the notaries for the protection of the bride. And she was always given some kind of dowry by her future husband. It seemed that the women were not as helpless as it appeared to the European community.

In actual fact there were two marriage contracts—the normal Moroccan document and another, British style, were drawn. The British document contained considerable additional dispositions than would have appeared in a normal Moslem document. Some of them proved to be unnecessary. Others were to prove very prudent as the years went by. It was a sensible contract and without it, Emily's situation in later years would have been an unhappy one.

She had very little money of her own, and Kirby-Green suggested that first of all, for her dowry, she should have the Shereef endow her with £100, half payable immediately and the balance in equal payments. This would give her some independence in case of any unforeseen difficulties arising. This came under the normal Mohammedan part of the contract, but in the secondary English contract Kirby-Green suggested that the Shereef also gave

Emily a dowry of £1,000 immediately and a further £100 per annum thereafter.

Moorish women were totally dependent on their husbands. There was no question of house-keeping, personal allowance, or any financial arrangements at all. He said Emily could not possibly be in that situation. She must have money of her own.

The most important clause of the contract was that the Shereef was to undertake never to take another wife—something he was quite entitled to do. If he did, he must immediately pay the sum of £800 to Emily providing he had no just cause to so treat her. Another clause, unusual though not unheard of in Mohammedan countries was that Emily had the right to divorce the Shereef—providing she had good reason. He could divorce her, but only with reason, and if he did so frivolously, he again had to pay her £800.

A simple clause, but an important one, was that she could go out, accompanied by a maid of her choosing or with the Shereef himself.

This was a vital addition to the contract. Moorish women, once married, if they were the wives of rich men, stayed in the women's quarters and it was not permitted for them to go out and about at all. The Shereef could insist on his traditional rights in that matter after the marriage, and Kirby-Green thought it wise to forestall any such difficulties.

Any children of the religion would be brought up in the Shereef's religion. It would have caused far too many problems to suggest anything else. The children would be Shereefs and Shereefas and therefore Holy. It would have been wrong and unfair to insist that they were brought up as Christians.

On the other hand, any children were to be educated in Europe but only because the standards of education were better outside of the Maghreb.

There was to be no question of Emily changing her religion, and she could not be compelled to live anywhere else in Morocco except on the coast because the interior was not safe for Europeans.

The final clause was that should she die before her husband, her body must be taken back to England for burial in her own family's plot.

Emily was rather embarrassed by the document, particularly as it had to be presented almost before she had time to prepare herself for the ordeal. The Shereef on receipt of her letter completely abandoned his son's marriage celebrations and came straight back to Tangier. He was jubilant at the news she would marry him, his normally rather melancholy face bright with smiles.

Very serious, she told him her conditions, and showed him the paper which Kirby-Green had prepared.

The Shereef ran a casual eye over it, and said that all the clauses were perfectly acceptable. He added that the document was unnecessary—he would never treat Emily as a Moorish woman. But without any argument, he handed the draft over to his notaries to draw up according to Moroccan law.

Emily was relieved that William Kirby-Green's assessment of the situation had been so accurate, but she felt that she must now return home and explain her decision to her parents in person. She was quite aware that they would be angry, shocked and disappointed but though it would have been perfectly simple to marry in Tangier and break the news to them later, she felt she must go back and discuss the marriage with them, even though they were certain to disapprove.

The Shereef was not pleased at the thought of his fiancée travelling alone, and insisted on sending his notary, Si Felus, and another man, one of Felus' assistants, a Portuguese, with her. He said that they could ask her father for her hand on his behalf.

Emily protested that she would be quite safe on her own, but he was determined that she should not leave Morocco alone. Perhaps he feared she might never return if he let her out of his sight with no one to guard his interests.

Her departure was speedier than she had intended. On returning to El Minzah, she went to see Mrs. Varley and explained what had happened. Ellen Varley was not only thunderstruck, she was angry. The scene between the older woman and the girl was not pleasant. Mrs. Varley said that she could not possibly be responsible for such a situation and that Emily must return to England immediately; on the first boat available. She would not have her living in Tangier and under her aegis in the circumstances.

'I am very distressed that you should have entered into such a relationship while living in my house,' she told Emily. 'You have behaved disgracefully.'

Perhaps feeling that people who lived in glass houses could be downright unreasonable, Emily packed and left immediately. She moved back to the Hotel de France while preparations for the journey to London were hastily made. The Shereef was no longer persona grata at El Minzah or the house on the mountain and their meetings were now deliberately furtive.

Just a few months after she had arrived in Tangier, Emily was again being carried on a hard-backed chair, across the shallows and into a rowing boat to board the little paddling *Hercules* for Gibraltar and the first stage of the journey home where she was to face more criticism and condemnation about the course of action she planned to follow.

But according to sister Helena, all was predestined, and the journey home itself dramatic, to say the least.

She wrote: 'An American crystal gazer had told her (Emily) that she would marry a foreigner and live in a strange land. Mother's song (The Moorish Bride) seemed to haunt her and it seemed as if Fate intended her for something unusual. England appeared grey and cold and the prison home excessively dull. So one day she agreed to marry her Moorish prince and wrote home saying that she was coming shortly to get her trousseau. The family was aghast, my father raved and mother wept. A fortnight later she arrived in London having travelled over land by way of Spain and Paris. It was December 1872 when there was civil war in Spain. The winter was severe, and the country was under deep snow in the north.

'Emily was accompanied as escort by the Shereef's

Moorish secretary, Si Felus, a dear old man of stately bearing and flowing robes, and a Portuguese old gentleman, who acted as courier and purse bearer. Outside Madrid, the train was attacked by bandits. The driver was killed and also several passengers. They entered my sister's reserved carriage, put pistols to the occupants' heads and demanded all their money and valuables.

'On hearing the commotion on the train, Emily fortunately had slipped her valuable jewellery into her stockings, and the Portuguese gentleman had attended to his banknotes. They explained they had nothing to give away. It was an awkward moment and my sister said the pistol point felt very cold. Fortunately, at this moment there was a cry that the soldiers were coming, and the bandits fled. There was sharp fighting and several were killed.

'The passengers had to get out of the train, which was considerably knocked about and the passengers waited for several hours in the snow before the relief train arrived.

'They had no further adventures and arrived safely in London, which was enveloped in one of its worst black fogs and continued so most of the time of Emily's visit.'

The fog must have made the trousseau shopping more difficult, in horse and carriage in London, but eventually the time came for Emily to return to Tangier for her wedding. Her parents accompanied her, and on January 3rd, 1873, her mother wrote home to Emily's sister, Alice, who had been left in charge of the rest of the family.

Gibraltar, January 3rd, 1873.

My dear Alice,

'Whoever thought mother would be such a traveller! First I will tell you I am exceedingly well and cannot say but it must agree with me. Now for a little news. We liked Cadiz very much. We left there Thursday morning at 7 o'clock and then we had to get into a small boat and be rowed to the steamer. We were rather late and the steamer started without us. The boatmen pulled off their coats, held them up and shouted. The man steering did not keep a good look out and we nearly went bump up against a large vessel. It was the nearest shave possible.

'At last they saw on board the steamer and stopped and took us on board. We had to be hauled up by the sailors. The sea was very beautiful, not at all rough, but the steamer pitched a good deal. The people soon got ill. Em laid down and did not move again. I was the only lady who was not ill at all and the only one who ate any breakfast. I enjoyed the trip very much and did not feel at all sick.

'Just before we got to Algiers it looked very stormy. We could not go on to Gibraltar and were obliged to stay at Algiers all night. Such a strange place. Of course we had to get into the little boat again and jump on some stones for a landing place. We went to the best hotel. I must describe the places when I come home. I should like to have the money it has all cost. It must be something enormous. However, it is very nice travelling and staying at the best hotels and have everything you want and nothing to pay.

'Papa has been very agreeable so far but this morning we came here by steamer, first getting into the little boat, of course. And as soon as the steamer stopped there was a boat with the Moorish Consul ready for us. Papa at the sight of him looked one of his dreadful looks and made Em fidgetty. I made Papa tell me what was the matter and he said at the sight of the Moorish Consul he felt as if Jack Ketch had come. He is a black man, so very lively, but quite nice in his manners. Is it not childish of Papa to dislike a man because of his colour?

'He is beginning to be doleful again. Says he never liked it and never shall. I was obliged to beg of him not to worry Em and now I think he will be all right.

'Our rooms were ready for us, our luggage and Lumley* here. She thinks Jack is the nicest gentleman she ever met, but I knew he would do all nicely.

'While we were at breakfast a letter came from the Shereef with such a nice message welcoming us to Gibraltar. We are to have a carriage at two to take us for a drive. We go to Tangier tomorrow. We are to have a grand

* Emily's maid, shipped with the luggage by brother Jack, over sea.

reception of which I will give you an account as soon as possible.

'So now, with my kindest, dearest love to you all, especially recommending my three little pets to your kindness, I am, dear Alice, Jack, Kate, Wal, Win, Horace and Gerty,

Your loving mother,
Emma Keene.'

Emma Keene was forty-six years old when she wrote that letter from her first trip abroad. It is clear from whom Emily inherited her fortitude.

Chapter Three

POLITICS TAKE A HAND

A month after the wedding the new Shereefa was sitting up in her bed, sipping an early morning cup of English tea, sent specially from Gibraltar, and reading a rather elderly copy of *The Times* which had been delivered early that morning to the house on the Marshan by the Jewish 'postman' employed by the Legation. All British mail went through Sir John Hay Drummond Hay, and it was the custom to pay a few pence for delivery which Emily thought iniquitous. Her husband, half-dressed, was sitting on the end of the bed, bending to button his long boots.

'It says here in the report of our marriage that the Koran enjoins you to beat me should I become disposed to be refractory,' she said, peeping at him over the top of the paper.

Her husband gave one last twist to a refractory button, and grunted.

'It is possible to make holy writings say anything you wish,' he said. 'Refer them to the 198th saying of Mohammed.' He quoted, 'I said, O apostle of God, what is my duty to my wife? He said, "That you give her to eat when you eat yourself and clothe her when you clothe yourself, and do not slap her in the face nor abuse her, nor separate yourself, from her in displeasure." Perhaps we should send them a copy of the sayings of Mohammed. What else do they write?'

'That I am an unfortunate Christian girl *who makes four wives* and has no protection from the law.' She pulled a mock woeful face at him.

'Do you think that you are an unfortunate Christian girl?'

'No, not at all,' she said.

Yet apart from the very deep love which she felt for her husband, the first few weeks of married life were not proving smooth. Pitchforked into Moroccan life, she found the furniture gaudy and not particularly comfortable and she tried her best to subdue the effect with antimacassars, jolly chenille tablecloths with bobbles, family portraits and all the other paraphernalia that gave an air of an English drawing room. A walnut piano, upright and with brass candle-holders had been acquired and placed in the main salon.

But the decorations were the smallest of her worries. It was proving difficult to become used to the way the house was run. She had an English maid, a Spanish cook and two Moorish slaves for her own personal service, but the place swarmed with slaves, secretaries, gardeners and servants of every description. It also swarmed with less desirable inhabitants, for Emily found she was living in a Zowia, or sanctuary. This meant that anyone, rich or poor, litigant or criminal, could claim the protection of the Shereef and Shereefa and remain under their roof, at their expense. Those seeking sanctuary were supposed to bring offerings, but these could vary from a little food—milk or meat—to large sums of money. It was possible for a Zowia to be highly profitable; it was also possible to go bankrupt running one. Whichever way, living there was not very comfortable. People would arrive for months at a time, and all their claims and complaints had to be investigated. Emily had no choice in the matter; the Shereefs of Wazan had run Zowias for generations; much of their prestige rested on this hospitality and help which they offered freely to their people. The new Shereefa found herself entertaining some very odd house guests.

Europeans in Morocco had hard things to say about the whole function of a Zowia, believing that they were another form of income and extortion practised by the Shereefs against the ordinary people. But Emily with her sense of thrift soon realised that the expense of feeding a Moroccan nobleman, his wives and all his retinue for months at a time, should he have claimed sanctuary, could become exceedingly expensive. A practical girl, it was not long before she was tactfully sending those who had no need to stay quietly on their way. She found it worked very well just to cut their rations a little.

There were other shocks. The Shereef owned considerable property around Tangier including orange groves and gardens where vegetables were grown. In turn, all of these were visited. They would ride out together, a picnic lunch being sent to follow them by the servants at the Zowia. At one orange garden, she met the Riffian wife of one of the gardeners. An attractive woman she wore an enormous straw hat with bright plaits of wool holding up the brim and attached to the crown. This girl, unveiled and wearing a bright red and white striped skirt and white *haik* was the possessor of an enchanting bright-eyed baby boy who took Emily's fancy. The mother, pleased by this attention to her offspring, made it clear by signs that the baby belonged to the Shereef.

Emily, despite her knowledge of the Shereef's three wives and harem ladies was shattered by the information and departed rapidly to sit under an orange tree and cry —where the Shereef discovered her, pink nosed and miserable and demanded to know what was the matter.

Emily feeling injured at first refused to tell him, but eventually blurted out that he might have told her if she was to find his children scattered all over Tangier.

He roared with laughter, and told her that she had a great deal to learn about her adopted country.

He explained that the gardener's wife had five daughters and they badly wanted a son. She had come to the Zowia to ask for the Shereef's blessing and prayers that she might conceive a male heir. 'So I did what I always do in these circumstances—gave her an amulet to wear,' he told her. 'The next baby was a boy—the one you saw. But because she believes it was my blessing that produced the boy for her, the son is mine. But only by reason of an amulet.'

He went on to explain how much power faith had in the Mohammedan religion. How barren women came to the Zowia for the same reason, and how any children they had afterwards were always considered his, and added that she would have to get used to it.

Emily was not entirely convinced, but made up her mind then and there to learn her husband's language. Without being aware of what was being said she realised that misunderstandings would constantly occur and she would never be able to communicate with the people with whom she was living.

She and the Shereef were finding life a little lonely, but being very much in love this was not too much of a handicap. Emily bravely passed off their lack of invitations and company to the fact that there was not much distraction in Tangier society at the moment, and they spent their evenings after the daily excursions enjoying music. The Shereef taught her many Moorish songs, and she accompanied him on the piano while he sang and played the violin. She dutifully went to Church every Sunday at the British Legation ignoring the stares and sniffs of the English women of the town. Chairs were placed in the hall for the worshippers and the Shereef would accompany her, sitting in the gallery upstairs, his head uncovered—unusual as a Moor covers his head in a place of worship—watching with interest all that went on and joining in the jollier hymns with gusto.

Towards the end of February, trouble started. By then news of the Shereef's extraordinary behaviour had spread throughout Morocco. The people were outraged. The Sultan's anger had been gathering, and finding his subjects so much in agreement, he decided to act; finding in the marriage the tool to limit the power of the Wazan family.

Emily realised that her husband was worried about something, but he would not tell her what the trouble was and it was perhaps as well that she did not know.

The main indignation felt by the Moroccans was that he had not insisted that his European wife renounce her religion and become a Mohammedan and their faith in him was considerably shaken. They had learnt to live with the fact that he liked to drink alcoholic drinks—explaining this away by telling themselves that the Shereef was so holy that as the liquid touched his lips a miracle occurred

—it turned to milk. He in turn was wily enough to drink anisette-type drinks which turned milky white when water was added to them.

This outrage of marriage to a Nazarene, attending her church services, and spending more and more time in European company was too much to pass off. The Sultan had sent a dispatch to the Governors of all the provinces expressing his indignation at the Shereef's conduct and then a letter arrived at the Shereef's home from the Sultan, written in the strongest terms. Sidi Muhammed commanded that the Shereef should send his newly married wife back to England immediately and he, the Sultan, would fulfil the terms of the contract and pay the £800 which the Shereef had undertaken to give her in compensation should he put her away. The alternative was that the Shereef should bring her at once to Wazan and that she must accept Moorish customs, particularly as regarded seclusion. In any case, the Sultan ordered the Shereef to reside every year for six months at Wazan on his large estates, three months at Fez, and the remaining three months either at Morocco City (Marrakesh) or Tangier, whichever the Shereef would prefer. In the meantime, the Sultan commanded that the Mosque tribute, a considerable annual sum always paid to the Shereef out of the religious funds, was stopped.

Sidi Abdeslam Hadj was quicker and smarter than the Sultan. He had seen that trouble must come once the dispatches had been sent out, and had made his own plans. He knew his influence in the Riff and the North of Morocco was temporarily damaged, but it remained as strong as ever among his followers in Algeria. And the French were having considerable problems in controlling the hill tribes of their colony who were constantly uprising and causing trouble. The Shereef was the one man who could quieten them.

He sent some dispatches of his own. There were some advantages in being the spiritual head and leader of the Brotherhood of the Moulay Taieb, the cult which his ancestor had founded. The brotherhood used 'messengers' to communicate between the geographically widely spaced units of the Moulay Taieb followers, and a system of secret badges, signs and codewords. No ritual of the order was permitted to be told to anyone who was not of the brotherhood. It was insisted that all members lived by self-denial, respect to superiors and with complete passive obedience to their leaders.

This organisation, always set up and ready was there to deliver Hadj Abdeslam's dispatches, no matter how far they had to go. A fleet of runners who would never divulge a secret of the Wazan family would carry them, running over mountains and plain; passing on the message until it reached its destination.

The Shereef's messages were addressed to the Shofa (Shereefs) of Algiers. All had less power than him, but all were followers of the Wazan cult. He asked them to obtain for him the protection of the French Government. They immediately sent a petition to the Minister of Foreign Affairs in Paris.

The French were not slow to offer their protection. They needed the Shereef's assistance with their problems of control in North West Algeria, and they had a longer range plan—the eventual annexation of Morocco to add to their North African colonies. The Shereef was the most valuable pawn in the game, and they cabled their consul in Tangier, M. Tissot, to afford all help and protection to the Grand Shereef and his English wife.

The first Emily knew of the intrigue was when the Shereef returned home in high humour after days of nail-biting and morose behaviour. On attempts to question him, he had snapped at her, so she held her peace. Now he told her to pack some clothes—they were leaving for the town immediately, to stay in the French Embassy.

'But why?' she asked.

Briefly he explained what the problems of the past few weeks had been.

'It seems no one wishes us to be happy,' she said sadly.

They left the Zowia quietly and at night. Bundled up in robes, riding down the scented hillside, buzzing with the noise of crickets and cicadas, and into the quiet, sleeping town. The horses clipped their way over the broken cobbles to the French Embassy, where, like phantoms, their riders slid inside with no witnesses.

The word went around Tangier that they had disappeared, and the Shereef was angry that the story was out. And more angry at the receipt of the March 18th, 1873 copy of the *Gibraltar Chronicle* which arrived in Tangier delivered by the *Hercules*. It said: 'The marriage of the Shereef of Wazan to Miss Keene, and the mode of life led by him subsequently, especially the fact of his not insisting on her renouncing her Christian tenets was so great an outrage on the most cherished precepts of the Mohammedan religion that however strong might have been the faith of the people in him and his exalted position, that faith has been greatly shaken by his last step. The intelligence of the marriage created, we are informed, a most powerful sensation at the Court of Morocco and the Sultan has sent dispatches to the governors of the Provinces expressing his indignation at the Shereef's conduct and ordering them in most explicit terms to warn him that if he does not immediately return to his possession at Wazan, conform to the precepts of the faith which he professes, making atonement at the same time for his past errors and lead a life of piety such as becomes the sacred (in Moroccan eyes) position which he holds, his estates will be confiscated, he will be deprived of his prerogatives and, if caught, thrown into prison.

'The news spread through Tangier at lightning speed, causing the most manifest satisfaction among the Moroccan community who though they have strongly condemned the mode of life led by the Shereef recently did not dare to previously express their feelings.

'That he himself is alarmed may be gathered from the fact that he and his wife have disappeared, no one knows whither, though the prevailing *on dit* is that they are concealed in some Foreign Legation in Tangier. To Miss Keene, the consequences cannot fail to be serious as she will certainly be regarded by the Moors with hostile eyes and her position will be a critical one.'

The story upset Emily whose one concern was whether or not her husband could be put into prison.

He explained it was unlikely. 'While we are under the protection of the French, they cannot touch us. They cannot touch my estates, my prerogatives, my money and nor can they touch you.'

She was not a politically minded woman. She could not understand why the French were able to protect them when the country did not belong to France, and was self-governed.

'Not entirely self-governed,' the Shereef explained. The Europeans had, it seemed, many fingers in the pie. They had loaned the Sultan money; they brought in trade. And they had agreements with the Sultan that any Moroccan citizen under foreign protection could not be touched by the Sultan's Government. It was a most complicated political situation, brought about by the fact that Morocco owed both France and England money. And it was a situation which the Shereef had every intention of exploiting.

Emily was disappointed that protection had not been offered by the British Consul. She did not know that her husband had approached Sir John Hay Drummond Hay before he went to the French. He had thought that with a British wife, Sir John would have immediately offered assistance, but he had not.

For very good reasons. France had the greatest acquisitory interests in Morocco. The British purely acted as a stumbling block to the French ambitions. Sir John gave the Moroccans his friendship and advice, but would not become too deeply involved in any political situation which would harm his good relations with the Sultan. To have given the Wazanni's British protection at that time would have meant that the Sultan and his Government would have lost some of the trust they had in the British Consulate.

The Shereef explained to Emily that he was of more value to the French interests than the Sultan himself, because of the Wazan power in the North.

'The French think they are using me—but I am using them,' he told her.

By the 19th March, 1873, everyone in Tangier knew what had happened and where the Shereef and Shereefa were hiding. Emily and her Prince were comfortably installed in the French Legation and enjoying the French cooking. She was over her original hurt and disappointment at the attitudes surrounding them and beginning to regard the situation as something of an adventure. Together they rode out in the town, boldly and uncaring of the black looks and muttered insults of the people in the streets.

'What are they saying,' she asked.

'They are being rather uncomplimentary about your ancestors,' the Shereef said lightly. 'We have a strong line in anti-Christian curses in this country.'

For all his soothing words to his wife the Shereef knew that the situation was a serious one for him. His religious influence had been shaken, and even more shaken when it became known that he had taken the protection of a Christian power. And by doing so set himself against the authority of the Sultan. What annoyed him the most was that though the Sultan had lost the exchange of wits, the Royal personal popularity had soared after the public condemnation of the Shereef's agreement to Emily's continued observance to the Christian customs. He knew that the Moors had already re-christened him *Insahrah*—a not too polite name for a Christian—instead of the term *el Santo* (The Saint) by which he had always been known. The ultra religious members of his community were trying to content themselves with the reflection that he must be out of his senses and were praying that Allah and the Prophet might restore to him his reason and enable him to see the error of his ways so that he could return to the paths of true Mohammedism.

And the newspapers continued to keep up the speculation and alighted unerringly on the truth of the matter. On the 23rd of March there was another issue of the *Gibraltar Chronicle* for Emily to read to him.

She translated it halting occasionally to stop for the correct Spanish words. The report read: 'The recent marriage of the Shereef of Wazan, or El Santo, the chief of one of the two most powerful religious Mohammedan brotherhoods with Miss Keene, a Christian, was such an unprecedented event that everything in connection with it has called forth more than an ordinary degree of interest, enhanced by the fact that the Princess, as Miss Keene must now be called, has apparently not surrendered any of the rights which she would have possessed had she married one of her own countrymen. In fact since the Shereef succeeded in placing himself under French protection both he and the Princess have been seen taking their daily ride with as much publicity as if he had been brought up anywhere but in Morocco.

'As we have already stated, the religious influence of the Shereef was seriously impaired by his marriage, and its decline was still further accelerated when it was known that he had solicited the protection of a Christian power in order to set at naught the authority of his lawful Sovereign. It may be remarked here, *en passant*, that as a Shereef of Wazan, he is superior to the Emperor, who is also a Shereef but of a lesser degree.

'As an instance of the authority possessed by the Shereef we are informed that about three weeks since several Moors from Gharbia (about a day's journey from Tangier on the way to Fez) were brought into Tangier with their horses and cattle, by some of the Pasha's soldiers, charged with cattle stealing, and with neglecting to pay the customary tribute. As to the latter charge there was no doubt, but nevertheless, on the representation of the Shereef that they were under his special protection, their property was restored to them and they were released from custody with no other punishment than, as is the custom of the judicial procedure in Morocco, being mulct in the costs of their own arrest.*

'There are certain political considerations involved which are worthy of special attention. By the Moors generally the action of the French Government in taking the Shereef under its protection is regarded as a piece of unwarrantable interference, and this view is adopted, doubtless, under the impression that the proceedings of France

* It is unlikely that the tribesmen had stolen any cattle. Their crime would have been to neglect paying the tribute because they had nothing to pay it with. Had the Shereef not intervened their cattle would have been stolen on a trumped up charge.

may extend to the re-instatement of the Shereef in his religious position in Morocco, from which the Sultan threatened to have him deposed.

'This however, can scarcely be the case. The action of the French Government, therefore, may be assumed to be purely political and the *raison d'être* is not hard to find. The majority of the Moors in Algeria belong to the brotherhood of Moulay Taieb, of which the Shereef of Wazan is the chief, and his influence in quietening the Algerian tribes cannot be overrated, inasmuch as in Algeria his prestige has not declined in the least; and as proof that the French Government is alive to this fact, it is even asserted that an offer has been made to the Shereef of an annual subsidy of $16,000, as is the case already with some other Algerian Chiefs, on condition that he will use his influence to the advantage of the French. All this is looked upon as the more important because the marriage of the Shereef with an English lady was considered as likely to have a beneficial effect on English interests in Morocco.'

English interests had indeed taken a knock by reason of the Shereef's action. At that time Sir John Hay Drummond Hay was assiduously cultivating both trade and friendship with Morocco. The British Government had no desire to add Morocco as another jewel to Victoria's crown, but had every intention of stopping France stepping in and gaining control of the country. The diplomacy game had been played with great skill by successive British consuls; sometimes the advantage would go to France; mostly it was with Britain, but no one was really winning.

Years before, Lord Nelson had said that it was essential that Morocco, and Tangier in particular, should never fall to a foreign power. If any country did move in to conquer the country he said it must be Great Britain. By this move Britain would have gained complete control of the gateway to the Mediterranean. Britain had already been in Gibraltar for over a hundred years, a site of considerable importance in days when warfare was mainly naval.

If anything Tangier was better placed than Gibraltar to police the entry to the Mediterranean with Britain's many gunboats, but British policy, however, was to keep Morocco independent, as Lord Nelson had recommended. Not out of the goodness of the merchant Britisher's hearts, but as a matter of diplomatic expediency. Morocco was a very useful piece of bargaining land with the French when other matters of more interest to Britain were raised.

Emily's marriage and the consequent upheaval it caused had dented British diplomacy badly and dealt the French a long wanted card.

The Sultan of Morocco, who was a far-seeing man where the French ambitions for annexation of his country were concerned, also realised how badly his own manoeuvre had misfired. His personal prestige was high with the ordinary people, but from a long range viewpoint for the retention of the independence of his country, the turn of events was disastrous. The situation was now stalemate. He could do nothing, having been made impotent by the combination of the French and the Shereef, who had made all his proclamations and demands quite worthless. He was forced to leave the Shereef in peace until another opportunity arose.

Emily did not care about the political to-ing and fro-ing. All she appreciated was that the final result of the French protection meant that all their personal plans were completely changed. Now, her husband told her, with the French backing him (to the tune of $16,000 a year) it was no longer possible to live in peaceful, civilised France. The money would not be paid to him unless he remained in Morocco. But as it was, his position was assured for some time; he no longer needed the Mosque tribute which the Sultan had stopped. They would remain in Tangier.

Emily's mother who had been un-nerved by the events of the past month was totally shattered by this news. She had been waiting for the day when they could pack up and leave what she felt to be a barbaric country. She could not believe that her daughter was now going to remain, probably to be murdered in her bed, as she put it somewhat dramatically to Emily.

But to Emily it was a matter of complete indifference where she lived. She had told her mother that she had a husband whom she loved and who seemed to worship the ground she walked upon.

'He is affectionate, and attentive to all my wishes, and I shall have a happy life with him I am sure,' she said. 'Where we live is of no importance. We shall stay here if he wishes it.'

And at heart, in spite of all the problems, she was happy to be staying. She had started a love affair with the country as well as with one of its leading citizens that was to last the rest of her life.

Chapter Four

AN ADOPTED DAUGHTER AND THE BIRTH OF A SHEREEF

The Shereef was quite right. All the troubles and agitations did very soon die down and Emily and her husband were left together in peace and quiet at their home on the Marshan. In fact, they were left very much alone. No invitations came from Tangier society, and neither of them felt particularly slighted. The newspaper stories of their wedding were too fresh in Emily's mind for her to be comfortable with Europeans.

It was like a prolonged honeymoon. The Shereef could not bear her out of his sight and it seemed that every day, thrown completely together as they were, she found more in him to love and admire. Life was idyllic. The persecution from the Sultan had ceased; there were no calls for assistance from the French, and the days began to take on a dreamlike quality as the hot summer months slipped away while they rode together in the scorched hills and walked on the lonely beaches beneath their home. Emily dreamily planted an English garden of marigolds, narcissus, verbena and roses, and found that whatever she planted grew with a springing strength and flowered boldly and brashly, greedily taking the endless stream of water with which she kept her garden green. She sat under the orange trees sewing, watching the glossy green fruit among darker leaves turning to pale lemon and then the bright orange coming through until the fruit was ripe enough to pick.

She was very much the housewife, trying to make some order out of the chaos of the Zowia, and she discovered in herself a talent for organisation. She asked to assist the Shereef in his role of judge and jury within their home, and learned that the working of the sanctuary were not as simple as appeared at first. Judgement had to be made when the murderer or the thief or the tax-evader took refuge, and if the facts told against him, he was taken to the Kaid for trial. Those who were judged innocent if perhaps the murder was unpremeditated, were sheltered.

Her life was uneventful now, and her habits still British. She drank tea, but in respect of the Shereef's religion, relinquished morning bacon. She made her private apartments on the first floor of the house more 'comfy' and continued to take her daily cold bath. The Shereef, finding her leaping from it pink and shivering one morning remarked that he had no idea that he had married a fish.

He was still fascinated with stories of her childhood; the thought of life in Britain was as exotic to him as the reality of life in Morocco had proved to be for his wife. She described the teeming streets of London; talked of the livery stables that her grandparents, the Wharrams, owned at Newington Butts, with the fine carriages, and the glossy black funeral horses with their plumes. Her brothers and sisters and the way of life became as real to him as they were to her.

She could not believe how lucky she was. Life was so peaceful and scented with all the warmth of the country and of love it seemed if happiness must be permanent. She was busy, too. Hating to be idle she was learning the language with the help of an elderly servant woman called Aisha who recounted tales in the style of the Arabian Nights. The stories themselves were fascinating to Emily for they generally concerned her husband's ancestors, and the history of the town of Wazan, the family's home. She would write down the unfamiliar words she had heard in her lesson and in the evenings when they were alone together, the Shereef would explain their meanings, help to correct her pronunciation and put her right about his family's history. She found it was not difficult for her to master the guttural sound of Arabic and blessed again her family's facility for learning languages.

She had also decided that as well as the language she must learn about her husband's religion, though she had no intention of changing her own. Indeed, no one had suggested that she did so. Study of the Koran gave her an insight into many of the Moslem attitudes towards the Christian and the Jew, and she began to understand that their entire mode of life was based not on secular law, but the laws which Mohammed had laid down. She found much of it sensible; much of it similar in respects to Christain teaching, but she could not help wishing that the prophet had been a little less positive in his anti-feelings towards Christians. It might have made the outside world a little less hostile towards her.

For she was encountering hostility. The servants were sullen and stiff, but she felt that the only thing to do was to wait and to hope that in time, once she had mastered the language, some kind of rapport might be achieved. She also had another plan. Before she and the Shereef had married he had mentioned to her a six-year-old daughter of his, Lalla Heba, who lived at Wazan, and had said that the child was sickly.

'Does her mother nurse her?' Emily had asked.

'Her mother is dead,' he said briefly, and Emily thought it as well not to press that point.

But the child was on her mind. She was missing her brothers and sisters. Used to always having small children around her, the thought of Lalla Heba began to obsess her, but her husband seemed determined to leave the little girl where she was. She coaxed him time and time again to bring the child to Tangier until he finally asked if she did not mind that the girl was his by another wife.

'Why should I?' Emily had said. 'I know that you were married before, and besides, she has no mother now. As your wife it is my duty to care for her.'

'Very well,' he said. 'We will send for her.'

It took a week to make the arrangements. Even a very small Shereefa had to travel with a fitting retinue, but eventually the child arrived. Emily was waiting at the door as the procession wound its way towards the house. There were at least thirty attendants, some on foot, some on mules with soft, red padded seats, surrounding a closed litter carried between two mules.

Emily stepped forward to pull back the brilliant striped curtains which enclosed the child and drew back shocked. The little girl was undersized to the point of emaciation, her cheeks flushed with fever and she lay motionless on the pallet, her eyes tight shut. Clucking and tutting, Emily picked the child up in her arms and hurried upstairs to where her mother waited.

'I fear we shall not have her with us for long, Mama,' she said. 'She is practically unconscious and has such a high fever.'

Together they undressed the hot little body, exclaiming at the way the child's bones jutted through her skin, as they slipped on a clean nightgown, especially sewn in the waiting period, and gently put the child to bed.

Emily was angry, and a ship in full sail had nothing on Emily when her temper was roused. She hurried down the stairs and sought out the women who had attended the child, demanding to know how long she had been in such a condition. The women were frightened by this tall, fierce eyed woman confronting them, and protested that it was no fault of theirs. The child had been ill with malarial fever for three months now.

Emily gave them a withering look, which set their hands fluttering to ward off the evil eye, and stamped back up-tairs. She was not too pleased with her husband either. How could he have left his daughter so ill and uncared for?

She tackled the Shereef later as to his part in the neglect of the child. He merely shrugged and said he had not known because the child was a daughter. Had it been one of his sons he would have been informed.

She understood the attitude towards girls in a Moslem society and accepted what he said. It puzzled her that the other wives had made no effort to care for the child, but the Shereef explained that each wife was concerned with her own children, and jealous for their rights. One of the disadvantages of polygamy was that the women did not really care very much if the child of another wife died. The death meant one less child to share any inheritance.

It was then, sitting by Lalla Heba's bedside that Emily

made a decision about her own future. If she had children who grew up to marry, *she* would make herself responsible for the children of all her children. And their children, too, if she was spared. She was prepared to accept much about the Moslem way of life, but neglect and downright cruelty to helpless little girls was not to be tolerated.

August crept to its end, the countryside became barren and brown and Emily hoping all the while to become pregnant turned her attention to Lalla Heba who had gradually been nursed back to health. The Shereef encouraged her interest in the child, and suggested that Emily sewed European clothes for her and taught her to read and to play the piano. He wanted his daughter to be as Europeanised as possible.

Emily, in agreeing, made a mistake that was to lengthen the time of coming to terms with her Moslem household.

* * *

History was taking a hand in the Shereef's destiny. At the British Legation on September 17th, 1873, Sir John Hay Drummond Hay working late by the light of a huge candelabra was wording a telegram to the Earl of Granville, Her Majesty's Foreign Secretary in London. It read: 'The Sultan of Morocco died on the 11th of September. His eldest son, Moulay Hassan, has been acclaimed Sultan at the City of Morocco.'

He then settled down at his desk to write a letter explaining in further detail the events of the past few days and the facts of the death. He began by telling how medicine for intermittent fever had been given to the dead Sultan.

'I do not suppose,' he wrote, 'that poison had been administered, for the greatest care was always taken by the Sultan and his confidential attendants to prevent food or potion being taken by his Majesty unless prepared by trustworthy attendants interested in preserving the life of his Majesty, but I should not be in the least surprised that some error has been committed by the Sultan himself or other persons ignorant of pharmacy in the preparation or administration of the dose which appears to have been followed by his death.

'The late Sultan was, I would think about 66 years of age. Moulay Hassan was absent when the Sultan died having been despatched some weeks ago with a considerable force to chastise the rebellious tribes in Hala.

'He (the new Sultan) is 24 years of age, has a good countenance and appeared intelligent, but was excessively shy which I attribute to the fact of my being the first European official he had ever met.'

Sir John's pen spluttered over the paper as he wrote on swiftly. The point of the communication was yet to come. Tactfully he explained that, should the Sultan not be accepted by all the tribes, the country could find itself at war, and the British subjects under his care would then be in considerable danger. In times of unrest, Christians were generally the first target for an excitable populace. He wanted ships sent to patrol the various ports where most of the British subjects in Morocco were living.

'I beg to add,' he wrote, 'that the appearance off the Moorish coast on such an occasion as the presence of a small gunboat such as the *Pigeon* or *Pheasant* would not be likely to produce a very favourable effect on the minds of her Majesty's Government to protect British lives and property. I therefore trust that some larger vessel than either of these two gunboats may be despatched on the service.'*

The letter was sent on the courier ship *Francis III* and within days Sir John's request was granted. H.M.S. *Aurora,* commanded by Captain Shalto Douglas steamed belligerently up and down the Atlantic Coast, hoving to off Magadore and finally arriving in Tangier on the 9th of October.

There had been no trouble. Sir John had made it his business to pass on the news of the Sultan's death to Emily and her husband and immediately the Shereef made preparations to leave on the journey in time for the installation of the new King.

Emily would have been extremely cross that she was not permitted to join in with him to see the colourful feudal installation ceremony, had she not been contented

* Records Office document.

to find that she was at last pregnant. The journey for the installation was a long hard one, and she did not intend taking any chances at all with the new baby on the way. The Shereef, in high good humour at all the news, was convinced that he would have a healthy son.

'It may be a girl,' Emily warned him.

'Impossible,' he told her. '*You* will never have girls.'

'There may be no choice in the matter,' she told him tartly, annoyed to discover another Christian cliché regarding the Arab temperament proving to be true.

Convinced he was about to become the father of a son, he rode off at the head of his enormous, richly dressed retinue, a proud man. The journey, which would take a week was to signify his approval of the King by placing his hand on the Sultan's stirrup. Privately Emily thought it was a long way to go for such a brief moment of glory, but then told herself that she would have felt quite differently had she been going, too. She had tinkered with the idea, but the Shereef had been adamant that it was no place for a woman. Even a European woman. There were limits he said. She was resigned to waiting a while before she could see more of Morocco than comparatively Europeanised Tangier. It was annoying—but there was plenty to do—baby clothes to make, and Lalla Heba to care for.

Unaccountably Lalla Heba was proving to be the only jarring note in what was otherwise a happy existence. The child had fully recovered her health, she plumped up like a little chicken and had become perfectly happy, quickly learning her letters and beginning to speak both a little Spanish and English. She was bright and had a real aptitude for music, easily learning the notes of the piano, but suddenly she had turned truculent and silent. She refused to speak anything but Arabic, would not look at the children's book Emily had had sent specially from Gibraltar and cried whenever she was dressed in the pretty, hand-embroidered, broad-sashed dresses Emily had sewn for her. Emily was bitterly disappointed with this failure and could not understand why. What made it worse was that the Shereef, though pleasant and affectionate towards the child, seemed to have little interest in her, and when his wife shed a few tears of hurt he merely said 'leave it alone. Forget it.' He was disappointed about the failure, but only on his wife's behalf. But for Emily, who adored children, to find one who seemed to actively dislike her was painful.

Emma Keene had long since returned home and now Emily sat down to write a long, happy letter to Newington, comforted by the knowledge that all her brothers and sisters were pleading to come and visit her. The Keenes seemed to have resigned themselves to her situation. Only her father was still concerned but she hoped that would pass. She added a tentative P.S. to her letter: 'Would papa permit mama to return for the birth of the baby? It would be such a comfort.'

With the Shereef away, she had time on her hands and she worked even harder at her Arabic. One morning her teacher, Aisha, her sharp eyes probably having guessed that Emily was pregnant, suggested that perhaps she might like to be present at the birth of a Moroccan baby. Emily was dubious about going; she knew that most Moroccan women believed Christians brought the evil eye with them and had anything gone wrong with the birth, her presence would be blamed. But Aisha said that as the wife of the Sidi, his baraka would be powerful enough to overcome the fact that Emily was a Nazarene. In fact, if Emily were to attend the birth, her presence might even ensure a male child.

It seemed an unlikely piece of reasoning, and somewhat late for Emily's presence to ensure anything, but Aisha went off to make enquiries, warning her mistress to be ready at any hour. Some days later in the early evening she hurried in announcing that a baby was to be born.

Emily rode by mule to a small mud house a few hundred yards from her own home where the birth was taking place. She was taken inside and led to the mother's room, accompanied by musicians and a group of women who held lighted candles. As she came into the chamber there was a buzz of excitement.

The candles had blown steady, once the door had closed

—and this meant a boy was to be born.

At a Moroccan birth of the period—and it has not changed in the remote areas even today—all the women sang dirge-like songs while burning incense increased the darkness and the extreme stuffiness of the house.

It was possible to make out the figure of the mother by locating the woman who was making the most noise. Long wailing cries and moans, breathless sentences asking for God to forgive her and saying that death would free her from all the pain, came from a dimly seen figure, sitting upright on the floor and covered with a blanket. Behind her another woman sat on a stool and supported the mother's back, while on the floor, half under the blanket, sat another woman, facing the mother.

The woman could not lie down and relax in case the *qabla* (midwife) saw the private parts of her body. That was not permitted. It was considered unlucky and indelicate. The *qabla* would deliver the baby by touch alone.

By deduction Emily proved the *qabla* to be the woman at the mother's feet. She sat on the floor, her feet stretched apart while her patient squatted in front of her, her buttocks resting on the midwife's legs. The woman who had been standing behind took the mother's place on the stool, supporting her and during the contractions, the mother placed her arms around the midwife's neck, resting her forehead on her forehead while the woman on the stool lifted her from the ground. A cloth was thrown over both the midwife's and mother's head, another on the mother's stomach while the midwife worked, quite blind, beneath it. Another woman occasionally brought some liquid in a basin and fed it to the mother who was now wailing louder than ever. Emily thought it all very primitive and thanked her lucky stars that the Shereef did not insist on things being done the Moroccan way in his own home.

She also decided that her mother or at least one of the elder sisters, must be persuaded to attend the birth of her own baby. She did not fancy the services of the *qabla*.

They were not very gentle with the mother. The baby was too long in arriving, and eventually the unfortunate woman was bounced up and down like a rubber ball before being sat on a hot stove. And to Emily's relief, the baby was born.

A thin, indignant howl rose above the other noises of the room, and immediately all the women broke out into a peculiar high-pitched sound—the zahrit, or joy-cry—which they made by trembling the tongue against the lips.

Emily went a little closer to look at the small bundle, with its enraged, crumpled face, topped with a fuzz of black hair. His indignities were not over. He was wrapped in a cloth and handed to one of the women, whilst the midwife helped the mother on to the bed and fed her a basin of broth. The woman busied herself with the baby. She wiped him with a bit of fabric before smearing the little body with a concoction of henna and oil. He was then rolled in linen and wrapped in a piece of old blanket and had a cord wound around him from shoulder to feet. At this treatment he yelled harder than ever, but the woman worked on. She wound a strip of linen across his temples and fastened it at the back of his neck.

That was to keep his brain from becoming dislodged explained Aisha.

A cotton handkerchief was then tied over the babe's chin and another piece of blanket completely covered his head. The woman then cleaned the screwed up eyes with rags, and applied Kohl to the eyelids and eyebrows. She washed out his mouth with oil, and the stiff and furious little mummy was handed to his mother, who was now sitting up.

All in all, Emily was feeling rather giddy and asked if a birth was always conducted in the same way.

Aisha told her the ritual never varied. But had the baby been a girl, a date would have been put between her legs to make her sweet for her future husband.

As Emily tottered back to her horse, grateful for the fresh air outside, she fully understood why the infant mortality rate was so high in Morocco. Something would have to be done.

She discussed her experience with the Shereef when he returned from the Sultan's installation and at first he was anxious in case the sight might have made her nervous about the birth of her own baby.

'Of course not,' she said. 'Birth is often difficult but with modern methods the dangers are so much less. There was no hygiene at all in that house. I cannot understand how either mother or baby survive.'

'Most do,' said the Shereef.

It was in matters of this sort that Morocco most needed to come into the nineteenth century, but the problem was to kill the superstition and fear that ruled the people. Emily believed education would be the answer and that her children might well be the ones to alter customs. But at that moment all she could think was that her husband had been born in the same way as the baby boy who might well still be yelling his indignation back at the stuffy little house.

'How lucky *you* survived,' she said.

He came and settled himself on the long, low couch that surrounded the room, lolling back with his head on her shoulder.

'Ah, but my mother was a woman of great fastidiousness,' he said. 'Her slaves stood around her to swish away the flies when she ate, and from all around where the food was cooked. If a fly touched her food the dish was immediately removed. Her appetite would quite vanish.'

It was an opportunity to bring up the story she had been told about his mother having been a slave, and, it seemed, the story was true. The Shereef explained that his mother had been one of the most beautiful girls that anyone had ever seen. His father had lost many sons, and was left with only two daughters when his followers in Fez saw a beautiful girl on the slave market. They bought her as a present for the old Shereef. At first she was merely his concubine and only fifteen years old when her first son—the present Shereef—was born. But the father loved her and eventually made her his wife.

His eyes had filled with tears and he was visibly moved, speaking of his mother. And Emily asked no more questions.

* * *

Emma Keene left London and returned to Tangier in May, 1874, accompanied by Gertrude, her youngest child, to be present at her daughter's confinement. The decision to leave Newington again was an unselfish one on the part of the Keene family as Emily's grandfather was contemplating retirement after 48 years in the service of Surrey County as a prison officer. It seemed most likely that his son would take over the post, but the appointment was not entirely decided and John Keene would have preferred his wife at his side during the period of uncertainty.

Once in Tangier, Emma Keene did not have long to wait. On the 6th of June, 1874, Moulay Ali came into the world in the British way with plenty of hot water, and a knotted towel to hang on to, and no superstitious nonsense. Emily's mother and a local European midwife were in attendance and the baby was born without any complications, leaving the Shereef thoroughly pleased with himself and Emily.

'I told you it would be a boy,' he said when he came in to kiss her and take a look at his son once his wife was tidied up and rested. 'And listen to how delighted the people are.'

'Listen!' said Emily who was feeling exhausted after all the effort of the last few hours. 'Listen! I am likely to be deafened!'

The birth of an infant Shereef was causing a prodigious din. Outside the house crowds of people had collected; the women making their zahrit cries, the men loosing off gunpowder from their long rifles.

The celebrations confirmed the completely feudal hold that the Wazanni's held over the population. The rejoicing went on for nearly three months. The birth of a new Shereef was an excuse for a continuous party—something the Moors never let go by. Enough presents to stock a home and a museum were arriving from all over Morocco as well as large gifts of money.

The object of the enthusiasm was a fit and healthy baby. Emma Keene, relieved that he was not too dark skinned—more a pleasant Mediterranean colour, inspected him carefully each day lest he should have turned darker in the night.

The custom in Morocco was for the father to name the baby, but the Shereef, knowing that in Europe the mother had some say in the matter asked Emily to choose their son's name. She would quite liked to have called him John, in the Keene family tradition, but reasoned that as he was a Moroccan child and would be living in a Moslem country, it was better to give him an Arab name. She had already suggested Moulay Ali for the Shereef's first grandchild, who had been born in Wazan a few months previously, and thinking it had a pretty ring to it, suggested the same name for her own boy. But she was to have problems in her attempts to bring him up European fashion.

In her memoirs she wrote: 'Not finding a regular nurse available, my mother and the midwife attended to the baby, and with the help of my maid all went on well. Mother always washed and dressed the child and a few days after his birth she invited an old retainer, a Moorish woman over eighty years of age, a woman whose mother and grandfather had also been in the service of the Wazan family to be present at the baby's bath. She squatted down and seemed to be interested in the undressing process, seemed to perk up when soap and sponge were applied, but when the child was placed in a bath, she rushed suddenly from the room, down the stairs with the agility of a girl of fifteen, and without any ceremony into my husband's bedroom. Though he was fast asleep she shook him vigorously, saying "Oh, Sidi, Sidi, do come at once; the Christians are killing your son!"

'A few minutes later the Shereef entered my room, breathless almost, and sat or rather fell into an easy-chair; he looked at me, and then at my mother, who, like myself, knew nothing of the old woman's visit to him. Mother was dressing the baby by this time and handed the child to him to be kissed. He began to smile, then to laugh, finally he fairly shook from head to foot with the exertion, the tears rolling down his face. We wondered what had happened to the Shereef, who at last found his voice and related the scene that had taken place downstairs. Then we all joined in the merriment.

'Meanwhile, I heard a scuffling outside my door; what was it? The household had been roused to such a pitch of curiosity as to what was really going on in my room, that the whole of the staff and many others who were there to assist in the making of cakes, etc., for the name day had gathered at the doors. They went off to their different departments quicker than they came, when they found a tragedy was not being enacted the other side of the door. Nothing less than the dead baby was expected, and I hope they were not too disappointed!'

The incident gave her cause to think. If she could convince the mothers of her own household that a dip into water did not mean instant extinction for a baby, it might be possible to begin to instil a little hygiene into the Moroccan methods of child-raising. She decided that bath-time should become a fairly public affair so that other mothers could see for themselves how a clean and well-kept baby thrived.

Moulay Ali's first few days were taking an entirely different direction from his infant compatriates. Moroccan new-born babies were generally kept well hidden, for fear of the evil-eye, until their name day, eight days after the birth. The infant then received a cursory wipe over with a little water, was wrapped in brand new constricting garments of the same type used at the birth, hands bound down to its side, and put to bed with the mother while the celebrations took place. Emily was determined that her baby would be comfortable and allowed to kick, and as neither she nor the Shereef were in the least superstitious, the evil eye was discounted. But the name day feast was to be conducted in the traditional manner.

The preparations were formidable. Enough food had to be prepared for several hundred guests, as well as for the poor. A woman whose job was that of an 'inviter' had been employed to ask the women guests. The men were invited by the Shereef himself. Emily was concerned that there would be enough food to go around as a Moroccan meal could consist of anything up to thirty courses.

On the morning of the day a large ram was sacrificed, slaughtered by one of the Shereef's distinguished relatives, who after slitting the animal's throat, announced the child's chosen name. Emily was not unhappy that etiquette demanded she remain in her room while this was going on, but her mother who had decided to watch turned faintly green and vanished inside the house and rejoined her daughter.

The party was very noisy. House and garden were packed with talkative Moroccans, and a band of female musicians were seated in the centre courtyard of the house, playing their wailing, primitive instruments non-stop. The women guests had been segregated into various rooms while the men were together in the gardens. Every now and then the door of Emily's room would open and a shy, feminine figure, gorgeously dressed and hung with jewellery, would come to the bed to offer congratulations. Dark-eyes darted to take in all the European details of the room and the special hangings round the bed which the Shereef had said were necessary for the occasion. Then murmuring traditional compliments the figure would scuttle out again, carefully shutting the door.

'Why not take the baby down?' Emily had said to her mother in a quiet spell between visits and when the lady musicians appeared to have temporarily exhausted themselves. The child was not supposed to be seen because of the evil eye, but she had a sudden thought that when he came through smiling, it might have some effect on that particular superstition.

Rather doubtfully Emma Keene carried the baby out of the room and a few minutes later Emily was startled to hear an enormous din coming from downstairs. There was an outburst of zahrits, which set her teeth on edge; the women musicians started up again with a crash and a screeching wail. About two minutes later her mother shot into the room, dignity fled, her cap tipped to an angle. The expedition had not been a success. Everyone had tried to touch the baby—for his untarnished *baraka*—and it had looked at one point as if the child might be suffocated until Emily's mother had managed to fight her way back to her daughter's room.

There were a few rumbles of protest regarding all this unorthodox behaviour, particularly from an elderly relative of the Shereef's. The old man was angry at what he considered the terrible dangers to which the Nazarene was subjecting the baby Shereef.

He demanded that Moulay Ali be sent immediately to the safety of the Holy City of Wazan. When Emily refused, he tried to insist that a Moslem wet-nurse should be provided for the baby, obviously having the gravest doubts as to the suitability of a Christian mother's milk.

The old man voiced the fears of all the family, grumbling to the Shereef, until he was told to mind his own business and that the mother's wishes in the matter were of the most importance. The old man went away shaking his head, and Emily, though sorry for his distress, was relieved that she was to be permitted to bring up her child in her own way.

At the end of June, Moulay Ali was progressing well, gaining weight and thriving. The Shereef was the proudest of fathers. He would sit most evenings with Emily at the baby's bathtime, watching the performance and handing over nappies and towels.

'I saw very little of my other sons,' he said one day when he was handed the baby for a goodnight kiss. 'It seems a pity now that they were such strangers to me.'

The Shereefa's life at this time was cosily domestic. With her mother for company while the Shereef was away, and her growing knowledge of the language, plus the fact that the servants seemed to accept her more since the birth of the little Prince, she was contented and relaxed. Sadly, Lalla Heba remained a mystery, running way from both Emily and her mother, still as sullen and withdrawn as ever, in spite of everything they tried to do to win the child over.

Then one morning nearing July, Emma Keene came in to see her daughter holding a letter. It was good news. Emily's father had been appointed Governor of the Gaol with a salary of £600 a year and generous arrangements as to house, coals and gas. The Prison Commissioners had given his father a pension of £900 a year and Emily's father had written to say that the old man was to move to a new house in the country near Croydon. John Keene Junior's family were to take over the prison house. This meant that the Keene family would have held the post of Governor of the Surrey County prison for over a hundred years.

It also meant that Emma Keene would have to return home to supervise the move.

After her mother had left for England, Emily found herself with plenty to do. She had told the Shereef that now they had Moulay Ali to consider it would be better to move house from the sanctuary where so many of his visitors were often diseased and ill. She feared the child might catch some fatal illness, for there were no precautions against any spread of infection.

The Shereef agreed and Emily found a house not far from the Zowia which he rented until they could find something permanent. She undertook to direct the move and wrote to her mother remarking that they were both changing homes at the same time.

Gradually the European community had started to call on the Shereefa again and she welcomed them with charm and pleasure. But the breach with the Perdicaris family was not healed. Emily still resented the abrupt way in which Ellen Varley—now legitimately Mrs. Perdicaris—had treated her and Mrs. Perdicaris was still incensed at what she thought of as Emily's underhand behaviour. But she and the Shereef had made some friends. A ball on the occasion of their first wedding anniversary when 80 of the European community attended had helped to break the ice, and the continued support and friendship of Sir John Hay Drummond Hay and the Kirby-Green family also encouraged others to be more cordial.

There was no shortage of money. The Shereef showered gifts on his wife and baby, and the number of servants seemed to grow all the time. Vast sums of money were spent running both the Zowia and preparing the new home; the Shereef liked to be surrounded by the best horses, the most efficient servants, the finest cooks and the most plentiful amounts of food and drink. Emily sometimes wondered where all the money was coming from, and was more concerned about where it all went. She resolved that at some point she would get her hands on the housekeeping and see that things were arranged a little more frugally. There was the child's inheritance to think of.

She had met two of her step-sons by now and not been particularly impressed by the eldest, Moulay Alarbi. Nor he with her, though she and the younger boy, Moulay Mohammed, made friends immediately. All in all she was fitting into her new life very well. But—was becoming restless. Still only twenty-four, she had boundless energy; none of her curiosity had evaporated. She wanted to see much more of her adopted country. The Shereef was cautious about taking her from the confines of Tangier, a little uncertain himself as to the welcome she would get from his followers in the more primitive towns, and for all her pleading, one day's shooting in the Angera Hills on the way to Ceuta was all she had been permitted to do.

It was not until Moulay Ali was sixteen months old that she finally began to travel in a way that was to make her the first British woman to be completely familiar with the interior of Morocco.

Emily a few years after her marriage.

The Keene family. Left to right, Alice, Katherine, John Keene, Emma Keene, Emily holding Walter. Front row, John Junior.

Emily surrounded by her sons (Moulay Ali right, Moulay Ahmed left) when she was nearing her ninetieth birthday. Her eldest grandson, Moulay Hassan with medals, stands behind his father, to the left. The remaining grandsons are standing behind, great grandchildren in the front row.

Chapter Five

A DANGEROUS JOURNEY

The one thing to be said for travelling in Morocco in 1875 was that for the rich, it did not matter how much superfluous baggage was carted along to make an incipient uncomfortable journey more bearable. There were plenty of slaves, retainers, mules, donkeys, horses to do the work, plus any number of solitary travellers who joined the cavalcade to shelter in the safety of numbers. Several changes of clothing were taken in boxes loaded on pack mules as the country though reasonably well-off for rivers and streams, was totally lacking in bridges. Crossing water, particularly in the winter and spring months meant everyone was liable to end up on the further shore wet through. And when it did rain in Northern Morocco the water fell in torrents. Wet or dry, by night the open countryside became very cold.

Though the actual journeying over fields, mountains and 'bled' (desert) was difficult, the enormous tents which accommodated everyone were more comfortable and clean than the average Moroccan house. Layers of carpets were carried to cover the ground under the tents—(Europeans took camp beds)—plus a great deal of bedding and hangings to make the tents more homelike inside and to keep out draughts. Once the tents were pitched, a high standard of luxury resulted, as Emily found out on her first trip from Tangier to Tetuan, Cueta and on to Gibraltar.

Mahmoud, the head slave, a tall and fine-looking negro, was in charge of the preparations for the journey and Emily was a little surprised to note in all the bustle that very little food was being loaded and enquired of her husband as to whether it had been forgotten.

'It is not necessary to take food,' he said, and added:

'Allah will provide.'

Pressed, he explained that it was the duty of all the villages and towns on the way to feed him and his party. 'We call it *muna*,' he said.

Emily was shocked when he explained that no money passed hands. The offerings were meant as gifts, and it was considered wrong to press payment.

He explained that when the Sultan travelled with his army, the Court, slaves and retainers, the retinue could amount to more than 3,000 people, all of whom had to be fed and entertained by the people. The villagers said that the Sultan 'had eaten up the land', and it was not unknown for whole areas to starve, left completely penniless after he had passed by.

'It is the way things are done here,' he said. 'The Sultan knows this is one way of controlling the people. Hungry people are too busy growing more food to interfere politically.'

The journey was to be in the nature of a state visit for the Shereef. He had decided that it was time that he presented himself to his people, hardly having moved out of Tangier since his marriage. Also, though Emily did not realise it, it was time for the family coffers to be replenished. The journey would bring in large sums of money in gifts from the faithful, as well as presents of goods. The tradition was that the local dignitaries made offerings to a man as holy as the Grand Shereef of Wazan when he visited or even merely passed by their town or village.

Preparations were made in great excitement, particularly as Emily's second sister, Kate, who was just nineteen had arrived to spend some time in Morocco and would accompany them. The Shereef also decided to take Moulay Ali, then sixteen months old. Gifts would also come the child's way. The English nanny was to join the party to care for the boy and the Moroccan retainer, a gentle, tall thin bearded man named Mohar who had looked after the baby from the time of his birth would travel with them.

Emily had had her difficulties with Mohar in the beginning. He was ruled by superstition and genuinely fearful when Emily disregarded any of the ritual he believed essential to Moulay Ali's survival.

He suffered greatly from the fact that the Shereef ran a Zowia as he firmly believed that if bread were given to a neighbour after three in the afternoon, Moulay Ali would break out in cold sores. When the boy was under two months, he would whisk all the nappies, wet or dry, off the line: leaving the laundry out after the magic hour of three in the afternoon, would mean that the child would cry all night and keep them awake. He had been most concerned that Emily did not meet another young mother for forty days after Moulay Ali's birth—because it could mean death for one of the babies, and it might be Moulay Ali who passed away. Most irritating was his insistence that if the boy drank water before he was a year old, his guardian angel would desert him.

It was not only Mohar. Emily's mother had found all the dust from her daughter's room swept into a pile under a divan nearly a week after Moulay Ali was born. When reprimanded, the servant had wailed that it was bad luck for the baby to take sweepings out of the room. And all protested when the baby's whispy hair was brushed and combed. His nurses explained that it was necessary to wait a year before combing a baby's hair, and now the poor child would have large teeth.

In time, Emily and Mohar had come to terms. She had great affection for the kind old man who cared for her son, and would not have contemplated going away without Mohar being one of the party. It would also have upset Moulay Ali who loved his 'nurse' very much.

They set off in mid-afternoon, Moulay Ali pleased with himself in a brand new European style suit topped by fez and burnous, the Shereef impressive in flowing white and green turban, and Emily and her sister in severe riding habits as they had chosen to go on horse-back instead of in an enclosed litter—the way a Moroccan woman would have travelled.

The trail was rocky but the spectacular views of the sea below compensated for the discomfort of being bounced about as the horses picked their way carefully over potholes and boulders. Three hours outside of Tangier the Shereef's private party caught up with the servants, slaves and baggage mules who had left earlier. The Moors could put up tents at a speed that would shame a field regiment and already a little encampment was taking shape, with the fresh smell of mint tea in the air. The camp was also buzzing with outside activity as the entire population of the nearest village seemed to have gathered on the spot to watch the arrival of their Shereef.

Emily's only other excursions with the Shereef had been within the town of Tangier itself where he was a comparatively familiar figure to the people. She was used to the way they would rush forward to kiss his feet or the hem of his robe as he rode through the town, and his complete disregard of the attention paid to him. She had asked once why he made no move to acknowledge these obeisances. He shrugged and said that it would take all day, and besides, they did not expect him to do or say anything. They were touching him to receive the blessing of his *baraka*.

It was only when they began journeying throughout Morocco that she realised fully her husband was considered a holy saint by the people and began to experience the problems of such overwhelming devotion.

On arrival at the camp they found a great crowd of people waiting. As the Shereef came into their view, conspicuous in his green turban, the women of the crowd let out the zahrits, shrill as a high-pitched whistle, until Emily and her sister tried to clap their hands over their ears and hang on to the reins at the same time. Someone started to bang a small Moroccan drum, and the headsman of the village came forward to greet the Shereef. He was followed by all the women who temporarily ceased the zahrits while each one presented a bowl of milk. Solemnly the Shereef dipped a finger into each basin, and nodded for them to move on. The women, their tattooed faces alight with curiosity, brought the basins to Emily, who, rather startled, decided that the best thing to do was to follow her husband's example. Surreptitiously she licked her finger afterwards, finding that the milk, though sour in taste, was not unpleasant. The bowls were then handed around the Shereef's retainers and slaves and returned, empty, to their owners. More women moved forward with offerings of eggs and chickens which were accepted by a wave of the Shereef's hand. Then his personal servants, moved the women back rather roughly Emily thought, until they settled themselves a short way from the tents though near enough to watch what was happening. Every now and then a few would creep in closer, until a servant ordered them back to a respectful distance.

They remained nearly all night and were waiting to let out their ear-piercing cries when after a surprisingly good sleep the Shereef's party moved off again towards Tetuan. The route was lined with a straggle of people. Obviously the word had gone out that their holiest man was to pass by and no one wanted to miss seeing him. Every mile or so the entire cavalcade had to stop for the Shereef to receive the gifts of the people and bestow his blessing on their villages.

It was not a long journey. The party reached Tetuan the next day and Emily was enchanted by the town. It was much less spoilt than Tangier, cleaner with a pretty market, a Kasbah of charming narrow streets with carved wooden doors, hiding secret houses. But it was impossible to walk about. The Shereef was immediately surrounded by a clamouring crowd frightening in their determination to get near him instantly he appeared.

They were received by the Khalifa and welcomed by a long flowery speech of which Emily understood only a little, though what she did catch seemed to be embarrassingly complimentary. At the head of the procession of their own people, the Khalifa's people and a vast mob, they were taken to a pretty house set in an orange garden, furnished with taste in the Moroccan fashion of long narrow rooms, tiled walls lined with many relaxing couches and cushions. The thing that pleased Emily and her sister the most was the remarkable quantity of running water spouting out of taps in a highly civilised fashion. She recorded with satisfaction in her memoirs that they were all able to take a good bath to wash off the dust of the journey.

All the dignitaries of the town had come to pay homage to the Shereef, and their small son came in for his share of worship. He was hugged, petted and caressed, and though as yet he spoke only English, he was not shy at all the attention, and wandered from room to room collecting love pats from everyone present.

The visit to Tetuan was a success and she would like to have stayed longer. As it was they left after the third day to push on to Ceuta, a Spanish penal colony, where they were to be guests of the Governor. Emily knew that her husband had distinguished himself in the war against Spain some years earlier and had been responsible for keeping the Spanish at bay. She wondered how welcome they would be.

The short journey to Ceuta took a long time. More and more people gathered along the routes and vast quantities of gifts were presented—fortunately some pack mules being part of the loot—otherwise carrying the presents would have been a problem. The headsmen of the nearer village begged that the Shereef and his retinue would be their guests for the night. On the first evening out of Tetuan it became necessary to pitch camp twice, in two different villages, so that no one should be offended, and it was fortunate that the retainers were so speedy in erecting and dismantling the camp. Emily was embarrassed by the generosity of the people, particularly when she saw the sordid hovels in which many of them lived and hoped that their caravan was not 'eating up the land'. She said nothing, though, having resolved long before not to interfere in any matters of custom until she was totally established in the country.

The welcome at Ceuta was tumultuous. At the frontier a guard of soldiers was waiting to receive the Shereef with military honours; the route to the Governor's house was lined with crowds controlled by troops.

'Now I know how the dear Queen feels when she goes out,' Emily whispered to her husband as they rode along, gravely acknowledging the cheers, 'but it does make one feel a little silly.'

'The Queen?' the Shereef said. 'Remember that in this country you are quite as important as your Queen is in her land. Probably more-so. By marriage to me—you are holy.'

Kate who was riding just behind had to throttle back a giggle.

Ceuta was one long celebration. There were fêtes, parades, official visits, including one to the local prison. Emily and her sister were polite but shocked when they saw the state of the prisoners, chained, fettered, obviously hungry and living in filth, and compared the conditions with those at their father's jail back in London.

The prison Governor had been told by the Shereef that the Shereefa's father was in the same line of business and asked questions as to how things were done in England. He particularly wanted to know if there were many deaths.

'Grandpa scarcely ever had a prisoner die,' Kate told him, perhaps feeling she could be more outspoken than her sister. The prisoners were very well fed, she told him. They ate bread from one of Britain's best bakers, the Aerated Bread Company, and they received a balanced diet of oatmeal, barley, molasses, preserved meat and potatoes. 'And,' she added as a parting thrust, 'there is a prison doctor on constant call should any poor felon be taken ill.'

Her blue-grey eyes gave a significant look at one poor Spanish felon who looked in very poor health indeed.

After three hectic days while Emily learnt what it cost in effort to be always in the public eye, a Government steamer arrived to take the entire party for the $3\frac{1}{2}$ hour boat trip across the Straits to Gibraltar.

The journey started badly. The sea was rough and the Shereef was a poor sailor. Emily spent the time in his cabin, administering to him as best she could. The trip was to end badly also. The Shereef had expected considerable attention on his first visit to British territory, particularly as he was arriving with an English wife. What he did not appreciate was that the welcome would have been greater had he not had the temerity to marry one of her Britannic

Majesty's subjects. The difference between the adulation of Tetuan and Ceuta and the Gibraltar welcome was obvious from the moment of landing on the mole. Only an embarrassed British Army lieutenant and the Moorish Consul Hadj Said Guesus, were waiting for them. There was no guard of honour, no parade, no fuss at all.

They could not have arrived at a worse time. Already in Gibraltar paying a state visit, was H.R.H. the Duke of Connaught, Queen Victoria's son, and the British Garrison's time was fully occupied in keeping their Royal guest happy. The Governor, Sir Fenwick Williams, was in poor health—he resigned from his post less than a month after the Shereef's visit—so when Emily and the Shereef were invited to the Convent, the Governor's House, they were received by the Acting Governor, Major-General Somerset. Both were mollified to find that with the Major General was the Duke of Connaught himself with Colonel Baynes, the Colonial Secretary and various other high-ranking officers. Emily's pleasure at actually meeting one of the Queen's sons was rather spoilt when she was smitten with the thought that perhaps he had only been there out of curiosity to get a close look at the English girl who had been so foolish as to marry a Moor.

After the visit to the Convent, Gibraltarian society closed its doors and the Shereef and Shereefa were left to their own devices, or rather those which the harassed Moorish consul was able to arrange. Happily there was a performance at the Theatre Royal by the Italian Opera Company of *Rigoletto*. This, for two music lovers was a rare treat, and although they returned to Tangier the next day, the Shereef in a very bad temper about the expedition, they consoled themselves that the Opera had been worthwhile, and that Emily's gown, especially brought for the occasion, had quite put the other ladies to shame. She had looked magnificent; her brilliant hair wound around her head, her always perfect carriage even haughtier as she hid any signs of injured pride from the rest of the audience.

She *was* hurt at the reception from her own people, but told herself that the British did not understand how important her husband was. If she still found his power and popularity surprising, it was to be expected that the ordinary English were unaware. And Major General Somerset, who had been charming, had explained his many problems—the shooting incidents that were taking place on the Spanish frontier between the Spaniards and his troops, causing trouble with the Spanish Government; the honour, but strain, of entertaining a Royal Duke. In an attempt to calm the Shereef who was very displeased with his reception she tried to explain all this.

But the Shereef was not convinced.

She was not sorry to be back in Tangier. In Gibraltar, surrounded by British people, she had felt shy and uncomfortable. The memory of the press's attitude to her wedding was too recent. She felt everyone must be looking at her, thinking that the Shereef probably beat her, and wondering about his three other wives whom, on the surface of things, he had callously divorced. It was an odd state of mind for her to find herself in. She was not shy, not timid, afraid of nothing, and yet the superiority of her own fellow countrymen; the condescension with which they had greeted her husband left her defenceless.

Not only defenceless—angry, too. She wanted to tell them about Sidi. About how kind and generous he was to her, and how far-thinking. No one realised what concern he had for his own country and the difficulty of his position. Europeans seemed to think him some kind of a monster. She wished they could see him playing with Moulay Ali, and see how his sense of humour was so funny and unexpected.

Gibraltarian society, though! Who were they? No one! All that mattered was that she and Sidi were happy together.

Back now in the protective atmosphere of Morocco, she thought out the attitudes raised in both her and others because of the brief journey to British soil. The results of her thinking were disturbing. In Morocco, disapproved of or not, she was a personage. She had her place as the wife of the most influential man in Morocco. The only comparable position would have been that of Sultana—

but had she married the Sultan, her life would have been shared with three other wives and many concubines. She would never have been permitted to appear in public. Her situation was entirely preferable, particularly now the Moroccans seemed to be slowly going half-way towards accepting her.

She liked her life. The kind of welcome that she and her husband had received in Ceuta and Tetuan had been very pleasing (if exhausting). What would it be like to go back to being an ordinary wife and mother in England? Or even France? It would be, she realised, an anti-climax. Instead of being *Son Altesse*, the wife of the Grand Shereef of Wazan, she would be known as that English woman who had actually married some Moor.

After the humiliating visit to Gibraltar, Emily saw her life and future in an entirely different way. She completely accepted the destiny which the encounter with the Varley family had led to and realising she was committed to Morocco and that any hankerings for Europe were pointless, set herself on the course of action that made her one of the real influences for good in Tangier in the nineteenth century and on into the twentieth century. She always kept her British friends, but she never let herself regret the loss of her status with the British again. And once she no longer cared, fickle public opinion eventually swung again in her direction.

It was two years since her marriage at the time of the Gibraltar visit in December 1875. After that date Emily saw herself as citizen of Morocco, though if anything her tastes and habits hardened into an even more British mould. This was one thing about herself she could not change. Her upbringing had been too positive. Morocco in some ways was going to have to come into step with her.

But it was still to be some time before the Moors began to trust her sufficiently for her to begin some of the small but important reforms which so helped the country take a few faltering steps into the modern world.

* * *

The Shereef was put out by Gibraltar and sulked. It

was admittedly provoking. The French and the Spanish treated him with deference and courtesy and the British brushed him off like a bluebottle. He was full of resentment, but fortunately for the peace of the Wazanni household, mollified by an invitation from Sir John Hay Drummond Hay to a boar hunt—locally known as pig-sticking—which was being mounted for the Duke of Connaught.

The Royal Duke had skipped from Gibraltar in his yacht, *Vega,* just four days after the Shereef and Emily had departed, probably as bored with the garrison town as they had been, and moved into Drummond Hay's comfortable Legation in Tangier which was a livelier resting place than the claustrophobic Rock.

The pig-sticking expedition took place thirteen miles from Tangier with an escort of Moorish hunters lead by a fearless, elderly man, Hadj Hamed. Emily was not invited to join—it was strictly a men's outing, but the Shereef promised that he would take her on another occasion.

He returned home in high good humour after the hunt. He was a fine sportsman and had acquitted himself well at what was a dangerous and unpredictable sport. Sir John had 'invented' the pig-sticking as far as Morocco was concerned. Then in his sixties he still led the Moorish hunters, who, wearing leather aprons and greaves to protect their legs would act as beaters through the thick woods, carrying bill-hooks to cut a path deep into the thickets where the boar lay. They used native dogs, ugly but fearless mongrels, that looked rather like a cross between a collie dog and a greyhound, whose noses were keen enough to wind a boar from a considerable distance.

The boar, when scented and driven generally made straight for the hunters. The animals would break in the herd, one following the other, separately and continuously. A man needed a steady hand, a cool head and a fine aim if he was not to be injured by the fiercesomely tusked beast. Guns were never used on these expeditions—there were complicated laws made by the Sultan regarding the use of fire-arms by Europeans in Morocco, to which Sir John rigidly adhered, to the detriment of his own popularity with his own countrymen. To get over the problem of how to kill Sir John had revived the principle of hunting with spears. Made of wood, these lances could prove unreliable. The hunter often found himself with a broken shaft in his hand, face to face with several hundred pounds of vengeful animal.

It had been a good few days sport, the Shereef said on his return. Many boar had been killed, they had sighted a panther and there were half-a-dozen brace of partridge in the kitchen. He also conceded that the Duke of Connaught was not too bad a fellow at all.

But the Shereef had come back troubled. There had been more than just the pleasure of his company to prompt Sir John Hay Drummond Hay's invitation to the hunt. He wanted something from the Shereef. M. Tisset, the French Consul, had approached the Shereef on the same matter, and failed, and the Frenchman had asked Sir John to try when the Shereef was in a good mood—on the hunting expedition.

What they wanted was for the Shereef to use his influence to capture a bandit called Si Sliman Ben Kaddour. The Sidi had agreed and now asked Emily if she would like to come on the expedition to Algeria, where Si Sliman was living.

Emily pondered. Obviously the time had come when the Shereef was going to have to begin to earn his $16,000 a year from the French. Now, from his expression and demeanour, it appeared that actually faced with the prospect of aiding them against his own co-religionist, he was not so certain that the arrangement was a good one.

Though France had seized and colonised Algeria in 1830, even forty-five years later there were those who still resented foreign domination and spent their time making life as complicated as possible for their conquerors. One of these was Si Sliman Ben Kaddour, the chief of the Oulad Sidi Sheik tribe. He, too, counted Mohammed as an ancestor, but his spiritual chief was Sidi Hadj Abdeslam, Grand Shereef of Wazan.

Si Sliman had settled himself with his tribe on the border of Morocco and Algeria well inland near the area called Ain Beni Matha. From here with his rebels mounted on swift horses, and well-armed with help from fellow Moslems in Morocco, he was able to make swift sorties into French territory doing damage to both the property and persons of those he considered collaborators. To the chagrin of the French Army, they had not been able to catch him; he was a fine shot, a fearless rider and cunning. He had once found himself in a house where French officers were in the next room and had escaped by dressing in women's clothes. The French authorities were thwarted and for some months had been trying to persuade the Shereef to intervene. Then Sir John had suggested that perhaps Si Sliman could be persuaded to settle permanently in central Morocco with his retainers—somewhere too far away for border raids into Algerian territory, and as an inducement, be given land and seed so that the tribe might have some means of living. The plan had been cleared with the Sultan of Morocco who was willing to give Si Sliman asylum. All that remained was for someone to persuade him to take up the offer, and the only one with sufficient influence was the Shereef of Wazan. The only snag was that Si Sliman would be required to surrender to the French which would require a great deal of persuasion indeed.

This then was the delicate mission on which Emily was to accompany her husband. His reasons for taking her, their small son and her sister Kate were that with them in the party, Si Sliman would know that he had come in peace.

Emily knew her husband was troubled and suggested that he refuse to go. He shrugged. 'It will be better for Si Sliman in the end,' he said. 'The French will catch him one day and kill him, and though he may feel for his honour there is no point in firing at the bird that is out of range. The French have Algeria and they will stay there. Si Sliman will change nothing.'

It took a month for the negotiations for the mission to be completed, and finally the instructions were received. The Shereef was to proceed to Oran in Algeria and negotiate with Si Sliman for his surrender to the Sultan of

Morocco and the French Government.

They left for Oran on a French man o' war *Le Cassard* on February 17th, 1876. Emily knew she was pregnant again, but kept silent in case the Shereef changed his mind about taking her along. She was excited by the idea of seeing more of North Africa and felt perfectly fit and healthy. There had been no problems carrying Moulay Ali and there seemed no reason why the same should not apply with this new baby. She had confided in her sister who expressed alarm that she should undertake such a hazardous journey *enceinte*.

'Oh really, Kate,' Emily said cheerfully. 'You know I have always been quite disgustingly healthy. Pregnancy is hardly an illness. Look at mama. Twenty times and still in such good health.'

Kate could be a tart at times. 'And look how many babies mama lost,' she said.

Le Cassard was a speedy boat and thirty-six hours later the Wazanni family landed in Oran where they were met by Government officials and taken to a central hotel. It seemed strange to be riding in a carriage again, and see paved roads and clean, modern looking buildings.

'It is hard to be too firm in one's feelings about colonisation when one looks at the difference between this town under French occupation and the conditions of our town,' said the Shereef very quietly in Arabic. 'There should be some middle way.'

The hotel was luxurious and comfortable; a suite of private apartments had been reserved for the Shereef's party, but in spite of all the modernity of Oran, one thing had not changed—the attitude of the Moslem to their spiritual leader. Within minutes of the Shereef's arrival the hotel proprietor was beginning to look as if he wished he had never let the rooms. A vast crowd had gathered outside his premises, swarming into the entrance hall, the women shrilling their joy cries, the men shouting to see the holy man. Finally in desperation the doors were locked and the proprietor called for the police to move the crowds, but like wasps, they merely swarmed in another place—at the back of the hotel.

He eventually appealed to the Shereef to do something, *anything* to move them away.

The Shereef suggested that if a few at a time were let into the hall for his personal benediction they might then depart.

The proprietor hurried away to ask the police to make an announcement to the crowds and the Shereef placed himself in the entrance lobby where handfuls of people were let in and then whisked out through the rear. Emily settled herself at the back of the room to watch the slow procession and found herself surprised and moved by the devotion of the people who were not even of her husband's nationality. Men cried as they touched his hand or the hem of his robe. Some of the petitioners carried small mysterious bundles which the Shereef blessed, and once they realised that the Shereef's wife and son were also present Emily had to retire quickly to her room and lock herself in. She was embarrassed by the amount of money and small gifts of jewellery which had been thrown into her lap, while the donors hurried away with a word. There had been no chance of refusing or even thanking. There seemed to be no resentment about her being a Nazarene in Algeria. Perhaps 45 years of constant contact with French Christians had broken down some of the Algerian's long-cherished hatred of the followers of Jesus Christ.

The system of *Yiasa*—gifts from the faithful—was to bother Emily's Victorian conscience for many years. The gifts thrown into her lap she could do little about on that first occasion, but she was furious when one of the Caids of Oran begged an audience to meet the Shereef and his son, presented Moulay Ali with some money and then thrust a bag containing 25 French louis into her hand.

Unable to speak the Algerian dialect of Arabic, she drew herself up to her full height, left her chair and demanded of her husband that he return the money.

'I find myself insulted by this gift,' she said.

The Shereef burst out laughing.

'Never reject the food the Gods have sent,' he said. 'Keep it.'

His tone was firm under the laughter and she made

hurried and embarrassed thanks to the Caid, then sat looking at the money in some dismay. No one could have been more thrifty and careful with money than Emily—in later years whenever any of her grandchildren required a new pair of shoes, she would insist on inspecting the old pair to make sure they were worn out—but like most money-conscious people she was extremely honest and proud, too.

Later in the trip yet another Caid presented her with a very fine diamond ring. She looked at the ring, looked at her husband, stood indecisive and uncomfortable.

'Go on, take it,' the Shereef whispered in Spanish, 'if you don't want it, I'll have it.'

She learned to accept *Yiasa* as the years went by, but managed to evolve a system of dodging it as much as possible by melting quietly away when anyone with money in his hand came purposefully towards her.

The Shereef had been firm that she must not refuse if any gift was actually presented. The donor would have been offended and possibly even afraid that by her rejection of the gift he would have lost the Shereef's *baraka*. Faith in that *baraka* was so strong, that the people believed any seed he blessed would produce a fine crop; that should he enter their home it would be a happy and prosperous one. Single women believed that a talisman from him would find them a husband. *Yiasa* became another custom of the country that Emily was forced to learn to accept, though years later, when her circumstances changed and her financial resources were strained she confided to friends that had she been less sensitive on the subject she might have been better off by at least £600 which then would have been very useful.

They remained some days in Oran while the Shereef received his briefings from the French authorities on his approach to Si Sliman. Emily and her sister enjoyed the stay; the pleasure of walking on streets where the pavements did not stumble one in ditches which promptly landed one's shins on a conveniently placed rock. It was pleasant to drive again in a carriage, and to see shops with French goods for sale.

It was as well they had the rest before setting off for Si Sliman's stronghold. The journey to Ain Beni Matha was a long and trying one although the pregnancy did not appear to be disturbing Emily's health. The weather was cold; the scenery monotonous at first and then wild and mountainous over tracks which plunged dizzily below and sometimes so high that peaks of high mountains lay below. They travelled by diligence—pulled by mules, and Moulay Ali slept most of the way lulled by the jingling of the bells attached to the mule's harness. Everywhere crowds waited and in the towns, the going became very slow as the people crowded round the diligence, almost overturning it in their excitement, defeating the police who tried to keep them away. Some of the *Yiasa* proved nearly lethal. Coins tied in rags were thrown in through the window of the carriage, one striking Emily hard on the forehead, and just missing the boy.

'Really,' said Kate, as she rubbed the bruise for her sister, 'who would have thought that being holy could prove downright dangerous.'

The Shereef was suffering also. One step outside the carriage and the clothes were torn from his back, a piece of the cloth of his djelabah being the most powerful of talismans. Pleasanter offerings were bunches of almond blossom and wild roses, and soon the inside of their conveyance looked like a bower.

By the time they reached nightly stopping places, they were exhausted and locked themselves in their rooms. In the mountain town of Tlemcen, which Emily would have loved to explore for its superb ancient ruins, the hotel was totally devoid of baths and it was necessary to use a nearby *Hammam*. Unfortunately the word leaked out as to where they were, and it became impossible to get back to the hotel and in desperation they took refuge in the Zowia of Mulay Taib, Kate remarking that she would have thought Emily had quite sufficient of the Zowia atmosphere back home in Tangier. The Shereef had vanished and Emily became anxious until a servant came with the news that he had remained in the hall of the *Hammam* in order to give his blessing to the crowd in the faint hope of dispersing them.

Great banquets were laid on, and Kate was hurriedly coached in the etiquette of eating Moslem fashion, Emily explaining that there would be as many as twenty courses. Sometimes more if the family were very rich. And that something must be eaten from each dish.

Kate said it was impossible—as it was. Even the Victorian English with their vast appetites could not cope with twenty courses.

Emily explained that all that was needed was to take a piece of bread, break it into the gravy and eat a little—that was sufficient to satisfy the host. She explained also how the food must be eaten with the right hand, which was washed by servants before the start of the meal and again at the end of the meal.

Actually Emily rather enjoyed Moroccan banquets. The food could be delicious; vast haunches of lamb roasted with herbs and nuts. Chickens cooked in honey and with raisins. The main dish kouskous—made with a kind of semolina topped by a savoury stew when properly prepared was good to eat and having a sweet tooth she had a weakness for the almond and honey cakes which were always served. She had become quite comfortable with the ritual of eating—the Moors sat on the floor to eat from tables about six inches high. She was accustomed to eating with her fingers, and understood the Moors' opinion of cutlery which they considered very dirty indeed. In fact, they considered it disgusting that anyone should put something in their mouths which had been used by someone else the day before. Their own clean hand going into their own mouth seemed considerably more hygienic. She never worried about eating food in any Moorish surroundings, having learnt that though their clothing might be grubby and bodies unwashed, every pot, pan or utensil used to cook was scrupulously clean.

It had taken longer to get used to the explosions of belches and burps which ended every meal. (Kate's face looked as if someone had made an improper suggestion the first time she heard the volley proceeding from the several dozen guests at a banquet) and it was odd being the only woman present. With Kate to sit beside her she felt less self-conscious.

On the journey from Marnia deeper inland the baby was taken ill with convulsions. The Shereef whom Emily knew to be as sentimental as a schoolgirl under his lordly and impressive exterior, cried over the child until eventually Mouley Ali was sick, proving the cause of the disaster to be too much hard boiled egg. Emily herself had been terrified at the signs of his illness. They had been crowded in by people with terrible diseases, blind, crippled and sometimes leprous. She feared at first that Moulay Ali had caught something from one of her husband's worshippers.

The mountains behind them, the route became treeless and waterless depressing with the only vegetation a plentiful crop of alfalfa. They were well inland and skirting the border with Algeria and Morocco when they reached the place intended as the rendezvous. There was no sign at all of Si Sliman. This put the Shereef in a very bad temper indeed. He was not accustomed to his subjects leaving him waiting in the middle of primitive desert country. There was nowhere suitable to pitch the tents, no water.The place was totally unprotected from attack. And there was no guarantee that Si Sliman would not abandon his religious scruples in favour of his patriotic ones.

'What now, MacDuff?' said Emily.

'We wait.'

The camp became very quiet and tension sharp in the heat of the day. The Shereef sat motionless on his horse, his face furious under the green silk turban. The diligence left behind long ago, Emily and Kate, dismounted from their horses and settled themselves on a convenient boulder, letting down the skirts of their riding habits and removing as much dust as possible. The soldiers stood quietly staring across the sand and scrub, waiting for attack or at least something to happen. Moulay Ali, who had been happily chasing a brilliant butterfly suddenly caught the scent of fear and began to grizzle a little. Emily busied herself amusing him.

Suddenly the silence was broken by a wild shout from

one of the Shereef's bodyguard. On the horizon, some miles away, was silhouetted the solitary figure of a man on horseback. He repeated the cry which echoed out over the desert and raised his arm in a beckoning gesture. A hurried consultation took place between Shereef and soldiers. Was it a trap?

There was nothing to do but go on. The man in the distance, seemingly alone waited there for a while and then galloped towards them, a cloud of dust hovering behind him as his horse's hooves disturbed the coarse sand. When he reached them he stopped his horse by rearing it up, then leapt from the saddle to salute the Shereef and explained they were in the wrong place. Ain Beni Matha was at least an hour's ride further on. Si Sliman was waiting there, as agreed, to receive his spiritual chief. Once again they pressed on. The horses were tired and the sand slowed them down, they dragged their feet through it like weary children going home from a beach. The men were hungry, dispirited and still fearful. The swollen horizon stretched on shimmering into the sky; there was no man, no animal to be seen in the distance.

It was nearly two hours later before Ain Beni Matha came into sight, but now the track curved so that it was impossible to see far ahead and the ground rose slightly. Huge gleaming blocks of stone caught the sunlight, dazzling the eyes but there was no sight of Si Sliman. The Shereef drew to a halt, and the troop of soldiers, slaves and servants stopped behind him. It was very still. A horse snorted, making Emily jump.

They waited, listening, the Shereef chewing on his finger, when the sound of the plodding hooves of horses was heard. Every man's hand went to his rifle as the jingle jangle noise of arms of all descriptions came from behind the rise of land. And then like a bugle call in the open desert a chant: 'There is no God but one God and Mohammed is his Prophet.'

The men of the Shereef's party, their hands off their guns, took up the call. It reverberated in the air, fervent and impressive, making a shiver run down Emily's back. Her husband's eyes had filled with tears, and they moved forward slowly to the top of the rise.

There was no warning of the appearance of a white-robed mounted figure which stood before them in carved stillness. The horse was magnificent in green and gold trappings and the man carried a long curved sword at his side, a gun on his shoulder. He so impressed Emily that years later she was able to describe how he wore a large turban, covered with the hood of his burnous, which was bound down to his temples with yards and yards of camel-hair cord in which was woven a little green silk and gold thread. Inside his numerous burnouses when thrown back, gleamed a green silk cord across his breast, falling under the left arm where the Koran was attached, wrapped in a silk handkerchief, and in his belt gleamed a couple of pistols.

The horse shivered for a moment, and then the man came at full gallop towards the Shereef, and Kate, behind let out a small scream, thinking that he meant harm. But a few yards from the motionless Shereef, the horse reared until he was almost upright on his hind legs and Si Sliman flung himself from the saddle, in front of the Shereef's horse, kissed the horse's forelegs and lay there, his face in the dust.

The Shereef looked down and gently pulled his beard, regarding the still figure, then he motioned two slaves to lift the man to his feet. Face streaked with tears and dust, Si Sliman looked almost bewildered and then he moved to the Shereef's side, took his hand and kissed it time and time again. The Shereef sat perfectly still, staring ahead, ignoring the sobs which shook Si Sliman. The noisy sobs were the only sound on the rise for some minutes; everyone seemed to be waiting to breathe and then on a deep sigh, the man found his composure, moved to Emily, took her hand and said a word of welcome in French. She felt sorry for him; he looked broken. But dignity recovered, he remounted the waiting horse, and courteously led them into a small valley which lay beyond the rise where he and his men had pitched camp. It was cleverly hidden by tall brushwood and boulders and would have been completely invisible unless someone had stumbled on it by accident. Emily began to have some idea as to how he had avoided the French for so long.

There were seven hundred men in the encampment, and they remained as still as the boulders surrounding them until Si Sliman made a sign that it was in order to greet their spiritual head. Then the men both mounted and on foot scrambled to surround the Shereef and Emily to touch them. Looking down at the fierce, bearded rebels at her saddle, Emily saw that most were crying; a look of ecstasy on their faces.

The celebrations began. Everyone fired his gun into the air, firing off shot after shot. The air was thick with the acrid smell of powder, and Moulay Ali clapped his hands with pleasure at the din, while Kate who was witnessing her first 'powder-play' was fighting not to duck.

The Shereef and his family were led with great respect through the crowd, while the gunfire still raised flocks of distressed birds. Kate was much alarmed even though Emily explained that she had never seen anyone killed yet by powder-play. They were taken to a handsomely arranged Marquee where all collapsed on the many cushions laid out for their comfort. Apprehension, plus exhaustion had finished them, except for Moulay Ali who was as lively as ever. A tea-tray appeared and the homely smell of mint brewing and the mint tea itself had considerable reviving powers, and the Shereef sent for Si Sliman to join them.

He came into the tent, a tall man with hard, direct black eyes and a very dark skin. His robes were white and clean—he had changed from the garments in which he had met the Shereef. Again he lay mute at the Shereef's feet and was pulled upright by the slaves. Still on his knees, he kissed the Shereef's hand and without rising, shuffled across to Emily to kiss her hand also.

'Be seated,' the Shereef said, pointing to a mattress. Si Sliman bowed and settled himself and a slave brought him a cup of tea. He took it, but his hand trembled so that the liquid slopped as he picked up the cup. Without ceremony the Shereef had produced two letters from under his burnous and he gave them to Emily to pass to Si

Sliman and then began chatting casually to his wife and sister-in-law ignoring the other man.

Si Sliman handled the letters reluctantly, and then he placed the one that was from the King of Morocco to his forehead, took a knife and opened it. He looked doubtful, frowned and then sighed as he read it and said: 'I am your slave; do what you think best.'

He then read the other letter which was from the Governor General Chanzy in Algiers, shook his head, and said sadly: 'What is there to do or to say except to tell you that I agree to conform to all the terms laid down in these letters.'

'It is well,' said the Shereef.

Emily had been impressed and proud of the way her husband had handled Si Sliman. His dignity had been almost chilling. She had not realised that he could be so princely. With her, except for school-boy sulks and tantrums occasionally, he was always amusing and loving; very much a kindly family man. And sentimental. His heart was easily touched. She had to look at him twice to recognise in the implacable commanding figure, lolling on a mass of cushions, but still rock hard, as her husband whose eyes would fill with tears if their little son cried out in any pain. And she felt sad that as manly a man as Si Sliman should be forced to subject himself in front of her and her sister, even though he was the author of many cruel deeds, had sent a bullet through a general's brain, and routed an army of superior strength to his own followers.

She could not help but like him as a man, he and she became friendly. He talked to her about his life over the past few years and insisted that he had not intended to oppose the Algerian Government.

'It started because one of my lieutenants disobeyed my orders and killed a man,' he said. 'They would not believe that I had nothing to do with the matter, so if the blame was to fall upon me, I determined to harass the Government, so that if punishment was to be mine, I should at least deserve it.'

Quite used to odd quirks (by European standards) of

Arab character and reasoning, Emily believed him. He had left the post that he held under the French and taken to the desert where no one had been able to catch up with him, though he was nearly caught on many occasions.

'I left Tlemcen with an armoury of bullets in my turban and my body encased in cartridges and escaped on a fine horse with the French after me,' he told her.

'Poor horse!' said Emily. 'No animal could carry such a load and as you describe gallop for dear life.'

He bowed to her.

'I called on God and Moulay Abdallah Shereef and patron saint of Wazan and Dar de Mana (the house of protection) and obtained spiritual aid.'

Emily acknowledged the compliment and asked: 'But why did you accept the terms to remain in Morocco? They might never have caught you?'

He bowed again.

'How could I do otherwise when Sidi Hadj Abdeslam came to fetch me and brought his wife and son so far from their homes for a humble slave such as I am. I am but clay. Mould me as you desire.'

'In thy strength,' said Emily, the correct answer to a compliment, and mentally congratulated her husband on his understanding of his opponent.

The worst of the situation was yet to come for Si Sliman. He had agreed to the Shereef's demands, he would surrender to the French, he would settle in Morocco and he would cause no more disturbance in the colony. But he had to explain to his many followers that he would lead them no longer in the battle for independence. It was in situations such as this that the really incredible sway that the Shereef of Wazan had over his people could be judged. Emily herself remarked that to be his wife was rather similar to being married to the Pope, and there is really no other parallel. Some previous Shereefs had throned and dethroned Sultans at will and therefore could perhaps be compared to the Bishops of Medieval England, but the power of the Bishops was nowhere near as great. The hold of the Grand Shereef of Wazan was emotional, superstitious, traditional and religious—a formidable combination—and even with men as intelligent as Si Sliman it was unbeatable. The Wazans did not solely rule the illiterate and unintelligent—but the educated and aware as well.

It was a state which could only apply to a deeply religious people—and the Moors were deeply religious; the tenets of their faith etched on their attitudes, their thinking and their entire way of life. Even their communication between each other was bound up with religion. The educated man would base his conversations on quotations from the Koran. Ordinary conversations between simple people were injected with a punctuation of 'God be praised'. And the sayings of their faith had acquired extra powers. To rid themselves of a too lingering guest the phrase 'God Give Thee Peace' would be a sufficient hint for the visitor to take up his djelabah and depart. A query for news brought forth the automatic reply: 'All right, thank God', if all were well, or should the news be bad: 'God knows. Everything is in the hands of God.' An odd situation which would cause an Englishman to exclaim: 'Well I never', brought a response from a Moslem of: 'Bless the Prophet.' It would be unthinkable to eat without saying the grace of 'In the Name of God'. In any kind of doubt the cry was 'I ask pardon of God the Great'. And the petition, covering all ills was 'I seek refuge with God from Satan, the stoned'.

Many of these phrases remain with present day Moslems as part of their lives. As Christians use 'God bless you', the Moors say, 'God hasten thee'. But today the sayings are, as in Europe, generally used as habit without the true religious thought behind. But in 1875 when Emily began to learn more about her adopted country these and many other phrases were used with meaning and portent. The religion was the anchor of the country, understand-

* Today Emily's descendants of the Wazan family are respected in Morocco and still considered holy by some of the population. But education, the gradual bringing of the country into the twentieth century has lessened their influence. They still hold positions of power, and are still in the service of the people as was Emily's husband in the days when Morocco was without proper government, roads, police and the appurtenances of civilisation and when the Shereef's word was law.

ably as without faith the people of what was then a backward land would have had little to carry them over the desperate problems of day to day existence.

What happened the morning after the meeting with Si Sliman gave Emily more knowledge of her husband's hold over the Moslem population. At his request Si Sliman was to return to Oran leaving his followers behind in the desert. They were to join him later in Morocco when the Sultan had granted land and seed. The followers appeared in hordes, some mounted, some on foot immediately after the tents were struck and the baggage mules loaded. They came silently and arranged themselves, squatting, in a semi-circle on the ground, making a rough theatre of the small valley where the Shereef's party had spent the night. Behind the seated Arabs were a ring of men on horseback. All waited until the Shereef appeared in the apron of the semi-circle and a huge roar rose from nearly a thousand throats. They then approached in dozens to receive benediction. The scene had a look of church; open sky and the rough grass within the small valley forming a natural Cathedral with the Shereef as the priest. When all had stepped forward for the communion with their spiritual leader there was silence for a moment or two, and then Si Sliman stepped to the fore. The Shereef with tact and courtesy fell back to stand beside his wife.

Si Sliman was impressive. He stood wrapped in his *burnous,* his turban wound about his head, fingering his small and rather shaggy beard. He carried a long staff like a Biblical shepherd which he placed in front of him as a support and then he leaned forward and began to speak in a clear, reverberating voice. As he spoke, explaining his decision, the people in front of him moaned and swayed and listened to every word. After twenty minutes, the speech ceased, and he stood, leaning resignedly on the staff. The people rose and rushed to touch him, anguish on their faces. Without him, their chances of freedom from the Nazarene had gone, but none questioned his decision. He had been commanded by the Shereef of Wazan who was holy and knew the word of God, and if *God* commanded, there was nothing to do but submit....

They tore at his clothes, until his turban tipped to one side. Kate, who did not really understand all that was going on remarked in a stage whisper: 'Doesn't he look funny!' Emily threw her a warning look.

It would have been a time of complete humiliation for Si Sliman. He had seen himself as the defender of his faith, but now the man who represented his faith on earth had told him that he must give the infidel a free hand in his own land. Head bowed and silent, he mounted his horse and took his place in the cavalcade which rode back towards Oran where he was to surrender himself to his enemies. His followers came too. They ran on foot, keeping up for many miles, anxious to lose sight neither of their spiritual chief nor their rebel leader.

The French treated Si Sliman with courtesy in Oran. He was to travel back to Morocco as the Shereef's prisoner. But now the Wazannis were in Algeria, it was proposed that the Shereef should return to Lalla Maghnia* and settle tribal disputes which had been raging between neighbouring towns in the area, in particular Oujda, a town just over the border in Morocco, which had been in a state of siege for two years. Not only the French were pressing for the Shereef's intervention; many of the Moslems from the area themselves were tired of the perpetual warfare and bloodshed. Si Sliman was left in comfortable apartments, but very much under an unobtrusive guard in Oran. The French would have preferred him moved immediately back to Tangier, but the Shereef pointed out he could not be in two places at once. In a day or two Emily and her husband set off again to the West, towards the frontier to try to make peace.

At the first stop, Marnia, the discussions with the chiefs went well. Negotiations were not easy. The mountain men with whom the Shereef was dealing would carry on blood feuds with other tribes and families for many years. Small boys would grow up with one aim—to buy a gun and avenge a relative who had been killed by a member of another tribe, and when that was done, another small boy from the other side inherited the ambition. Like a picture

* Now Marnia.

pictured in a looking glass, the war went on and on endlessly.

Marnia settled the Shereef decided to go on to the town of Oudja. A strong escort was provided by the local tribes, a fearsome-looking rabble of cut-throat mountain men, and after a great deal of quarrelling and arguing as to which was the best route, they eventually set off over the violent, brown Atlas mountains for the three hour ride to Oujda.

Emily and her sister were beginning to become blasé now about the powder play, the screeching noises and the incredible displays of devotion which met them whereever they went. As they came down the mountains from Algeria, the 'bled' of Morocco lay ahead, fair with corn, and fruit at this early season of the year, the frontier marked by a small stream which ran alongside the mountains. Wearily the horses and mules plodded through the water, stopping to nuzzle some of the brown, brackish stuff, and then on into the heat of the land. 'Powder play commenced outside the town,' Emily remarked briskly in her description of the journey, 'and continued to the gates of Oujda.'

Today Oujda is a pleasant, busy little town; then it was a sprawling series of hovels, guarded by a wall and surrounded by olive groves. The road was ill-kept and wound about so that the visitor tripped upon the town walls by accident. As they neared the gates of the town, the crowd became dense, people were trampled under foot and screams of pain mingled with those of ecstasy. 'But,' pointed out Emily, 'they would die for the sight of their religious chief. If it was written, such was their destiny.'

Quite a few of the population of Oujda were to meet their destiny that night.

They arrived within the town walls, tempers and clothing frayed. Emily's riding habit had been torn by the constant tugging of the crowds, and the horses were restive and bad tempered with some reason. A hair from their tails was as good a talisman as anything. The Shereef had lost most of his djelabah and Kate was suffering from hands pulling at her clothes.

People were eating the ground from where the Shereef's

horse's hooves had been, and those who were not making a meal of mud, were smearing it over their hands and faces.

It took head-cracking from the heavy sticks of the escort before an entry into the town and a path to the house where they were to lodge could be made, and somewhere in the last few minutes of the journey, Moulay Ali and Kate had disappeared. Emily was rarely disturbed except at the thought of danger to a child, and most particularly her child. She was frantic, but one of the escort hurried to reassure her that all were safe. They had taken another route to the house and managed to arrive with little fuss. Mohar, always mindful of his charge's safety had left the column, leaving the burden of welcome on the Shereef and Shereefa. Moulay Ali and Kate were already installed safely in the house.

Emily immediately got to work to make the place livable. The outside had depressed her but inside it was not as bad as she had expected, and she busied herself demanding carpets and rugs and arranging the furniture that they carried with them. She was a determined homemaker, no matter where she was put down, and two years as the wife of an influential man had re-inforced her natural authority. She demanded what she needed for comfort for her family and always got it.

But in spite of the comfort within the house that she managed to arrange, the night was to be a bad one. As the sun went down, dropping behind the plain like a penny in a slot the moon rose, full and clean, lighting the town, and casting weird shadows. The night was very quiet at first, except for some desultory firing at the edge of the town which they decided must be a continuation of the celebrations in the Shereef's honour. This proved to be wishful thinking. The noise increased, the sharp cracks rattling the cool night air. There was some kind of battle going on.

Outside the town in the olive groves, the men of Oujda thinking themselves protected by the Shereef's presence in their town, were settling old scores. They had left the town, gone to the cafés which clustered on the outside walls, and there met some of the men from the interior who had followed the Shereef to Oujda. These men were of the tribes who had been holding the town of Oujda at siege. A quarrel began, which turned to blows which turned to gunpowder. In the same way as in gun battles in the newly discovered West of America, everyone joined in. The authorities panicked, the town gates were closed and those outside refused admittance.

Emily was just ordering the mint tea to finish their meal when an official of the town arrived to see her husband.

'Oh Lord, what shall we do?' he asked, 'the men of the town are outside the gates and they fight with the men from the hills. But the mothers and wives of the men cry out to let back their men, for if we do not open the gates, they will surely be killed and if we do open the gates it may be that we shall all be killed.'

Emily was about to see another aspect of her husband's character. He had a reputation as a fine soldier, warfare was his hobby, and the opportunity to direct a small battle was not to be bypassed.

Even as a small boy, the Shereef's favourite game had been to make soldiers out of clay in the Sultan's garden at the family home in Wazan. He would divide his wobbly armies into regiments of Moslems and Europeans, and out of sheer perversity always made the Europeans win as it amused him to watch the rage and fury of his personal slaves and attendants. The old Shereef, his father, Sidi el Hadj el Arbi, thought his son's mud-battles were amusing and would remark: 'That child will have more to do with the Europeans when he grows up than we think.' Sidi el Hadj el Arbi was known as a miracle worker. It is possible that he had the gift of second sight also!

After the war with Spain in the 1850's when the Shereef had distinguished himself in battle, he had turned his own slaves and retainers into an efficient regiment, until the Sultan, fearing perhaps that these organised troops might be used on *him*, made such a fuss that the Shereef abandoned the hobby for the sake of peace and quiet.

He was pleased to take over the situation in Oudja. 'We keep the gates closed,' he said, rising to his feet and beckoning a hovering slave to bring his djelabah. 'The entire safety of the town depends upon it. Mahmoud—' he called and his head slave came into the room and stood waiting for instructions. The Shereef crossed to a table where he hurriedly wrote a letter. 'Mahmoud, you will take this to the people outside the city walls and return with an answer.'

Mahmoud bowed and slipped quietly from the room, the letter white in his black hand.

'What did you write?' Emily asked.

'That I am disgusted with their behaviour, and that if the firing does not cease *immediately*, I shall leave the town tonight.'

In the streets there was chaos. Women and children huddled round the walls wailing and crying. Some of the men whose relatives were outside fought and struggled with the soldiers in an attempt to open the gates and let in the men outside. Other men tried to climb on to the ramparts of the town and fire on the crowds below, but on the Shereef's orders they were quickly pulled down as the hillmen would have returned their fire and perhaps charged the flimsy town-gate. The moonlight lit the scene; turning dirty white robes spotless, illuminating the open-mouthed, wailing women who in grief had let their veils fall. The red flashes of fire from beyond the walls gave a look of some bizarre firework night. It took an hour or two before the gunfire, stammered, hiccuped, stopped, and shortly afterwards Mahmoud, dignity intact, returned, bowed low to his master and said: 'It is done, praise be to God.'

'And those outside can stay there,' said the Shereef.

The gunfire ceased but the wailing went on all night. An Arab woman's grief is a very vocal thing. She huddles herself to the ground, body swaying rhythmically, and the wail begins, rising to anguished shrieks. The swaying movement induces a form of self-hypnotism until she tears her face with her nails, rolls in the road or bangs her head time and time again. Even today a mourning woman's hands are tied to prevent her from causing herself harm, and the banshee cries disturbing the night gave Emily and her family little sleep.

In the morning they arose tired and haggard except for the Shereef who was in his element with something positive to take care of. He sent out his own personal bodyguard of soldiers to open the gates, round up the wounded and began to arrange for the burial of the dead. It was not a climate in which bodies could be left unburied. Then he sent for the chiefs of the various factions and their followers who humble as caught-out schoolboys stood before him; bearded men with hang-dog expressions. The Shereef dealt with them firmly. He laid down the rules and allowed no period for discussion. All hostilities were to cease. Men were to live in peace in the name of God. The Chiefs offered apologies for the disturbances of the night before. It had been the shepherds and the keepers of the camels and the cattle who were responsible. It was all a question of misunderstandings between the lower orders of the tribes. The Chiefs themselves were not responsible. They could only apologise and pray that the Shereef and God would forgive them and their people.

'You will make a truce,' said the Shereef, 'and it will be kept. Now give hands....'

The chiefs and the men who had crowded into the room with them who had been doing their best to blow each others heads off a few hours previously, solemnly held hands; the younger men kissing the heads of the older men.

'I want to hear of no more trouble from these lands,' the Shereef said dismissing them.

Emily was anxious now to leave Oujda. It had not been a pleasant night, and their hurried departure was not enjoyable either. All along the road back the way they had come the day before were bodies. Some were covered with djelabahs—others, bloodied, the limbs twisted lay exposed to the burning sun. And in the cemetery just outside the town the work of burial was going on as fast as possible while the wailing of the women never ceased. She and Kate averted their faces from the worst scenes, and breathed a sigh of relief when they were at last past the scene of the night's battle and were back

Emily with her father and brother John.

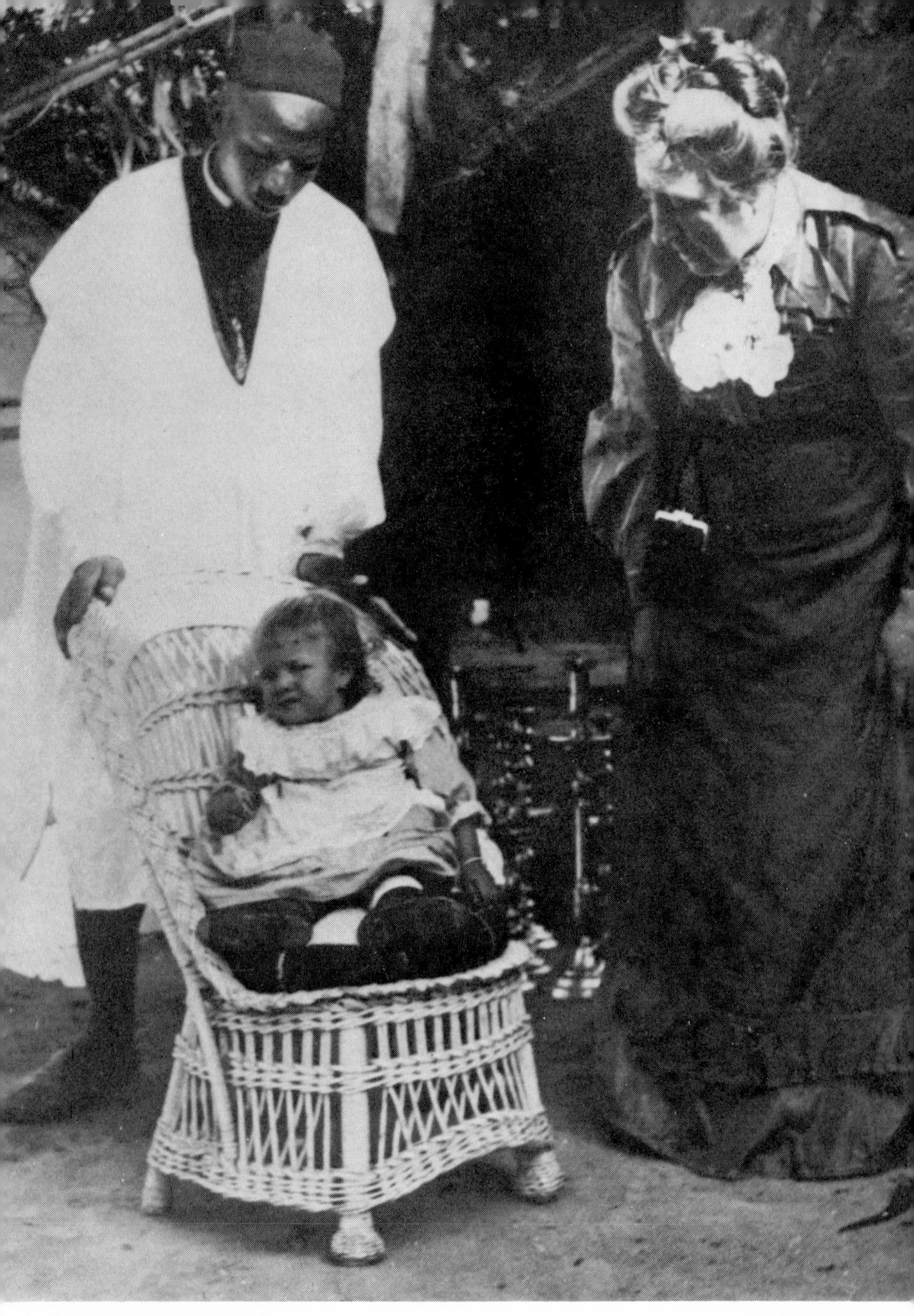

Emily when in her seventies with her granddaughter, Minni—always called Mini the English because she was so fair. The child was born lame and died before Emily. They are buried close to each other.

in the open countryside with the sweet smells of the fruit trees and the pale green of the young corn to dim the earlier picture. It became a pleasant journey. Every small, flat-roofed house bore a great untidy nest where the 'red-legs', the storks lived, and their young were poking inquisitive long beaks outside the security of their homes and waiting to be fed. The storks were a good omen, Mohar told Emily and Kate. Their presence meant that there would be peace in the land. The red-legs, as the Moroccans call the stork, were lucky birds.

Once near a town or village the same wearisome attentions from the people accompanied the party all the way back to Tlemcen. There Si Sliman was sent with one of the Shereef's secretaries and an escort to travel back to Oran by land and then by sea to Tangier to await the arrival of the Shereef. The Shereef and Emily with the rest of their party were to carry on to Algiers where he was to report to the Governor General, General Chanzy, on the success of his mission.

That night Emily told her husband that they were expecting another baby—news which put him into great spirits. At first he was anxious for her health after the tiring six weeks they had just spent, but once reassured he began to plan.

'How would you like to go on from Algiers first to Paris and then on home to England?' he asked. 'We will all go together and you can tell your parents our news in person.'

Emily was excited by the suggestion.

'It is settled then, God willing,' said the Shereef. 'The secretaries shall arrange it immediately we reach Algiers.'

From Oran the journey was not so difficult. They were able to travel by carriage and it took fourteen hours. Emily was perturbed by the number of Arabs who ran alongside the carriage for miles to stay at the side of their chief. They ran, faces contorted, feet moving automatically until quite suddenly they fell down exhausted on the trail. They made Emily anxious, but the Shereef told her not to fuss. The runners were in a kind of trance, and felt nothing.

They made plans for their journey all the way back to

Oran. The morning after their arrival the Shereef visited General Chanzy, and returned to their hotel a thwarted and cross Prince. He marched up and down the room, refusing to say what was the matter. Emily after two years of marriage knew that if cross-examined, he merely exploded. He would tell her what was wrong when he was ready.

She busied herself fussing with their small possessions which she carried everywhere to make hotels more home-like, while he paced. He eventually sat down and was deep in thought when it was announced that General Chanzy had returned the Shereef's visit and awaited him in an ante-room. 'Good!' said the Shereef. 'I shall settle this business now. Perhaps you had better leave us.'

Emily prepared to leave the room, but before she had gathered up her reticule there came another message requesting that the Shereefa would call upon Madame Chanzy immediately. Obviously the French authorities as well as her husband wanted her out of the way. *Men's* business was to be discussed. Emily put on her hat and called for a carriage and took herself off for tea with the Governor General's wife.

It was later that evening when her husband explained what had been troubling him. The French Government had dug in their heels when he announced that he wished to proceed immediately to Paris and England from Algiers. They were not taking any chances with Si Sliman breaking his promise. They wanted him delivered by the Shereef to the Sultan of Morocco as soon as possible—and that meant returning to Tangier immediately to complete the mission.

He was furious that his plans were spoilt and his word disregarded.

'Well, never mind, McDuff,' Emily said. 'We'll go home first. We can always go to Europe later.'

She was thinking that the French were making her husband earn the money they had been paying him for the last two years, and to her, it seemed quite just. But it was hardly the moment to voice this viewpoint. He was thwarted, and when her husband, who was used to having his own way in everything, was thwarted he sulked. While the French paid him, he had no choice in the matter. They had to return to Tangier.

General Chanzy was also slightly perturbed by the outcome of his polite request to complete the mission. The Shereef's manner had become cold and autocratic; but the general had his orders from the Quai D'Orsay. Si Sliman must be rendered harmless. On the other hand, his brief was to keep the Shereef happy. He was too valuable an ally to the French to offend. Any falling out with the Wazanni's could disrupt the French Government's long-range planning.

Hastily the man o' war *Le Cassard* was prepared for the journey back to Tangier and a formal invitation given to the Shereef and Shereefa to spend some days in Algiers as the guests of the French government. The Shereef declined. He had, he said, pressing business which needed his presence in Tangier immediately. If he was being made to go back to Tangier he would make it look as if he had intended to go anyway.

The Shereef's refusal to accept French hospitality concerned General Chanzy. He made a great display of the farewell ceremony, having as many of the Government staff as he could round up to accompany the Shereef and Shereefa to the ship. Preparations were made for a champagne lunch to be given on the sea between Oran and Algiers when the Shereef was decorated with the Order of the Grand Officier de la Legion d'Honneur by the Commander of the *Cassard* on behalf of the French Government.

This was an unexpected honour and somewhat lessened the Shereef's fit of pique. He was delighted with the scrap of red ribbon, but, not entirely mollified, said: 'It would have been better if Chanzy had presented it. Or—' a light in his eye— 'Marshal Macmahon when we arrive at Paris.'

'They probably wanted to present it to you as quickly as possible and in dramatic circumstances,' said Emily, tactfully. 'After all, it is very unusual to receive such an honour at sea. Don't you agree?'

'Maybe you are right,' he said.

Chapter Six

ANOTHER SON AND A VISIT HOME

Emily was exhausted when they reached home again. She was now nearly six months pregnant and the increasing heat of the town was exhausting. The journey had tired her more than she would admit. She had lost much of her vitality and looked drawn with dark shadows encouraging the grey of her eyes. The Shereef was perturbed. He blamed himself for taking her on the trip and cossetted her with loving attention.

He had at last found them a permanent home. A villa which both had admired for some time was put up for sale and the Shereef purchased it as a surprise gift for his wife. The house, situated on the Marshan, was a pretty one, on two floors, set in a large garden and with views of the sea from the first floor windows. But it lacked many necessities—running water had not been installed and most of the rooms needed completely redecorating to suit Emily's taste. There would be some delay before they were able to move in.

In the meantime, Si Sliman who was eventually to be conducted by the Shereef to the Court of Sultan Moulay Hassan for discussions on his future, was quartered in their present home. He spent his time in voluntary captivity, and having given his parole, wandered around the town, always accompanied by one of the Shereef's secretaries or some kind of guard. He seemed resigned to the situation and showed no signs of attempting to escape from Tangier to return to the bled where his followers still waited for word of what they were to do and where they were to go.

The Sultan, the French Government and even Sir John Hay Drummond Hay were not entirely happy at the idea of Si Sliman at loose in Tangier. Sir John, the *éminence grise* of the town did not care for the presence of so dangerous a rebel on his territory; the Sultan wanted to settle the matter, having lent his name to it, and the French were in a fidget in case Si Sliman cut and ran. They knew he would find support from the men of the Riff had he cared to carve his way through their mountains and then turn for the South where his people waited. But he seemed content to stay in Tangier, enjoying the hospitality of the Wazannis.

The Shereef himself was doing nothing to speed events. He had not forgiven the French for thwarting his intention of visiting Europe and had decided that they could now wait for him. He had complete confidence that Si Sliman would not break his word. For the Europeans the same trust did not come so easily. The power of the Shereef over Si Sliman had admittedly been proved, but they did not appreciate just how much the Shereef's word was law and how a promise given to him by a Moslem was like a promise given to God.

So the situation hung in abeyance as the summer's heat made Tangier a somnambulant town. The Shereef amused his wife; attending to her comfort and helping her plan their new home. He lingered quite deliberately and whenever he received another and more impatient request for the mission to be completed made various excuses. His wife was not well. The house was not ready. He was required on his own personal business in Tangier. But the real reason for the delay was Emily. He was more in love with her every day and could not bear to leave her. She was unaware of the extent of his procrastinations and had actually been encouraging him to finish the Si Sliman business. She felt that her husband was not entirely proud of himself for having broken Si Sliman and once he was delivered to the Sultan that would be the end of the matter and the Shereef could then relax.

Emily was therefore upset to receive a letter from the French Government couched in as tactful terms as possible, but asking her not to stand in the way of the completion of the mission, and when she showed the Shereef the letter, he exploded that they dare blame her.

She kept silent for a moment or two while he paced the long length of their sitting room, then she said mildly: 'Perhaps it would be better if you cleared up the matter and then we can forget all about it.'

'I want to be here when our baby is born,' he said.

She considered for a moment. Then she said: 'Why do you not go to Mequinez as soon as possible with Si Sliman and return immediately. The baby will not arrive until September. That will give you two months—quite time enough.'

He settled himself beside her on the cushions and put his arm around her shoulder. He said: 'You do not understand the workings of the Court. Once I am there, the Sultan will find a thousand and one things for me to do. There will be tribal wars to suppress; I shall be sent over the land like an eagle. It may be as much as a year before I can return home, but if you will promise me that after I have been away for two weeks you will send a special messenger to say that I am urgently required at home, this, God willing, will be my excuse.'

It took a week to ten days to arrange the caravan for Mequinez and then the Shereef was on his way, Si Sliman, a glum figure, riding at his side. Emily then busied herself with preparations for the new house and after two weeks had elapsed sent Mamhoud to bring her husband home again. Even though Kate had returned to England she was contented. It was good to have some time to herself, to recuperate after the long journey and enjoy the feeling of quickening life within her. She was growing very big; much more so than she had been with Moulay Ali, and she found that whatever she did was done trance like and slowly. But as her tiredness evaporated under the hot sun and in the long drowsy afternoons when she slept alone on their four-poster bed she began to recover her energy and look forward to the time when the baby would be born and she could travel with her husband again.

She was happy that the hostile atmosphere of her household was beginning to melt away under enthusiasm over the advent of the second baby and with approval of the way she was bringing up Moulay Ali. Though he spoke little Arabic, he was being taught the Moslem faith, and the people were pleased. Also, to her great delight, Lalla Heba without any prompting was making tentative gestures of friendship. Nothing was said and Emily herself proceeded delicately in case these shy flutterings towards resumption of friendship should be spoilt. The child, now nearly nine, was growing very pretty. She made no explanations, but picked up where their relationship had left off nearly three years previously. She asked to be taught English words and indicated her desire to start relearning the piano by tinkering with a few notes and asking casually: 'What happens after that, mama?'

It was all very mysterious, but pleasing, particularly with the Shereef away.

He returned home in early August excited by the success of his visit to the Court. Sultan Moulay Hassan had received him with great honour and it looked as if the feud between the two families might have diminished to some extent. The Shereef was full of confidence. The Sultan had even asked kindly after Emily, and there had not been a word about sending her home or insisting she lived in Wazan. Everything seemed changed.

Emily was curious to know what the Sultan was like.

'He is very tall and elegant. His skin is pale and he is handsome. But he looks sad. Most important,' the Shereef added, 'he is intelligent. I almost wish that it was possible to break with the French, leave myself free of their demands and join with him.'

This was a step the Shereef was unlikely to take. It paid him to remain a French protégé, particularly since the protection system was part of Moroccan life. It had begun after the Moroccan Government had made treaties with most of the European countries agreeing that Moorish subjects in the service of foreign diplomats and consuls were exempt from taxation and did not come under the jurisdiction of the country's authorities. Over the years the system had got out of hand as more and more people, particularly traders not specifically in the service of any foreign power claimed, with the connivance of foreign residents, exemption. This meant that the Sultan was deprived of the tax revenue from most of his wealthier subjects and the country's economy suffered accordingly.

The Sultan had been co-erced into guaranteeing any debt owed to a foreign trader by a Moorish subject. He set up a system whereby the local Governors were responsible for the debts of their own towns and provinces while the Sultan in turn was responsible for the Governors. It was a very easy system for greedy and dishonest men to exploit, and unfortunately for the treasury of Morocco, most of the Governors were both. They would present a bill to the Sultan for considerably more than the debt; the Sultan would pay the bill to the Governors who lined their pockets with the excess. But the debt was finally paid by *all* the inhabitants of the area, all of whom were held equally responsible. The Governors levied dues on the population until the full amount was raised and repaid to the Royal treasury. A situation that did not make Christians any more popular with these Moroccans who were not fortunate enough to be protected.

The Shereef of Wazan was not in any way involved with trading protection, but as an 'employee' of the French Consul, he and his people were automatically exempt from Moroccan taxes and jurisdiction. And as he was the wealthiest man in Morocco, his becoming a French protégé had done little to endear him to the Government of his own country.

In fairness to those Moroccans who placed themselves under the system, they had justification. The method of tax-collecting was cruel and extortionate. The tax-collectors would ride out on the Sultan's behalf, calling at every town, village and small house. They would take away as much from the people as they could find. A farmer's entire hard-worked-for crop of grain would go, carried off in sacks on the backs of the tax-collector's pack mules. A shepherd would lose his whole carefully built up flocks of sheep and goats. A small business man's savings would be taken. The harder a man worked to improve his lot, the more attention he would receive from the tax men, who were hated by the people throughout the country. Rather than be left to starve, the people would try to hide their savings; present themselves in their oldest clothes, hoping that they would be passed by. For it was not a question of taking a fair portion of a man's assets. It was a question of taking all he had.

Not surprisingly anyone who could afford to would pay foreigners large sums of money in return for becoming a foreign protégé. Unscrupulous Europeans became rich quickly, selling protection. And meanwhile, in order to fill the Royal Treasury, the Sultan extracted more and more from those who had not been fortunate enough to find a Christian to bribe or genuinely work for. It had become a vicious circle.

Emily's husband knew that the moment he ceased to shelter under the umbrella held so conveniently for him by the French Consulate that the Sultan would descend on him for both revenue and help in the interior. His assessment of Moulay Hassan was correct—the Sultan was intelligent—and tough. He was ruling his country with an iron hand and yet endeavouring under the promptings of Sir John Hay Drummond Hay to take some steps to bring Morocco up to date. The protection system was his biggest handicap, and the British Minister was solidly on his side in the fight against it. So much so that Sir John had never permitted anyone who did not have genuine qualifications to become a British protégé. He had even refused the Shereef protection after his wedding to Emily, declining to break the self-made rule he had obeyed for the entire time of his service in Morocco.

Sir John's honourable behaviour on this and other matters had helped the Sultan to trust the British, and though Moulay Hassan was ruthless where his people were concerned—he put down any sign of uprising with the utmost ferocity—he was open to suggestion. Sir John himself approved of ruling with a firm hand and the Sultan's forays into 'eating up the land' did not shock him.

Moulay Hassan had agreed with Sir John to permit more freedom of trade between Europe and the coastal towns. He had given his permission for a mole to be constructed at Tangier to ease the problems of landing. He had given his consent to a cable being laid between Gibraltar and

Tangier, though in actual fact the work was not done until 1886. He would not permit any form of telegraphic work in the interior, putting forward the reason that his subjects would certainly destroy the cable. Moulay Hassan would have liked to acquiesce to more of Sir John's suggestions, but he struggled with a corrupt Government and a people who would think he was preparing the country for the Christians if he progressed too quickly with reforms.

He realised his father had made a blunder at the time of the Shereef's wedding, a blunder which drove Sidi Abdeslam into the outstretched arms of the French, and he took the opportunity of the Shereef's visit to Mequinez to put the damage right. The Shereef was easily flattered and the Sultan's attentions were gratifying. The attitude of the French in blocking his decision to leave Algiers for Europe had provoked him considerably. He swung back on to the side of the Sultan—a change of heart that was not to be made public.

The Shereef was back well in time for the birth of his second son Moulay Ahmed, who arrived on September 6th, 1876. A twin-sister was still-born, reinforcing the Shereef's prophecy that his wife would never bear daughters, and confirming an earlier and stranger prophecy.

In 1872, about the time when Emily was first seeing the coastline of Africa, from the deck of the *Hercules*, Sidi Abdullah Ben Ahmed, a doctor of law, one of the Wazan family and living in the interior town of Zeroni, being 'very much troubled in spirit by the rumour that his Sheik, his Spiritual Chief, Lord and master was thinking of contracting an alliance with a European', set out for Fez to visit the holy shrine of Muley Dris, 'hoping to obtain some inspiration to enable me to understand what was passing in the life of my much beloved Sheik'. There he had a vision which he described in a book of the period. He wrote: 'Knowing his (the Grand Shereef of Wazan's) sympathies with European customs one had become accustomed to his ways of thinking and acting, but certainly not to the extent of taking for a wife a Roumia (European). The constant rumours worried me so much that at last

I determined to set for Fez for the purpose of visiting the holy shrine. Arriving at Fez, the (then) Sultan Sidi Muhammed Ben Abdurhaman, engaged me in long conversations on the subject of this projected marriage. In the sacred writings, which I searched, there was no prohibition to such an alliance. I then carried out my intention of visiting the holy shrine of Muley Dris to commune with him in spirit.

'Having made my ablutions and recited my prayers, I sat down to ponder and seek inspiration on the subject so dear to my heart. I fell asleep, and dreamed I was in Tangier, on the borders of the blue sea and watching a vessel thereon.

'Presently, I perceived a large gathering of people, but on closer scrutiny, I observed that it consisted of all the holy saints of past and present. Those from the East were evidently discussing with those from the West some momentous question to which neither side could find an acceptable conclusion. Ultimately it was suggested that lots should be drawn to decide upon which side the onus of discussion should fall.

'The subject of this was not revealed to me, and I could only learn that it was a heavy responsibility to be borne, both sides professing their inability to sustain its weight. The casting of lots being agreed to, two small sticks of unequal length were produced, and the lot fell to the holy Western Saints to bear the burden. So overwhelmed were they with the great responsibility thrust on them that the arrival of Sidi el Hadj Abdeslam el Wazanni in their midst was unseen, until he saluted each one by name. After the exchange of the usual salutations, he inquired the cause of their dilemma, and upon learning the same, begged them one and all to trouble themselves no more upon the subject, of which I, the dreamer was ignorant. Sidi el Hadj Abdeslam, ever ready to take other people's burdens on himself, announced to this holy assembly of Saints from East and West that he would be responsible for all they chose to impose upon him, upon which the holy assembly were aghast, as one clause in the compact whatever the body of the same contained, had not been communicated.

"Tell me, I pray you," said my Sheik, "the whole of this secret compact between you, which I accept, even before it falls from your lips."

'Said one, "It behoves the bearer of this heavy burden to marry a Roumia."

' "Even that I will do," said my beloved Sheik and master, "allow me to make but one condition regarding this proposed marriage, to which this holy assembly of Saints must be sponsors."

' "Speak, Sidi; we can acquiesce in your desire before you put it to us, so name the one favour you require from us all," they said. Whereupon Sidi el Hadj Abdeslam asked to be assured that the Roumia he was to take to wife should bear him two sons, the first to be named Ali, after Sidi Ali ben Ahmed, of glorious memory and the second Ahmed, after Sidi Ahmed Ben Taibe of revered memory.

' "Such it shall be, by God's blessing," replied the assembled holy Saints from East and West.

'At this particular moment in my vision I saw a carriage come in the midst of all the holy Saints. In it was seated a young girl dressed in European costume. The sun, as it were, shone on her right cheek, and behind her were the two tall candlesticks of pure gold. She was fair to see, and in my heart of hearts I inquired whether this young girl would accept our creed of Islam. Still debating the subject in my mind, I looked up at her, to see her beckoning to me with her finger. I rose and went to her. She leaned forward until her mouth was on a level with my ear and whispered....

'At this moment I awoke from my slumber and found myself in the most holy shrine of Muley Dris in the city of Fez.'

With the birth of Ahmed the prophecy made four years previously was fulfilled. The reference to the sun and moon meant that Emily was worthy to be the wife of a Shereef and the two golden candlesticks represented the two sons she bore. The curious aspects of the story are that Emily only learnt of the prophecy after her husband was dead and that there was no doubt that the dream had taken place and been published before she and the Shereef had met—though his earlier engagement to the French girl would have put the thought of an alliance with a European in the minds of the Moroccans.

Perhaps her marriage was predestined. The roumia described in the dream was fair. Emily was fair. The discarded French fiancée, dark.

The birth of the twins, even though the girl had died, established Emily's acceptance by the Moorish people. Particularly the women. Any mother of twins, according to superstition, had the *baraka* plus. This time there were no complaints, even from Mohar, about bringing up the baby in the European way and gradually the women of the household and those of the town began to come to her for advice about their own babies.

When she was an elderly woman, Emily said with pride that most of the men of Tangier had received their first bath at her hands, but it was in 1876, when she was twenty-six years old, a vital, athletic girl with the bright hair that so fascinated her husband, that she started to give instruction to the Moorish ladies. She taught them basic and rudimentary hygiene. She made them wash their baby's bottles, insisted that the children were weaned at the proper time, instead of the usual custom of breast-feeding until the child was well over a year old. She undoubtedly saved many lives as the infant mortality rate was very high in Morocco then. Her clinic began almost immediately after the birth of Moulay Ahmed and when they had moved into their new house. She had exchanged a Zowia for an emergency ward!

Her biggest problem was that the people had almost too much faith in her medical abilities. They would bring children suffering with hernias, ophthalmia, dysentery and malnutrition. They could not afford the European doctors of the town; their native methods were usually nauseating forms of magic, which sometimes worked by sheer faith, but more often did not. And besides, once it was decided by the people that the Shereef had passed some of his *baraka* to his wife, her services were more in demand than ever. Quite shamelessly, she cajoled the local doctors into giving her advice and even medicines. They grumbled a little about the bread being taken from their mouths, but the personality of the bright, lively girl, arriving on their doorstep, jumping from her horse and demanding information was formidable. They told her all she needed to know. And her 'practice' grew from caring for children to caring for adults as well. She did her best for everyone; never turned anyone away and in the town the people began to regard *es senora,* (the lady) as their friend, conveniently putting aside the thought that she was an infidel.

This was the happiest period of her life. The love affair between her and the severe, dignified seeming Moor she had married blossomed, strengthened by the two sons which they both adored. She was the firmer of the two; her babies were not to be spoilt. She was determined that they should have the best of education, speak as many languages as possible and be brought up as good Moslems. But she was still a most loving mother. A far-seeing girl she already had her eye on the future and was determined to protect their heritage. As Holy men, they must be as Moroccan as possible while learning and retaining all that was better in the European way of life. The Shereef, however, was a doting father, and she was always begging him not to spoil the boys. Demonstrative, he would pick up the sleeping baby from his cot 'because it looks so sweet'. He liked to walk in the garden carrying the child, while a disgruntled Mohar, deprived of his task, walked behind. And if one of the children were ill, he would become distracted and cry; tears streaming from his dark eyes down his dark cheeks. Emily herself wrote: 'No one suspected the tender heart that beat under the rather severe and very dignified exterior of one whose conversation in public was carried on by a third person. Rumour has it that his voice had never been heard in public before we were married, nor had he been seen to smile even. I have been told that when the Shereef first came to live in Tangier, the impression was that he was dumb, consequent on his carrying his silence to such an extent. He ultimately became a fairly good conversationalist, full of anecdotes, and made the most atrocious puns. The transformation which was permanent, was appreciated by his co-religionists, and his sayings are quoted to this day.'

Quite apart from her marital happiness she felt loved and useful. Now when she rode the streets of Tangier it was not only the Shereef's robes that the people flocked to touch. The hem of her riding habit was also considered holy, and she was greeted everywhere with affection. She had become used to being surrounded by slaves, though she did make efforts to see they were comfortable, even to the extent of erecting rather tinpot, but adequate little homes for them on a piece of waste ground outside the villa.*

Soon after Ahmed's birth Emily's sister Kate, who was now nearly as enamoured of Morocco as the Shereefa herself, arrived to stay until after Christmas. The Shereef had promised that he would now take Emily on the long-discussed boar hunt, and with Kate and the English nurse to take care of the boys, she felt it was safe to go. When it came to the point of departure, it was the Shereef who could not bear to leave the children. He fussed as to whether they would be all right putting off the expedition at the least sign of teething sniffles from Ahmed or slight indisposition from Ali. With all these alarms it was getting on into December by the time they finally left for the Angora Hills where the best hunting was to be found.

They were away for ten days, sending daily couriers back to Tangier for news of the children and Emily, who enjoyed any open-air activity, thought the sport exciting and well-worth the journey. Her nose pink in the cold, muffled up in her furs, she watched her husband bring down several boars. He was a good shot, but regretted that the expedition was not a pig-sticking one, Emily having persuaded him to use a gun rather than the wooden spear which she thought far too dangerous a method of hunting for a married man with two children.

His persuasions nearly cost her her life. At Djebel el Habib while the undergrowth was being beaten to rouse the boar, a beater, perhaps careless, perhaps resentful at the presence of a Christian woman in his hills, let

* These houses exist today.

fly a stray bullet in her direction. Fortunately she had chosen that moment to duck under a branch. Had she not, the bullet would have gone straight through her head. As it was, it whistled on harmlessly and lodged itself in a tree.

She straightened, her face white. The Shereef was white, too, with the thought of what might have happened, and he supported her for a moment, for the shock had made her shake. Then he exploded into violent rage. The other beaters, wanting no part of the blame, dragged forward the culprit, who swore it was a mistake. They stood, clamouring for forgiveness, in a circle around the Shereef and his wife, the branches dripping dismally with mountain mist, aghast that one of them should have angered their holy man. It was a serious matter; they believed that his fury would bring bad crops and general disaster. They feared he would take his *baraka* from them. Soon the inhabitants of the entire village, women and children, all ranged on the damp, cold hillside, to beg that the Shereef would forgive them and permit the hunt to continue, for he had decided to return to Tangier immediately.

'We will punish the man in any way you wish,' the headman said. 'May we shoot him for you? Or will you send him to prison? It shall be as you will.'

Emily, her nerve recovered, thought it best to make light of the affair.

'But I *will* have him shot,' the Shereef said. 'He could have killed you.'

The man, bearded and rough in his coarse brown shepherd's robe cringed before them. Emily shook her head, relieved it was still in place. She said: 'Let us pardon him, go home tomorrow and forget all about it.'

'If you wish,' he said, his eyes filling with tears. 'But if I had lost you. . . .'

* * *

In summer of 1876, before his second son was born, the Shereef received a letter which surprised him and startled Emily out of her usual composure. It was from her father, and a totally unexpected document. Emily said flatly that it sounded nothing like anything her father could ever have written, but the Shereef was of the opinion that the letter was a great compliment to him, John Keene having gone to great lengths to compose in the Moroccan style. It was even written in Arabic and said:

'To his much esteemed son-in-law (on the original draft of the letter the word "beloved" had been used in place of esteemed and then crossed out. This, it seems, was going too far for John Keene's natural Victorian reticence.) "I the undersigned send my greetings and cordial blessing. Know, oh worthy Shereef, that I have long since desired to send you a letter in the beautiful language which you speak. This desire of writing to you in your native language became still stronger when I found your Highness is so faithfully united with my beloved daughter and that you, the father of my dear grandchildren showed such kind feelings towards me on the day when I celebrated my 50th birthday. I felt that your heart indeed belongs to your wife who came from a Northern country and to her kindred who still reside in the North.

'Now you must know I have some good friends among the Sons of Israel who in this country suffer no restrictions and in consequence of their freedom are just as respectable as all other good citizens of this Empire and among those Jewish friends I found persons well acquainted with Arabic and who can thus be the true interpreters of the cordial feelings I entertain towards you.

'First of all I tell you that I value and esteem your filial affection which has been shown by yourself and which will pass on from you to my little grandson, Moulay Ali. A token of that affection I find in your contribution towards the gold watch given to me on my fiftieth birthday. This gift unites in equal love you, your wife, my daughter and my grandchild to my seven other children in England.

'I also thank you for your adherence to your solemn promise to let my daughter on becoming your wife, continue worshipping our Heavenly Father according to the custom of her people. Perhaps you will say a man ought not to thank his fellow man who keeps his promise given in the presence of God and even to his own hindrance. But history tells us that even in the name of religion many wrongs have been done and many acts of oppression have taken place in order to injure those who happen to be born in different religion.

'O my honoured son-in-law, my heart rejoices when I think that you stand far and high above such religious prejudices. You allow my daughter to satisfy the pious wishes of her heart and to follow her Christian religion. I look upon such a tolerant feeling as the sign of a noble mind, of a mind that is not the slave of tyrannical opinion, such a mind is on the contrary a master ruler that spreads benevolence and mutual love all round about it.

'I esteem such noble feelings, for I myself could make no difference in my kindness to a man whether he be a Moslem or a Christian or a Jew, and I feel that you are convinced, as I am convinced, that those whom God has placed at our side, and to whom he has given a desire to enjoy happiness, should not have their lives troubled and disturbed by any unkind prejudices of their fellow mortals.

'Recently travellers of well known veracity who visited the Moorish dominions, came into provinces where murders and outrages were committed upon Jewish traders, and such crimes are of frequent occurrence. They made known those sad events in newspapers which are printed in this country and which are read by hundreds and thousands of men. Then I thought to myself: "Oh, that I could speak to my excellent son-in-law and that I could ask him to use his wisdom and the great influence which he deservedly enjoys in his native land in order that he might give council in the assemblies of the best men in the Empire. Oh that he could find some means by which the Governors of the land might be made to enforce more effectively than at present equal justice amongst all dwellers in the land without differences of creed, so that murderers should not rob their victims, paying a part of their spoils as ransom for their own lives and keeping another part of the spoil as a profit and as a residue of a criminal enterprise which God cannot forgive and which remains unatoned upon the guilty conscience."

'I feel that my interests and affections are drawn to the fair land which is now the home of my children and in which my son-in-law is so great an ornament and then wished that to my son-in-law should belong the everlasting glory of helping to put an end to constant sufferings which lawless persons inflict upon defenceless Jews and I thought within myself even I do know that among the leading men in Morocco there are those who can add to the honour of that country and can save it from becoming a byword to other nations of the earth who may perhaps say that there are more than anywhere else murders and outrages can be committed freely and with impunity. I just as you, love all men alike and I would wish to prevent the throwing of obligy upon the principles of religion.

'I honour all religions because they teach men to discover in outward ceremonials and observances a divine advice that all men should love and protect each other. I found in the Scriptures of the Jews the beautiful and universal lesson "Love thy fellow man as thou loves thouself." I learned the same lesson in the sacred books of the Christian creed which came later into the world than that of the Jews.

'I read the same beautiful lesson in the translation of your sacred volume which announces to millions of men that grandeur of divine mercy and the holiness of unity amongst all children of men. Indeed, I read in all books of religion that men should tolerate the benevolent opinions of their fellow mortals, that they should make their own religion respected by doing good deeds and by preventing evil doings; therefore I resolved to write to you in favour of unity, peace and good deeds.

'The idea has therefore occurred to me to inquire whether anything can be done (not solely on the part of foreign Ambassadors, but generously and gloriously on the part of the great and good men of your country) to make the Governors of the land more responsible and to put to an end such cruel acts of inhumanity.

'I entreat you to let me know your opinion about the mitigation of the evils arising from the ill-treatment of the Jews and whether any advice can be given by you to the chief men in the country in order to place all inhabitants under the strong protecting arm of equal justice and equal treatment.

'Pray write to me an answer on this subject in order that I might give comfort to the hearts of some of my friends and that I may be able to show them how good are the best men of your country, and how faithful your ruler is to the great firman which the last Sultan of Morocco granted to the Jews 21 years ago and which firman was lately confirmed by the present noble minded Sultan as I can show you by copies of Arabic letters which have passed between representatives of His Majesty the Sultan and some of the Jewish representatives of my friends here in London. The firman and the correspondence promise that the Jews shall enjoy that liberty under which men thrive and prosper as plants prosper under the bright and cheering rays of the sun.

'My dear son-in-law tell me also your opinion how in your country education and trade which are much needed everywhere can best be promoted. In my opinion the buildings of roads which connect cities with cities and manufacturers with purchasers is the great want to which public attention might be profitably directed. If you have prisoners who are chained down in idleness make them work for the construction of the roads, if you have robbers guilty in any way, either of murder or of other misdeeds, make them workers on the roads. If you have idlers who will not earn a living in an honest manner, make them workers on the roads. This would be one of the means to diminish crimes committed under the mask of religion. In a similar way we, in this country, employ shiftless persons and I must say we are not unsuccessful in our endeavours to improve the corrupt classes.

'And now last. I beg you to let me see my daughter and grandson this summer. You remember that you said you would bring her to England two years ago; come now, you shall be heartily welcome. If you cannot come yourself, send them. On the word of an Englishman they shall be well cared for and they shall return at the time when you wish it. I want to see that boy whom I love so much and you will not refuse me this wish. Bless this child for me, salute my dear daughter your wife in my name and I pray in my innermost heart that God, the all powerful, our Father which is in Heaven, ever have you and them in his watchful care.'

The Shereef was somewhat apathetic about the political suggestions and sentiments in the letter from his father-in-law, remarking that unfortunately people in Europe had little idea of just how feudal Morocco was, and how impossible it would be to build roads without the Sultan's permission. The Sultan was none too enthusiastic about any road building project as he realised that this could open up the country for the foreigners to take over. The remoteness and difficulty of travel in Morocco were in themselves a guard against any form of overseas domination.

But the Shereef was most touched by the personal messages in the letter, and he set about making arrangements to visit England. But it was not until July 1877 that the trip took place. The Shereef had wanted to leave in the early spring, but arrangements had to be made, mainly receiving the Sultan's permission to leave Morocco. This was eventually granted, and the French Consul on hearing the news was delighted that his Government in Paris would at long last have the opportunity of re-wooing the Shereef on their home territory. He was tired of naggings from the Quai D'Orsay as to why the Shereef seemed to have cooled in his friendship towards France.

French diplomacy was having a thin time in Morocco. Sir John Hay Drummond Hay had the Sultan's ear and was blocking French tactics. A new French minister, M. Lesourd, had been sent to Tangier in the January of the year to see if he could improve the French position. Even so, Sir John had managed to pull off two diplomatic coupes. On his suggestion, the British were training Moorish soldiers for the Sultan at Gibraltar with the approval and co-operation of the British Government. There were 112 Moorish soldiers in tents on neutral ground on the Rock, being trained by the Garrison's Colonel Cameron. The experiment was successful and the Sultan wanted more men to be taken under the scheme. Sir John, cock-a-hoop, wrote to the foreign secretary, the Earl of Derby, saying: 'The fact of this wild people being brought into contact with the civilised world, the instruction that will be imparted, and kindness and goodwill which are shown to them by the Garrison and inhabitants of Gibraltar will be a great step to promoting civilisation in Morocco as on their return to this country they will spread far and wide their knowledge of the power and goodwill of the British Government and people.'

The training of the troops was the first step to a more important coup. Sir John had been working to get a Britisher into the Court of Morocco. Foreign representatives were not permitted to live in the royal, and therefore Holy, cities which was irksome as all business had to be done by courier. An informer at court would be helpful, if it were possible to plant someone there....

He found his man in Lt. Harry A. de Vere MacLean of the 9th Regiment, then stationed in Gibraltar. Harry MacLean had been engaged in training the Moorish (Askar) troops on the Rock and seemed to have an affinity with them. He was a Scot, considerably more intelligent than the average soldier and ambitious. Sir John suggested to the Sultan that as the training scheme in Gibraltar was proving so successful, it would be an asset to have a British officer stationed actually at the Court, training the troops. Sultan Moulay Hassan liked the idea, and in March 1877 Harry MacLean resigned from the 69th Regiment.

Sir John bided his time, and on April 14th, sent a despatch to the foreign office, stating that Mr. H. A. de Vere MacLean, Lieutenant in the 69th had retired and been engaged by the Moorish authorities to aid in instructing the Askars as regular troops. It was a *fait accompli*.

The French were disconcerted by both of these moves and made offers of training facilities in Algeria. They also complained bitterly (as they were to complain for many years) to the Sultan about the presence of Harry MacLean at Court. The Sultan ignored their protests. He liked the good-looking soldierly young Scot, particularly as the army became more efficient within weeks of MacLean's arrival.

With the Sultan more and more pro-British, the Shereef and Shereefa's visit to Europe gave the French the opportunity to regain some lost ground by at least ensuring the Shereef's loyalty to France. M. Lesourd pulled out all the troops in arranging their reception in Paris. The French policy still leaned to the view that the Europeanised Shereef would be of more political value than the independent-minded Sultan. British policy through Sir John continued to rely on the Court and Moulay Hassan to block France's ambitions.

Emily was most anxious that the visit to London would not turn out the same way as the Gibraltar trip. She decided to take some precautions and went to see Sir John to ask his help.

She was faintly embarrassed and hesitated for a moment before giving the Gibraltar disaster as her reason for coming to see him.

Sir John interrupted to save her more discomfort.

'And you would like me to inform the Foreign Office in London so that some arrangements can be made for your visit to England?'

He began to rummage among the papers on his desk. 'It is already done.' He handed to her the draft of the letter addressed to Lord Derby.

'Read it,' he said.

She settled down to decipher his tall, spiky handwriting.

'My Lord,' it began, 'the bearer of this letter is His Highness Sidi Hadj Abdeslam al Hasany el Wazanni, the Great Shereef of Morocco, whose spiritual authority is recognised by the Mohammedans of this country, in Algeria and even in parts of the East. His Highness is a branch of the present reigning family and therefore a distant relative to the Sultan Moulay Hassan.

'Sidi Abdeslam is married to an English lady and has no other wife.'

'His Highness is distinguished for his charitable and liberal views and friendly feelings towards Europeans and the readiness he has always shown to aid in ensuring their safety in travelling in this country.

'His Highness has obtained permission of the Sultan to visit Europe and intends to travel with his wife and family in France and England.

'His Highness is greatly interested in military matters and in the fabric of arms of all kinds.

'I have the honour to request that your Lordship may have the goodness to give the necessary directions that His Highness be admitted to all the Government factories of arms, dockyards, Woolwich Palaces and other places which require a Government Order.

'I have the honour to remain,
'Your Lordship's very faithful,
Sir John Hay Drummond Hay.'

'Will that do?' he asked as she put the paper back on his desk. He watched her, waiting for her reply. His own feelings were that the Shereef meant little politically, yet even if Britain backed the Sultan, it was as well to show no discourtesy to the Wazannis. An astute diplomat, he believed in covering every eventuality.

'You have been more than kind, Sir John,' Emily said. 'I am grateful to you.'

They left on one of the Paquet Boats for Marseilles in July with both the children and an entourage of eleven servants. The Shereef, always a bad sailor, retired to his cabin, saying he remembered the journey too well from the time he had made his pilgrimage to Mecca, and thereby gained the title 'Hadj' (pilgrim) in his list of names.

'The French gave me a man o' war for the voyage,' he said, 'and it pitched and rolled all the way.'

'A man o' war!' said Emily. 'All to yourself?'

'Yes,' he said. 'But I had to give it back afterwards.'

Emily recorded that on arrival at Marseilles the Commissioner of Ports with a Professor of Arabic came aboard in the name of the French Government to conduct them to the Grand Hotel, where luxurious apartments had been reserved. The Prefect's secretary called when they arrived at the hotel, and the Moorish flag was hoisted. Then the Moorish merchants who resided in Marseilles came to pay homage in cash and kind to their spiritual leader.

They stayed in Marseilles for four days, inspecting the city, but the *pièce de résistance* was a visit to the *Yan Tse*, an enormous boat which had been newly built by the Messageries Company where the Chinese domestics aboard served refreshments. The Shereef who had never seen a Chinese before was enchanted by these odd looking people and on his return to the hotel sent all the servants to the ship so that his fellow Moors could see them, too.

The servants, including Mohar and Mamhoud, were full of wonder at everything they saw, and Emily enjoyed watching them and their reactions to this new civilisation. At first the train terrified them. They were hesitant about boarding such a monster and their long, black eyes widened into near circles as it began to move, and every lurch and jolt made them grab for safety. As the train picked up speed they held on, rigid with fear and at the first stop, all said a fervent 'El Amdollilah'. (Thank God!) Once they realised that this puffing, strange vehicle was not going to kill them, they settled down to watch the fertile organised scenery outside the windows and tried to count the telegraph poles.

It was as well that Emily had her servants to watch, as the trip must have been an exceedingly dull one. On arrival at Lyon, the same ceremonies took place as in Marseilles and they were whisked around the town as fast as possible to be shown all the sights as the party was leaving for Paris on the night train.

In Paris everything possible was done to impress the Shereef. They were met at the station by a first secretary and an interpreter and taken to the Grand Hotel du Louvre. That same afternoon the Shereef called on the President of the Republic, Marshal Macmahon, the red ribbon of the Legion d'honneur bright on his djelabah. Later the Duke Decazes, the Foreign Minister at the time called, and the rest of the evening and the next day were fully occupied in meeting the most influential people in France. Marshal Macmahon loaned them his box for a visit to the Opera, and they were entertained by M. Gabeau, the chief interpreter to the French Army, while Marshal Macmahon was represented in the party by General Marquis d'Absac.

The Shereef was pleased with the attention even though he felt it was only his due, and left Paris reluctantly. Emily had enjoyed the shops and caught up with the latest fashion, relinquishing her bustle in favour of the new slimmer gowns, and she had bought a great many enormous befeathered hats which sat well on the curls and puffs of her piled-up hair. The Shereef had thought their four day stay enchanting; particularly his meeting with the girls of the corps de ballet whom he had met backstage after the performance of the Opera. He had never seen such a display of female legs and for a moment the Frenchmen accompanying him had thought that a difficult situation might develop. Fortunately, his wife they said afterwards, had appeared to be more amused than perturbed by her husband's reaction to all the pulchritude, and after letting him look and actually *touch* for a minute or two, had gently drawn him away.

The British did their best, but their heart was not in it. Everyone got the Shereef's names and titles wrong, including Doctor Leared an expert on Morocco from the Foreign Office, who met them at Charing Cross Station and escorted them to Conduit Street where an apartment had been taken for their stay. The finished copy of Sir John's letter to the Earl of Derby was produced and Emily helped one of the secretaries in their party to compose a letter for the Foreign Secretary. It read:

11 Conduit Street,
Regent Street,
August 10th, 1877.

My Lord,

I have to acquaint your Lordship with my arrival in London and I enclose a letter addressed to your Lordship by Sir John Hay Drummond Hay, Her British Majesty's representative at Tangier.

Will your Lordship kindly inform me when and where

it will be conveneint [*sic*] for me to call upon you.

I am, my Lord,
Very faithfully Yours,
Abdeslam Ben Alaibi,
Prince of Morocco.

Once Sir John's letter was received, the Foreign Office went into action, sending copies to the Lords of the Admiralty, the Lord Chamberlain, Her Majesties Dockyards and Her Majesties Palaces, asking for facilities for the Shereef and Shereefa to visit the various establishments.

The Admiralty sent back a testy letter asking for clarification of the Shereef's name, and received an equally testy reply, quoting the names given in Sir John's original letter. The one letter of the many which would have gratified the Shereef and Emily herself had they seen it was from the Foreign Office.

'The Queen has given directions that the gentleman whom the office keeper here calls the High Sheriff of Morocco should have a Royal carriage whenever he wants it. The Lord Chamberlain's office will give you the necessary orders.'

The carriage arrived, complete with coachman, footmen, and Royal coat of arms, and was put at their disposal for the entire visit. This quite altered the attitude of the inhabitants of Newington Butts when Emily with her bearded, robed husband appeared in it. It became very chic to know the Shereefa of Wazan.*

Emily was seeing the prison Governor's house, as furnished with her parents' belongings for the first time. She was sad not to have seen her grandfather again—on his retirement he had moved to the smart suburb of Brixton, but he did not have long to enjoy his £900 a year pension. He died on February 9th, 1877, just a few months before Emily and the Shereef arrived in England, and her parents were still in semi-mourning.

* Emily was quite aware of the effect that the carriage had on her erstwhile neighbours and friends. The story of the expression on the faces of the inhabitants of Newington Butts when she appeared in the Queen's coach has become a part of the Wazanni's family history.

She and the Shereef attended services at her own parish church of St. Mary's, Newington, and more grandly, at Westminster Abbey, and St. Pauls. The Shereef accompanied her on all three occasions, uncovering his head during the services, and mightily bored he was, not understanding a word of the long sermons. He found the Surrey County Gaol where Emily's father gave him a guided tour, much more interesting, and was amazed at the way it was run compared with the prisons in Morocco.

'Now you know why Kate was so sharp with the Governor of the prison at Ceuta,' Emily told him. He was tasting a bowlful of skilly at the time, and nodding at her remark said: 'This is good. Do they give it to prisoners?'

'And to me when I was a little girl,' Emily said. 'I used to creep into the kitchen and persuade the cook to give me a bowl smothered in sugar.'

They had been in London for four days when a deputation headed by Baron Henry de Worms arrived at Conduit Street from the Anglo-Jewish Association. They had come to intercede with the Shereef to approach the Sultan re the treatment of the Jews in Morocco. At that time, the Jews were forced to live in 'Mellahs'—special sections of Moroccan towns set aside for them. They were not permitted in the Moslem part of the town unless barefoot and always had to wear a black robe and cap. They suffered considerable persecution. Improvements in their condition had recently been made at the town of Azimour. There the Jewish population were now allowed to wear their shoes outside of the Mellah. But the Sultan had rather spoilt the effect of this gesture by digging up the ancient Jewish burial grounds at Fez in order to extend his Royal Palace. Only pressure from foreign sources had persuaded him to give the Jewish community a new burial place.

The Baron, along with a Leopold Schloss, the Reverend Lowry and Hyman Yuly of Mogador, one of the many Moroccan merchants who had settled in Britain at that period, crowded with various other members of their organisation into the apartment's receiving rooms where the Shereef waited to meet them.

It was an uncomfortable atmosphere, the Shereef knowing perfectly well that there was little he could do to help their cause.

The Baron spoke first, an elegant figure, very different from his co-religionists in Morocco. He cleared his throat and asked if the Shereef would please take the thanks of the Anglo-Jewish Society to the Sultan for the relaxation of conditions in Azimour.

'Unfortunately,' he said, Human Yuly translating into Arabic, 'in some parts of Morocco the Jews are still obliged to go barefoot; they have to give way in the streets of the cities to Moslems, and, in spite of the example of Turkey, their testimony is not received in the courts of Justice. Nations, or those who profess particular creeds cannot expect sympathy if they themselves oppressed persons of other religions. I hope that your Highness will use your influence as the Spiritual Chief of Morocco to cause toleration to be preached to the people, as well as ordained by the Emperor.'

The Shereef nodded gravely, and waited while Schloss and the Reverend Lowry said a few words.

He then said: 'With the help of God, I trust that the objects of this deputation will be achieved.'

And retired into another room. The interview was at an end.

'That was rather abrupt, Sidi,' Emily said after the deputation shuffled away, the Baron looking outraged.

'What can I do?' he said. 'Absolutely nothing.'

The Shereef was in fact genuinely concerned, and unhappy that there was nothing he could do. One of the remarkable things about him was his complete tolerance for other races and religions, unusual in a citizen of a country more bigoted than most. He enjoyed being asked for assistance, and liked to use his influence, but this particular problem was a greater one than he could possibly control.

Emily herself had a problem. The more gossipy papers had dug up the story of her marriage on her return to London, but had got most of the facts wrong. They reported that she had been Governess to Sir John Hay Drummond Hay's family on her arrival at Tangier. She was afraid that Sir John might object. She decided to issue a disclaimer to the story which *The Times* printed, headed 'The Shereef of Morocco'.

'We are asked to contradict a statement which we are informed has appeared in several papers to the effect that the wife of the Shereef of Morocco, now visiting London, was formerly governess in the family of Sir John Hay Drummond Hay. We understand that the lady was not acquainted with Sir John until the day he married her to the Shereef, according to English law, in the presence of Admiral MacDonald and other officers of her Majesty's fleet.'

Emily was satisfied, when she found the statement well-placed under a letter from Florence Nightingale, supporting the Indian Famine Relief Fund.

The day had started well, and it was to be the best day they spent in London. A visit had been planned to the new Alexandra Palace—the place of popular entertainment for the working classes of the North of London. The Palace had recently been rebuilt after a calamitous fire which burned down the original building just fourteen days after it had opened.

As they set off accompanied by Emily's father and the two children the Shereef announced he did not propose to stay long, but as it turned out, Emily had great difficulty in getting him to leave, he so enjoyed himself.

The Shereef was grumbling slightly about the distance they had travelled when they came up to Muswell Hill in their imposing Royal carriage, and then he saw the vast mass of the Palace on the hills with its four towers, fine arched doorway and dome. The green grounds fell from the grey building down to ornamental lakes, the grass dotted with the promenading figures of women in elegant flowing dresses making bright splashes of colour. It was a charming scene. When told it was the Alexandra Palace, he grew more interested in the outing.

Mr. Jones, the manager, was waiting at the Muswell Hill entrance to receive them and the entire party was immediately whisked off to a tent where they were to watch some bicycle races. The Shereef and his sons found these most exciting, and Moulay Ali whispered to Emily that he would quite like to own a bicycle himself.

'It would not be very much good on the streets of Tangier,' she whispered back. 'You would be spilled off in no time.'

After watching nine races, the Shereef's interest had begun to cool, he was finding it all a little repetitive. He fidgeted in his seat until the manager led them away for a guided tour of the palace and grounds. The Shereef was impressed. The grand hall was capable of seating 12,000 people and an orchestra of 2,000, as Mr. Jones explained when he took them into the huge area.

'Tell me what you would like to see,' Mr. Jones said. 'The concert room?—we are very proud of that. It will seat 3,500 visitors—the Italian gardens? The Conservatory? Our halls for the display of art? The bazaar department where there are many things to purchase? The trotting ring, the race tracks, or perhaps our Japanese village? And, of course, you must see our modern Moorish house.'

They decided on seeing the various gardens and the conservatory to please Emily, and the Shereef said he would like to see the race tracks and the stabling for several hundred horses. They took in the Moorish house which the Shereef pronounced rather more elaborate than the genuine article, but quite accurate, and he tried his hand at the game of billiards in one of the many billiards rooms.

The tour took quite some while as the Palace covered over seven acres, and then the manager said perhaps they would like to sit for a while and took them into the theatre —'It seats more than 3,000 people,' he said proudly—to see a performance of the latest play—'Black Eyed Susan'. Without understanding what was going on on the stage the Shereef found it all fascinating, and as he showed no signs of wanting to leave, a dinner party in one of the smaller banqueting rooms was hastily arranged, with guests including Emily's father, Sir Edward Lee, Dr. Leared from the Foreign Office, and Sir Edward Currie. And Emily felt a stab of triumph on realising that her father was impressed at all the attention that was being paid to her husband.

After dinner they were taken to a circus performance in the Central Hall where the Shereef was almost embarrassing, he laughed so much at the antics of the clowns, and was delighted when a baby elephant was brought into the ring and named 'Shereef' in his honour. The evening was rounded off by a firework display by the well-known Mr. James Pain, and the guests of honour watched the performance from a balcony connected to private rooms which had been placed at the Shereef's disposal for his visit. James Pain included a grand set piece with an Arabesque motif in honour of the Shereef, and the evening was ended with a portrait of Princess Alexandra in fireworks.

'Quite the best day we have had,' said the Shereef as they climbed back into their carriage.

'I wish we could have entertainments like that in Tangier,' Moulay Ahmed said sleepily. Emily smiled at her family. After over five years in Morocco she was accustomed to the enthusiasm shown by the Moslems for the toys and marvels of the West. In some ways her husband was no more sophisticated than the humblest of his subjects or his own sons. He had enjoyed himself like a schoolboy.

She enjoyed the day better than others. For the rest of the time, the British Government had laid on a programme of visiting Woolwich Arsenal. Her Majesty's dockyards and military establishments which even her enquiring mind found stultifying. The Royal Gunpowder factory had been slightly worse than the Royal Small Arms Factory, but the last straw had been the Royal Clothing Factory at Pimlico. But at least there had been the consolation of visiting Windsor Castle and Buckingham Palace, even if the dear Queen was away at Osborne, and they called upon the Earl of Derby, who had been most affable, which she thought a very great honour indeed.

But she was not all that sorry to be catching the 8.50 a.m. tidal train to Folkestone from the Charing Cross Station on August 24th. The South Eastern Railway would have them on the way and back in Paris by 6.30 that evening, via Boulogne and Beauvais. Then there was only

Moulay Ali at the French Military Academy in Algeria.

Muley Ahmed Ben Abdeslam,
Shareef of Wāzen (1898).

Emily in Algerian costume.

a visit to Madrid where they would be received by the King—and then, by private steamer from Cadiz back home.

The children were looking a little peaky, she thought, London life was so different to the open air existence they enjoyed in Tangier. They were missing the sunshine and their horses in spite of all the modern marvels and wonders that there were to see. It was time they left.

Chapter Seven

THE LAST OF THE HAPPY YEARS

As the steamer from Cadiz rounded the point and sailed into Tangier Bay, Emily was standing at the bows, her arm around Moulay Ali who was perched on a jutting beam, watching for the town to come in sight.

'Look, mama, we are nearly home,' he shouted excitedly as the town appeared, shimmering white as a freshly iced cake under the brilliant afternoon sun.

Across the water, the town looked so pristine that it was impossible to believe the filth and smells of the streets, but Emily was pleased with the view. Tangier *was* home for her now. There had been no pangs on leaving England; London had become alien, it had grown so big and so impersonal. The Shereef had disliked the city, thinking it cold and grey and the people sad-looking. Emily did not entirely agree, but seeing the beautiful African coast in the distance, the purple mountains crouched like guard dogs, the great broad stretch of beach where miniature people on miniature horses were riding for pleasure and above all the sun—burning and blazing from a sky so blue it seemed white, England seemed another world. It was good to be back.

The trip over she settled herself comfortably back into everyday life. Moulay Ahmed was a delicate little boy and required a great deal of love and attention. And then there was the clinic to cope with.

'I really don't know how you manage it,' Lady Hay Drummond Hay said one day when she was visiting. They were taking afternoon tea, a custom never abandoned by Emily, in the pretty garden, bright with beds of spring flowers lovingly coaxed into bloom. 'All those people requiring constant attention. And I am sure they can be very difficult.'

Emily laughed.

'Not difficult,' she said, 'just suspicious.' It never ceased to amaze Emily that her patients came at all. She knew how the population had been brought up to believe that the Christians' one aim in life was to wipe out the Moslems. Nearly all her pills and potions were tried out on some unfortunate dog first to make sure they did not contain poison. In the early days of the clinic Emily might have been offended had she not known that it was the custom of the country for the host to taste all food first at meals to reassure his guests on the self-same matter. She said as much to Lady Hay Drummond Hay who smiled, and then grew serious.

'I fear you may be even busier. Sir John says that unless we get rain soon, there will be much disease and suffering in this land.'

The weather had been unusually hot all through the late summer and winter and there had been hardly any rainfall at all. Sir John's prediction proved correct. By the middle of June there was famine in the interior. Cattle were dying and the people starving. In Tangier the price of bread rocketed, but apart from a small outbreak of smallpox—and there was generally a small outbreak of smallpox—health in the town was good.

It had become a family custom at the Shereefa's home that when the papers were delivered, Emily would put on a wrapper, sit by the window and read the news to her husband, who remained stretched out comfortably in their bed. He liked to keep up with European events so that he could converse more easily with their European friends.

'It says in the *Times* that there is to be an appeal for the starving people of Morocco,' she told him one morning. 'Sir John's son, Robert, has written to ask for aid. Lady Hay Drummond Hay was telling me that Mogador is worst hit and there is to be a subscription got up here in Tangier for the Mogador poor.'

Robert Hay Drummond Hay was consul at Mogador, and

the Shereef said: 'Give them something then, I leave it to you how much. But make it generous.'

Emily shook her head at him. Where money was concerned the Shereef was a problem. He gave it away with as little thought as if he were parting with an orange or two from their orange groves. He spent it as if he had the power to manufacture it. Emily, whose state of mind regarding money was quite the reverse, tried her best to stem the flood; save and budget, but it was a losing battle. She could not even manage to have him keep a new djelabah on his back for any length of time. If he went out without her in winter and saw that one of his followers looked cold and needy, more often than not he would take off the garment, hand it over, and come home shivering himself.

It was not just that he was generous. He had a feudal attitude towards money and possession. Money was to be spent, used and enjoyed. When it had gone—he would make someone give him some more. A quick trip around the tribes and he would start back with plenty of *Yiasa* to start the spending and the giving all over again.

Nevertheless, she still loved him, though his profligate way worried her. She could see her children left with nothing. An appeal to be more careful for the children's sake did sometimes work. It would have more effect than an appeal on her own behalf for these days he did not seem to be as interested in her as when they were first married. He encouraged her to take up her own pastimes, and as she could not often leave Moulay Ahmed for fear of his health, the Shereef frequently went off on hunting trips with Sir John and Hadj Hamed, leaving her to organise the home, care for the children and run her clinic.

He was still proud of her. His possessions meant very little to him. They could aways be replaced, but this European wife, so intelligent and different from the Moorish women he had previously married, still fascinated him, though his dark eyes had rediscovered the pleasure of looking on younger, graceful girls of his own race and religion. Emily herself had become a little Moroccan in her ways over the years, which disappointed him. It made her less unique. She liked to wear the intricate, beaten silver and gold native jewellery and being good mannered, felt that when with Moorish people she should observe their customs. They believed footwear to be unclean; shoes were never worn in the house, but the women had sandals 'stencilled' on to their feet using the dye, henna. This could look quite pretty, with delicate tracery of 'straps' drawn on the top of the foot and a sole of henna which hardened the skin. Emily had her feet decorated in this fashion so that she could leave off shoes when in Moroccan company and the Shereef would always lift her on and off her horse and carry her to doorways so that her bare feet never touched the ground. This sight never failed to astonish his fellow countrymen who considered it demeaning to show attention to a woman.

The house on the Marshan was still a happy one. Ahmed had plenty of playmates and any child could be sure of a welcome from Emily. Foundling children, though rare* would be brought to her.

It was about 1879 when a small baby girl was delivered to her home in the middle of a smallpox epidemic and she asked the Shereef for permission to keep her.

'Do as you wish,' he said, exactly the answer she had expected.

There was a problem. No one had any idea where the child had come from, and Emily felt she should be vaccinated against smallpox. She did not want the boys or Lalla Heba to be exposed even though they had been vaccinated themselves. The Shereef suggested that the family medical attendant did it, but he was away. Emily thought for a moment. 'You know,' she said, 'I think I could do it myself if I had the vaccine. Did I ever tell you that when I was a small girl at boarding school I saw the principal's baby being vaccinated. I was so fascinated that on the eighth day after the doctor's visit when I found the lymph was still exuding, I took a darning needle, carried the baby into the orchard and vaccinated myself. Not very well I am afraid. I still have the mark to this day.'

* There was and is no adoption system in Morocco—any child is usually taken in and loved by someone of the family.

The Shereef was intrigued and inspected the mark.

'Could you do it to this child then?' he asked.

Emily did not see why it should not be possible if they could get the vaccine. 'Do you suppose that Hadj Said Guesus could obtain it for us in Gibraltar?' she asked.

The Shereef liked the idea. He agreed to send for the vaccine and added that if Emily was successful with the foundling, perhaps it would be possible to vaccinate more children.

The vaccine arrived from Gibraltar a day or two later, between two pieces of glass. But when it came to the point of operating on the little girl, Emily found herself trembling and feeling rather sick. Supposing it went wrong? How responsible she would feel!

Carefully she took a needle from her sewing box, dipped it in boiling water and made a scratch on the girl's arm. Then, offering up a small prayer to both God and Allah, applied the lymph.

It proved to be successful.

'Now,' said the Shereef peering over his glasses at the scratch which was satisfactorily exuding, 'you must try it on other children.'

He only needed to make the suggestion to the mothers of Tangier for them to arrive at his home with children of every age. Emily, courage increasing, sent away forty patients on the first day, all of whom returned voluntarily eight days later to make sure that the vaccination had taken.

That small scratch on the arm of an unwanted baby girl was to save 50,000 Moroccans from the disfigurement of smallpox. Emily's second batch of patients numbered seventy and it was only a short while before people were coming from all over the country, days' journeys, for vaccination. Her 'practice' grew and increased through the years right up until the time of her death, many years later. Apart from the children and adults, some with grey-beards, whom she vaccinated herself, she instructed others on how it should be done. She would send the lymph, gathered from treated patients, to outlying districts with carefully written instructions how to use it.*

Within a year of starting the service she was unable to cope with the requests and had to teach women of her household to help. The patients were satisfied as long as the lymph itself was provided by her and as long as she actually saw them. This gave the treatment the benefit of her *baraka,* inherited from the Shereef.

Between all this hard work she had some relaxation. There was another trip to Cueta where she had made friends, both European and Moroccan, including a pretty little fair haired girl. The child could have been a little English girl with her blonde hair and blue eyes and she had engaging, charming manners. Emily always made a point of taking her some present whenever she visited the town.

She would occasionally go on a hunting party when Ahmed was well enough to leave, but she was more often at home, and it was on an occasion when she was alone that she had a very strange experience.

Whenever her husband was away she slept with both Moulay Ali and Moulay Ahmed in her room and on this occasion, Ahmed, always a light sleeper, was restless and kept her awake. Ali was sound asleep in her bed. She recorded what happened that night in her memoirs.

'About 1.30 a.m. I was dozing,' she wrote, 'and thought I would just give another look at the child. Finding him in a nice sleep, I thought I could settle down, when all at once a bright star seemed to be hovering over the chimney piece. I had put out the candle and only a night-light remained. I looked again, and this light moved towards the foot of my bed, gliding along quite slowly, and then stopped. I looked again, trembling from head to foot, when suddenly the form of a man appeared. It was a venerable

* The wife of one of the present Shereefs of Wazan—H.H. Shereef Moulay Driss (a grandson of Emily's) who lives in the Shereefa's old home still gives vaccinations to the local people, in spite of the fact that the Tangier hospital is across the road from her house.

Shereef Moulay Driss said: 'The people get their compulsory vaccination at the hospital, wipe it away and come to my wife for it to be done again. They believe that coming from a descendant of Emily Keene's, the vaccination is holy, and therefore more effective. This house is still a sanctuary, and while any member of the Wazan family lives here, we shall no doubt continue to give vaccinations.'

face with a long white beard. The body was wrapped in a white garment, draped over the shoulders (haik is the Moorish name) the forehead and head were indistinguishable, as though a mist surrounded them. I took the baby into my bed and covered both of them and myself under the bedclothes. I wanted to call out, but feared to awaken the children. Then a little courage came to me so I peeped to see if there was really anything when I saw the apparition pass through the locked door.

'After it had disappeared, I lighted a candle and made a tour of inspection, which revealed nothing. I told no one, fearing to scare my English nurse and not knowing how the Moors would take my statement. When the Shereef returned from his hunting expedition, I related all that had happened, naturally expecting him to sympathise with me, but instead, in a very calm way, he replied: "Oh did you see him? It is my father. I often see him, so don't be alarmed if he comes another time."'

Emily saw the ghost of Moulay Alarbi on several more occasions, and in spite of the Shereef's matter-of-factness on the subject she was still frightened when he made one of his unexpected appearances.

In 1880, she acquired another child, Moulay et-Touhami, the Shereef's son by a previous marriage who was then nine years old. The boy had written asking to come to Tangier to be with his father—he lived with his mother in Wazan but was the responsibility of his two elder half-brothers. Moulay et-Touhami had tried twice to come to Tangier after running away from home, and had been taken back until giving in to Emily's persuasions, the Shereef finally sent for the boy to come and live with them.

He had not been well-treated by his half-brothers and proved to be a problem. The Shereef did not care for the boy and grumbled if Emily appeared to be paying him more attention than her own children. Sometimes she did just that, feeling that he required more love than her own cheerful, normal sons. She kept tales of his mischief away from the Shereef for fear that the boy would be sent back to Wazan. It was obvious he had been very unhappy there. The slightest suggestion that he might have to leave

Tangier was enough to make him behave himself for several days.

Her family was growing. There was Lalla Heba, now nearly twelve years old, Moulay et-Touhami, her own two boys and the foundling little girl. Emily was in her element surrounded by children. Every festival was observed, both Moslem and Christian, and she was always able to find an excuse for a children's party. A big event was the day in September when the Christmas puddings were made, ready for Christian Christmas. The making of the puddings became a family ritual. Every child had to wish and stir, and by the beginning of November they were all launched into making Christmas presents. Emily did not believe in bought gifts; she felt that love and effort put into a piece of work made the gifts of more value. No child was ever lonely or unhappy once under her capable wing. In years to come the 'dormitories' stretched to take as many as two dozen grandchildren, for she never went back on her earlier decision to make certain that all children of her family were treated equally.*

However, in 1880, there were only five to care for—quite a small family by Victorian standards—and the only problem was Moulay et-Touhami. Emily had a suspicion that his bad behaviour was caused by drinking. There was always plenty of alcohol about the house and it would not be hard for him to obtain. Although all the evidence was there she could not accept that a nine-year-old boy drank, particularly one as intelligent as Moulay et-Touhami. He was impressively bright. He had learnt to speak both English and Spanish within a few months of his arrival in Tangier and he swallowed facts and information like an intellectual ostrich. But there was a possibility that even so young he had a weakness for alcohol. The Shereef's drinking was becoming heavier and steadier; she knew that his eldest son, Moulay el Arbi also drank; it seemed as if there might be a family weakness.

* The Christmas pudding ritual and the present making form the clearest memory for the living grandchildren and great grandchildren. Some of her grandchildren hardly knew their mothers at all. They were completely brought up by their grandmother.

She talked over her problem with M. Lesourd, the French Consul, who had become a friend, saying that she felt Moulay et-Touhami should be going to school. One where there was plenty of discipline.

M. Lesourd suggested that he might go to the Lycée at Algiers if it could be arranged.

Emily had hoped that the Consul might suggest the Lycée. If Moulay et-Touhami was helping himself to the household alcohol there would be very little chance at a French run school for the habit to continue. Also she wanted very much to send her own boys there when they were old enough. If the Shereef agreed that Moulay et-Touhami could go, it would be the thin end of the wedge for Ali and Ahmed.

'If the Shereef will permit it, I think it would be a good idea,' she said.

The Shereef agreed, remarking he wished he were young enough to go himself, and added: 'You had better take the boy there. I've no intention of travelling with him, but it would be a poor compliment to the French Government in Algeria to pack the child off alone.'

Emily therefore made her first trip through Morocco and into Algeria without the protection of her husband. It was the first of very many journeys she was to make alone.

The truth was that by 1880 and seven years of marriage to the same woman the Shereef was less dependent on his wife. Her Victorian rectitude was beginning to pall a little, especially as his drinking habits increased. Emily would not tolerate drunkenness and he was forced to drink only in moderation when she was about. He began to search for excuses to send her away. Though he still loved and respected her, she fettered his inclinations. Also there were young and pretty girls among the slaves and servants of the house who were very willing to respond to his attentions. John Keene's words on her wedding day were beginning to blossom into truth. Emily was nearly thirty, and though still handsome, her hair magnificent as ever, she was not able to compete in youth and freshness with the teenage slave girls and servants of the household.

She knew that the climate of her marriage had changed,

but she was still contented with her children and her charges. Her husband treated her with respect and affection, never giving her cause for complaint in her own home while she was there. She was saddened by the shift in his attitude towards her, but she was not unhappy and being practical she put the situation down to that malaise which comes over any marriage after several years.

Time drifted on. In 1882 Lalla Heba celebrated her fourteenth birthday with cake and candles. The girl had grown so pretty with long dark hair and candid olive eyes that Emily sighed that this birthday had come. The custom was that now she must be betrothed, and would be married very soon. She seemed no more than a child, squeaking and squealing with pleasure at the lighted candles, her round childish cheeks puffed out, the nape of the neck so smooth and vulnerable where her hair parted as she bent her head to blow out the spears of light. She was childishly happy with her presents, and it seemed barbaric that she could not have the privilege of falling in love and choosing her own husband as a European girl would. But Emily said nothing. She had learned in her nine years as a Moroccan's wife that some things could not be changed and it was wiser not to try. And she had seen that the arranged marriages could and did work out very well.

Lalla Heba herself had endorsed Emily's policy of non-interference a few days before the birthday party. She had settled herself at Emily's side on one of the long divans in the first-floor salon of the house her head on her step-mother's shoulder.

She said: 'Mama, do you remember long ago when I first came here I would not speak to you and hid when you came and ignored your lessons?'

It was a subject that had never been mentioned and carefully Emily said that she remembered.

The child explained hesitantly that she had been afraid. The servants, Aisha, Mamhoud, even Mohar, all of them had said Emily was turning her into a Christian and that once she was used to Christian clothes and spoke Emily's language, her step-mother would make her change her religion.

She had lost her suspicions and the servants theirs when Ali was born and was brought up a Moslem. They realised they had been wrong.

'That was when I changed, if you remember, mama,' Lalla Heba said. 'Will you forgive me?'

One happy ending, Emily thought. Not all her encounters had finished so well. She was thinking of poor Si Sliman. The Sultan had not kept his promises to Si Sliman or his people, and gradually the tribe had become restless and begun to pillage and raid again. A price of $2,000 had been put on Si Sliman's head by the Sultan. One night when the rebel chief was at dinner, one of his own followers had killed him for the reward and ridden off to Court, in Fez, presenting Si Sliman's head to Sultan Moulay Hassan. Emily imagined, it, still bearded, the fierce eyes closed, the thin mouth silenced, the brown skin livid, and shuddered. The worst and the best that could be said for the man that he was a patriot and a religious. All his troubles stemmed from what were two admirable qualities.

She voiced her feelings to the Shereef, who grunted and said: 'And apart from all that, the Sultan never paid the reward.'

It was just about this time that Emily received an unlikely visitor. Robert Spence Watson, a contemporary writer, had arrived in Tangier with the intention of achieving something that no Christian writer had managed before —visiting the Holy City of Wazan.

To do this he needed help from the Shereef and Shereefa and had arrived in Tangier with a letter of introduction to them from Sir John Hay Drummond Hay, who was at that time holidaying in Scotland.

Robert Spence Watson's book contains a pen-picture of the Shereefa and her husband which shows all to clearly how the European attitude had changed towards her. His sentences ring with awe that such an important, titled, charming lady should deign to spare him her time.

He rode to her home on the mountain, his letter of introduction safe in hand and wrote of the meeting:

'When we at length reached the Shereef's domains we had to descend a short, steep lane, and found ourselves in a sort of yard where we were greeted by a whole pack of yelping curs, something between collies and jackals. Several Arabs and Ethiopians were lying about, and donkeys (both Spanish and Barbary) mules and ponies stood in lines tethered together by the fore-feet. I handed my letter to one of the Arabs who informed me that the Shereef was not at home. I desired him to give it to the Shereefa, and he went away into the house, leaving me to look about me for twenty minutes, when he returned with a fine little boy, six years old, who said to me in good infantile English: "Mama says you come with me into the garden." I took his hand and he led me away to a charming garden where I found the Shereefa and her companion. There was something reassuring in a kindly greeting from an English lady, and I was at once made to feel at ease. The Shereef, she said, was in the city; he had spoken about my going to Wazan, but she did not yet know whether he would encourage it. He wished to know why I was going, and by which road, and many other particulars before he decided....'

Emily then walked him around her garden and he was 'particularly pleased with some remarkably fine variegated verbenas which the Shereefa gathered me' and then:

'The Shereefa apologised for not asking me in to the house, but explained it was contrary to Moorish custom, especially as her step-daughter who was engaged to be married was staying there. She showed me her two fine boys, four and six years old, with warrantable pride. The younger is the sturdier of the two, but the elder already speaks English, French, Spanish and Arabic, as a child speaks, of course, but in each case with understanding and good pronunciation. I was sufficiently surprised to find myself walking about and talking without restraint to the Shereefa, just as though we had been in our native land, and felt a little uneasy as to what might happen if the Shereef were to return and find me there. Just as I was about to take leave I heard the trampling of horses, and the Grand Shereef himself rode up on a fine cream-coloured, white-faced barb. He was accompanied by two attendants, also on horseback. He at once dismounted and came slowly towards us. It was a fine scene. A stately, very portly, very dark man of 50 years, with an altogether typical face—firm, fixed and impassive—a man whose anger would be terrible and without remorse; but of evident power and quiet dignity; this man silently and calmly coming along to where I was standing, a palpable trespasser and interloper. He was richly but plainly dressed, wearing the fez and blue djelabah, but European waist-coat and trousers. I had plenty of time to observe him, for he came slowly, and I wondered whether behind that immovable face lay the command which storytellers would assuredly have put there, "Sew this dog of a Christian in a sack and cast him into the depth of the sea."

'However there was really no need for any kind of apprehension. The Shereefa introduced me, the Shereef shook hands with me, and told one slave to bring three chairs, and another to set the fountains playing, and then we sat down, and I explained to him exactly what I wished to be at, the Shereefa interpreting for me. He pondered over the matter a little, and then told me that he thought I might safely go, and he would give me a letter to his son who was now the Shereef at Wazan, his lieutenant in fact. He added, that I must clearly understand that I went entirely on my own responsibility. He did not think that I ran much risk unless I met with a fanatic, but, that as I was the first European to enter the Sacred City as a Christian, he wished that I would adopt at least the turban, djelabah, and slippers of the country. He thought that I should find them comfortable to travel in, whilst I should also attract less attention....

'I came away highly pleased with my kind and courteous reception. I was much impressed with the great tact and ability of the Shereefa, who is certainly a woman of remarkable power. It was pleasant to see how thoughtful and polite a husband she has got. I found afterwards when speaking to some Arabs about it, that they were more than surprised that the Shereef should give her his hand to mount and that he should accompany her to hear the

English church service. As I rode home, I could not but think that the fact that an English lady of so much ability occupies her peculiar position may one day be of importance to both Morocco and England.'

Mr. Spence Watson made his journey to Wazan safely and in fact was greeted with astonishing cordiality by all he met. This was explained later when on his return to Tangier he went to say his thanks and goodbyes to the Wazanni's.

'When we reached the house,' he wrote, 'we found the Shereef and Shereefa seated on chairs under the shadow of a great rock, their fine boys playing merrily about, and a number of Arabs grouped round upon the rugs. They received me with much cordiality, the Shereefa addressing me as "Brother". I asked her if that had become my title as of right since I had visited the sacred city. She said that she had never been there, but she had ascertained a day or two previously that the Shereef, partly in fun, and partly to ensure me a cordial reception, had told his son in my letter of introduction that I was her brother! He asked what we were talking about, and, on its being interpreted to him, he laughed heartily over it, and seemed to consider it a capital joke. I need not say that it was a fortunate one for me.'*

Robert Spence Watson made less impression on Emily than she did on him. She never mentioned him in her memoirs, perhaps because both she and the Shereef were concerned with Lalla Heba's betrothal. The Shereef had arranged a husband for his daughter—a relative from Wazan, and she was to marry in October. The news had been announced in March. And his problem was that someone had to go to Fez to make the customary arrangements for the wedding presents, and also that his aunt was arriving from Wazan, with the presents from Lalla Heba's future husband. She had to be properly entertained and made welcome, and there was the trousseau to prepare.

The aunt arrived shortly afterwards with the usual dozens of people to attend her, all of whom had to be housed and fed. The presents she brought were impres-

* *A Visit to Wazan*, Robert Spence Watson, Macmillan and Co.

sive—beautiful jewellery, lengths of superb silk, goods for the future home. And the trousseau was begun. Lengths of silk were cut into the flowing kaftans that Moroccan women wore belted at the waist with gold chains, and seamstresses were hired for the work of sewing them together. It was important, the aunt explained to Emily, that the women of the household were present while the cutting out took place, and that they sang to the rhythm of tom-toms, clapped their hands and gave the joycries. Each garment as it was cut must be sprinkled with aniseed for good luck, else the marriage would not be a happy one.

The problem of the journey to Fez still remained and the Shereef, who had quarrelled with his two elder sons in Wazan did not wish them to undertake the trip for their sister. To set his mind at rest Emily offered to go.

Her husband looked at her consideringly.

'You will?'

'Yes—and I'll take Moulay Ali. It's time he saw some of the interior of his own country.'

She waited for his decision anxiously. For seven years she had wanted to go deeper into the South of Morocco. She now knew the coastal strip down to Cueta and Algeria well. The interior was still a mystery; the area that only a few Christians had ever seen. The question was, would the Shereef permit it?

He was only too willing, not wanting to go into the interior himself. Events were moving in Morocco. Nearly two years previously after much pressing, Sir John Hay Drummond Hay had managed to call an international conference in Madrid on the subject of protection. His aim had been to abolish the system but he had failed. For once the French had won a diplomatic battle concerning Morocco. They had fought for the retention of the protection system; the Italians had backed them, and the international powers had brought pressure to bear with threats of trade reprisals on the Sultan if anything were done to alter the status quo. If anything the situation was now worse. Any foreign merchant could appoint any Moroccan as his factor and as Sir John pointed out, these factors, generally rich men who paid for the privilege of protection, were not selected from angels but from what he called erring Barbarians. There was no limit to the number of people who could become foreign protégés; the situation was entirely out of hand, and the Sultan was helpless. He was also angry with the Wazan family whom he felt had assisted the French machinations.

For these reasons the Shereef thought it would be better to stay in the safety of Tangier than venture into any of the Royal towns. And a little time to himself while Emily was away would not come amiss.

Preparations were well on the way before Emily began to get slightly chilly feet about the journey. When she told Sir John and William Kirby-Green about the proposed trip, both were horrified.

'You cannot possibly go into the interior alone,' William Kirby-Green said. 'What can the Shereef be thinking of to permit it?'

Any faint criticism of her husband made Emily bristle. Her cold feet rapidly warmed.

'If Sidi thinks it is safe, it is safe,' she said. 'After all the people in the environs of Tangier are perfectly well disposed to me.'

'That is as may be,' said Sir John, 'but you are not known in the interior. I say it is foolhardy. At least you must wear native clothing so that you will not be so conspicious.'

She suggested this to the Shereef who squashed it at once.

'All of Morocco knows that my wife is an Englishwoman,' he said, 'and as such you must travel.' Sauce for Robert Spence Watson was not to be sauce for his wife.

The journey to Fez should have taken ten to twelve days. In fact, it took twenty-seven, so many villages begged Emily to stop overnight with them in order that they should receive the blessing of her *baraka,* and that of her son. Their halts must have cost the people dearly in provisions. Emily was travelling with twenty pack mules, sent from Wazan, six saddle horses and four mules from her own stables. Mahmoud was in charge of the advance guard with half-a-dozen men under him; the Shereef's house-keeper travelled to attend to the Shereefa's comfort, the house cook with his assistant was in the party and also forty men who were to guard Emily and Ali.

The Shereef rode out with her for the first hour of the journey with the rest of the household making a procession of all the important men in Tangier to see her and her son off. The ordinary people of the town who could never resist a celebration joined in to listen to the fife and drum band which chirped and boomed them on their way. Followers of the Shereef's from the South carried gay flags and it was a fine send-off. Before they turned back, Emily hugged and kissed Moulay Ahmed, instructing him to be a good boy and mind his father and Lalla Heba, and then waved until he and the Shereef were out of sight.

She caught up with her advance guard four hours' ride from Tangier and found the tents already set up, the fires lit and the local villagers waiting to welcome her with gifts of eggs, chickens, flat loaves, vegetables, haunches of lamb and milk.

The countryside had been disappointing. Bleakly flat, nothing grew but the skeletons of fierce looking thistles. The ground was parched and cracked, parting under the hooves of the mules as they trudged on. A few hawks swayed lazily in the sky and every now and then they would disturb a brilliantly coloured goldfinch. They rode over marshy plains towards the sea and later past forests of cork trees. Every now and then there were fine views of the long Atlantic beaches and the slow white rollers smashing on to the beautifully smooth sands. Then eventually they came on to a broad plain which stretched on interminably into the distance.

It took nine days to reach the town of Ksar el Khebir, a distance of approximately sixty miles from Tangier. They were to stay there two days for man and beast to rest. Provisions had to be checked, saddles tested and missing horses' shoes replaced. Emily was offered a house in the town but preferred to stay in her tent, knowing it was clean and comfortable.

More presents were bought, many for Lalla Heba, and

hospitality was offered by the Pasha and other notables of the town. They left for the next stage of the journey intending to skirt the next important town on the way, Mequinez, but deputations from the Pasha of Mequinez were so persuasive that Emily agreed to visit there.

After a brief stay in Mequinez, a claustrophobic town of dark and gloomy alleyways, they were riding to regain the correct road to Fez when Moulay Ali who had been cantering ahead of the party, came back at a gallop.

There were, he said, people waiting to see them over the rise.

'Oh dear,' said Emily. 'At this rate we shall never get to Fez. We must try not to be held-up this time.'

Moulay Ali had seen several horsemen who were waiting, turbaned and armed in a small valley. They galloped towards Emily's party, threw themselves from their horses in obeisance and announced in a way that allowed no argument that they had come to escort the Shereefa and her blessed son to their village. Emily looked at their fierce, bearded faces and decided that perhaps it was as well not to disagree, though Mahmoud, the other forty retainers and twenty extra men who had joined them for safety on the journey, were fidgety and ill-at-ease.

'Es-Senora, these are the men of the Beni T'Mir tribe,' Mahmoud whispered to her. 'They are not to be trusted. It is not safe to go.'

There really was no decision to make. She had to go with these men.

Keeping Moulay Ali close by her side she cantered her horse up to one of the tribesmen. 'Where is your village?' she asked.

He pointed just over a hillock.

The hillock never seemed to be the right one and for one of the few times in her life, Emily was frightened. All sorts of unpleasant prospects ran through her mind as she rode along, upright and regal in the saddle.

At least she thought as they plodded on, the six horsemen ahead letting off their rifles and filling the clear air with the acrid smell of gunpowder, it would be a lesson for Moulay Ali on the disadvantages of his position. She only hoped it would not be his last lesson.

Eventually they arrived at a spot near to a village where the brushwood grew very high and the area was dotted with olive trees. It was a sleepily peaceful place; a perfect camping spot—and also a perfect spot for a massacre. Her own people had the same thought, and began to remonstrate with the tribesmen who led them.

Emily told them not to fuss and not to anticipate trouble.

They subsided, muttering, while the men of the Beni T'mir swiftly set about putting up tents and preparing fires. Emily's men were not permitted to work, the tribesmen said. They were guests. From the village nearby steaming food arrived with the women who also carried milk. A symbol of peace, and thank heavens for that, Emily thought.

The Shereefa's men still feared some kind of treachery even though when the villagers left for their homes that night, they went with dignity, kissing Emily and Ali's hand or head and asking for a blessing. Mahmoud thought it best to mount a guard of twenty-four men who in order to reassure themselves that the Beni T'Mir were not going to leap out of the brushwood and slaughter them all, did their own form of whistling in the dark and kept a raucous din going all night. Emily did not have the heart to tell them to be silent. She was far from sleep herself in any case.

'We will leave early,' she told Mahmoud, 'before the villagers are awake.'

At daybreak tents were hurriedly taken down and mules repacked, but the plan failed. The Beni T'Mir villagers appeared and refused to permit the Shereefa and her son to leave. A deputation arrived at Emily's tent to beg that she stay one day longer. There seemed no point in refusing. They might physically prevent them from going, Mahmoud said. Bowing to the will of Allah in true Moroccan fashion, Emily made a gracious speech of thanks for their hospitality. Immediately the deputation had gone, her own women burst into wails and tears, declaring they smelt treachery. But the sun came up, the villagers reappeared with food and no violence was done. As the day went on, the atmosphere lightened and by mid afternoon Emily was amused to see how her people threw off their suspicions. Suddenly everyone, Beni T'Mir and Wazan retainers were friends and a feast began.

She made a point of explaining to the headsman that they must leave the next day because the Shereef would be angry if they were late in Fez and suggested that perhaps his people would escort them on the road.

The headsman delighted with the request went off to choose his best men for the journey. He reappeared at sunlight with twenty men who took down the tents and presented her with two extra mules in order to carry the *Yiasa* offered by the villagers. Moulay Ali was made a separate present. A dirty linen bag was handed to him. It contained $100—the tribe's offering to the Zowia of Wazan.

Fez provided the usual exhausting, noisy welcome that by tradition, courtesy and genuine enthusiasm had to be given to the family of the Grand Shereef of Wazan. Moulay Ali took first place in the cortège riding into the magnificent old town through the great arched gateway, while Emily, as was etiquette, remained slightly behind. She was proud of her boy as he sat his horse with dignity, looking very young to carry off the Royal bearing he had adopted for the occasion. Every class and sect of Morocco was there in the streets to greet them and the people shouted: 'Thank God that Sidi el Hadj Abdeslam has remembered us by sending us his son.' Emily found the crowd fascinating and more colourful than in Tangier. The citizens of Fez were the most preponderant, rich and dignified. The Fezi were the aristocracy of Morocco and far ahead in learning from the people of other towns.

Foremost in the crowd were the Taibians and Tehaumis, both sects direct followers of the Wazans who outdid all the others in enthusiasm. The din was thunderous. Powder-play, chanting priests, zahrits from the women, native bands, cheers from the men. The heat was unbearable. Fez set in a great bowl of land was like an oven, and Emily who was wishing she had left her stays off, felt that she was rapidly being cooked even though her riding habit was of a light-weight linen.

It was some time before they could find any peace. Even quartered in the pretty house made ready for them the people pushed into the gardens and pressed inside, appearing through every opening. After leaving behind gifts they did disperse and Emily and Ali were able to eat. Much too late both went to bed and got some rest, though neither slept as well as they did at home in Tangier where a fresh breeze from the Atlantic relieved even the hottest night.

The shops in Fez were a revelation to Emily. The most beautiful things were for sale and were to be purchased for Lalla Heba's trousseau and dowry. She ordered ear-rings of gold, looped with five pendants and ornamented with coral and wondered how on earth Lalla Heba's small ears would ever support them. She brought a fifteen strand pearl necklace with another necklace of hanging gold fish to outline it. A scented black necklace was made up of amber, musk and other sweet smelling substances mixed to a paste, dried hard and then pierced before stringing. The jeweller assured her that the perfume would last for years. She chose gold bracelets, anklets and rings, silks, belts of gold thread, velvet slippers gold embroidered, fine silk scarves and veils of raw silk so lightly woven that the husband would catch a glimpse of his wife's pretty face.

There were things for the home to buy as well. Wall coverings in crimson and green cloth—much prettier than wallpaper, she thought. Cooking pots in brass and copper, finely chased trays and Moorish pottery.

More presents arrived from the townspeople, particularly from the Tuat tribe who had provided the gold for her own wedding ring and would do the same for Lalla Heba. Emily began to understand why she had trudged over plain and mountain with twenty pack mules. It was beginning to look as if she would have to purchase or borrow more pack animals.

Her ride home was an energetic one. She visited a friend of her husband's, Shereef Sidi Dris of Blidah el Wazanni, who lived three miles out of Fez and he presented her with a magnificent four-year-old black stallion before she left. Stroking the glossy nose of the animal she said: 'Oh! He is magnificent.'

'Magnificent—yes, but a son of Satan,' said Sidi Dris. 'You must not ride him.'

Emily did not care to be given orders.

She beckoned to Mahmoud to order a slave to change the saddle from her own horse. 'I shall call him M'Barak,' she said, and immediately her own side saddle was in place, nodded to Mahmoud to help her up.

Sidi Dris was extremely perturbed and his face lengthened as he looked up at her laughing down at him from the great height of the horse. He could imagine the wrath of his spiritual leader if any accident should happen. Already the horse was dancing from side to side restively while Emily held the reins and whispered: 'Whoa, boy! Whoa.'

He could not order the Shereefa down, but he did the best he could by sending several of his servants to conduct Emily back to her lodgings in Fez. M'Barak was not used to being ridden and frolicked all the way back to Fez. Emily was glowing with excitement as she controlled him. She was quite unafraid and enjoying the battle which was more than could be said for the men surrounding her. Each of them was convinced that he personally would be blamed when the Shereefa fell and killed herself. What woman could control a horse of that spirit?

She not only rode him back to Fez, but all the way home to Tangier and though the horse submitted to her when she was in the saddle, he was a mean, bad-tempered animal. He pranced with rage and fury when a couple of miles from Tangier a large and noisy procession, led by the Shereef joined his own cavalcade. The powder-play, the music and the waving of banners made him snort and rear until Emily was forced to admit temporary defeat and ride a quieter horse for the rest of the journey.

The Shereef was happy to see her home again. He had missed her, the pleasures of freedom palling faster than he had thought possible. And when he saw the big, black horse, kicking and bucking as one of the men tried to hold its head, he had hard things to say about Sidi Dris' lack of commonsense.

'Has no one told him that my wife is a mad woman?' he said. 'That to offer a challenge is to offer corn to birds.'

'Oh, don't fuss, Sidi—' Emily said. 'He'll be tamed soon enough,' and she slapped the horse's flank who tossed his head, rolled his eyes at her and blew down his nostrils like an insulted dowager.

She, too, was pleased to be home again. The Shereef looked tired, she thought, but Moulay Ahmed was well and Lalla Heba hopping with impatience to inspect all her purchases. Moulay Ali was standing a little apart, shy after the separation, but looking richly brown from his weeks in the saddle.

'Where did you get that little nigger?' the Shereef wanted to know, hugging Moulay Ali.

Her absence appeared to have sealed the crack which had been appearing in her marriage. The Shereef was his familiar, loving self, and the house on the Marshan curled around her. She was busy with more preparations for the wedding, putting her garden to rights and learning new pieces of music which the Shereef had had specially sent from Gibraltar. And she was determined to master M'Barak. Every morning she slipped off to ride him, and each time the encounter was a battle. Sidi Dris had been right—the horse was a devil. Then one morning she went to the stables and M'Barak had gone. His stall was empty. The grooms were all trying to look as if they were somewhere else, and the more she questioned them as to where her horse was, the more evasive they became.

She ran back to the house where the Shereef was just stirring in the depths of their big bed.

'M'Barak has gone,' she said, 'and they won't tell me where—' and burst into tears.

He dragged himself awake and sat up sleepily, putting out an arm to pull her towards him.

'Now listen,' he said, 'I'm not tired of you, and the children are too young to be left motherless. We'll get you another mount.'

He was as good as his word, but as Emily said petulantly, it wasn't the same. The new docile horse was just dull after M'Barak.

* * *

Lalla Heba's wedding was to take Emily to Wazan for the first time and she was nervous. The visit would mean that she must meet all three of the Shereef's ex-wives, and she found that prospect unpleasant, but felt that if she looked her best it would help her through the ordeal and so she was sewing herself a new wardrobe. Fortunately the latest fashions would suit her. The bustle was back, a blessing as it became her so well. The styling though was very complicated and she hoped she would be able to cope with the sewing. She had some fine silk for herself that she had purchased in Fez, and on a basic sheath skirt of taffetta was draping this in swathes below a fitted waistline and bodice which would show off her fine bosom. The swathes came round to the back of the gown to add body to the bustle.

The departure for Wazan with all the Tangier wedding guests including thirty Moorish ladies was sheer pantomime. Emily had planned to leave immediately after breakfast, but once the thirty ladies, muffled up to the eyebrows in case any man should catch a glimpse of their faces, emerged suspiciously into daylight, all became confusion. They were over-excited and squabbling amongst themselves. Their mules waited patiently, but most of the women had never ridden before and after the fourth had come a cropper, landing like a bundle of expensive, tangled silk on the hard ground, lamenting her fate, Emily had to retire indoors to hide her mirth. They would have been hurt had they seen her laughing at them.

Eventually the procession got under way in the inevitable din of gunpowder exploding, music and joycries, the ladies clinging desperately to their big comfortable Moroccan saddles and showing in every line of their shrouded figures they were certain their last moment had come.

There were over two hundred people in Lalla Heba's procession which rode into Wazan after an exhausting day and night journey. The bride-to-be had travelled the entire way squashed into a litter, heavily draped so that no one should see her, and Emily winced at the thought of the heat and discomfort which she must have endured. She had tried riding in a Moroccan bridal litter a few months after her own marriage and apart from nearly stifling had had the greatest difficulty in getting in and out. The Shereef had been helpless with laughter watching her struggle to emerge, saying he thought at first she would have to stay in the contraption for life. However, Lalla Heba was quite cheerful about the incarceration, enjoying being the centre of attention and with no qualms about marrying a man she had never seen.

From a distance Wazan looked enchanting with red-tiled roofs different from any houses elsewhere in Morocco. It was nestled amongst beautiful mountains and surrounded by fast running streams, but once they neared the town walls it became impossible to get any impression of the place at all for over two thousand people had gathered to watch the cortège arrive. The small town, perched on the mountain side, surrounded by cool arbours of trees, was so packed that it was only possible for the procession to move a few feet at a time. Emily's personal slave, sweat pouring down his face, was forcibly dragging her horse through the crowd, and as docile as the animal was, he was beginning to back and swing his hind-quarters nervously.

Suddenly she spotted her husband, towering above the crowds on his white faced barb. He was beckoning to her, and with great difficulty she manouvered her way to his side, dark faces pressing around her saddle and hands reaching out to grab at her robe. The heads bobbing at her thighs, some shaved, some turbaned were so crammed together it would have been possible to have walked across them.

As she reached the Shereef he cupped his hands over his mouth to shout over the roaring of the crowd and bellowed: 'Follow me, we are going a different way.'

He led her off the rough road, and the horses glad to stretch their legs, galloped wildly through gardens and over hedges at such a speed that they were soon alone, their servants left behind. The last hedge took them into a charming garden where the Shereef pulled up his horse, jumped from the saddle and was ready to lift her from her horse as the animal stopped. Then holding her hand, he dragged her behind him into the nearest house, along a passage, up a staircase until they were on a roof where all of Wazan was spread out before them; the crowd was so thick that the picture seemed still, framed by surrounding mountains.

The house and its surroundings were known as 'The Sultan's Garden' and were to be their home while they stayed in Wazan. Lalla Heba was living at a cousin's house in the town itself. There was time to relax and rest before the boys, excited by the performance they had just been through, arrived three hours later, not a bit tired and full of stories of how they had nearly been crushed and unseated. They then wanted to explore their new quarters. The gardens surrounding the house were superb. The terrace was lined with flower pots bourgeoning with lilies in full bloom, scenting the air marvellously. Below the terrace was the garden itself with flowerbeds full of verbena, geraniums, stocks, sweet williams, dahlias, roses, fuchsias, as well as more exotic Moorish flowers. Emily was entranced. All those English flowers growing bravely so far from home; all blossoming at any old season—she could even see some crocus. They made a blaze of colour, better even than her own garden at home in Tangier.

The trillings of canaries and goldfinches imprisoned in cages suspended from the trees hung on the cool evening, and in one corner of the garden, clear, cold water fell into a bowl which overflowed into a marble tank with a pretty fountain where goldfish swam. From this tank the water flowed in little channels down every path. As well as the birdsong there was the constant sound of moving water, pure and restful.

Emily remarked that it was just how she had imagined the gardens of the Alhambrah at Granada.

'Well, we did create those, too,' her husband said dryly.

The house had equal charm. Long rooms were furnished with great taste and luxury; low divans covered in fine silks; recesses that held big comfortable beds. The tiled floors were particularly fine and spotlessly clean.

'This is my own house,' the Shereef said. 'If we choose to live in Wazan, it would be your home.'

But there were good reasons for not living in Wazan. Reasons like three ex-wives. Emily was to meet the first of them that evening. She rested and after a cool wash down with water ladled from a huge earthernware jug put on her best new gown, twisting and turning in front of the mirror to check the fit and style. It suited her very well, she decided, and pinched her cheeks and bit her lips to give herself some colour.

The ladies of the harem would all be looking very exotic, covered with jewellery, but their gowns, though graceful, did make them look like bundles tied up in the middle. The curving fit of the European style emphasised a full bust and a trim waist. It was hard to guess whether a Moroccan woman was a skinny eight stone or a full-blown twelve stone under their gowns. She gave a last critical look at her reflection, took a deep breath and set off, accompanied by half-a-dozen of her ladies for the first visit.

The eldest wife came as a pleasant surprise. The Shereef had divorced her several years before Emily had even arrived in Morocco, but she was much loved and admired in the town of Wazan and Emily understood why the moment they met. A great crowd of women had gathered at the Shereef's cousins house where Lalla Heba was staying and where the first and present Shereefa were to meet. Emily had to fight her way through as the women crowded to get a better look at the Nazarene, chattering not entirely complimentary comments to each other until they fell back and she was thrust almost into the arms of her husband's ex-wife.

The old Shereefa *was* elderly. A very tall, masculine looking woman of over sixty. Very kindly and sweetly she took Emily's face in her hands, kissed her on both cheeks and said: 'Please look upon me as your mother.'

Emily was quite overcome with emotion. She had been imagining an unpleasant encounter and had not expected to find warmth and friendliness. The interview, an informal one, was over in a moment. There was to be a longer meeting the next day.

'She is nice,' she said to the Shereef that evening.

'I suppose she is,' he said. 'She is my cousin, you know. We were married when I was very young and she is years older than I am. But the family wanted the marriage.'

'She said I was to think of her as my mother.'

'She is old enough to be your mother,' he said.

The reception the following day was even more of an ordeal. So many women of the Wazan household had gathered to watch Emily's arrival that she had to fight to even get into the garden of the old Shereefa's house. Chattering figures, bright robed, smelling of heady sweet scents, crowded around her. Henna-dyed hands reached out to touch her bustle and the lace trim around the neck of her gown. Chirping and trilling like an aviary of inquisitive birds they hemmed her in, but somehow she pushed through them and managed to get in to the vestibule of the Shereefa's home, where she stopped to draw breath, mop her wet forehead and recover dignity.

Somehow the servants were able to close the great wooden doorway behind the surging mass of women and she was led through another door and into a large patio where hundreds of pigeons wheeled above, darting through lofty arcades. The patio was full of more women who all gave the joycry as their new Shereefa appeared, frightening the birds who scattered with a great fluttering of wings.

Emily hesitated, uncertain what to do, when she saw the tall, thin figure of the old Shereefa coming towards her, followed by a troop of younger woman attendants, all of whom carried lighted candles. The old lady again kissed Emily, adding for good measure some hearty pats on the back and led her to sit down in another room where all the important ladies of Wazan all in their best kaftans completely covered by fine silk haiks, waited. All hurried forward to greet her, and wish her and her Lord health and long life, which had to be repeated to each one before adding the accepted courtesy: 'Thank God and you.'

It was a pleasant friendly tea-party, chatting about children and the servant problems, rather like any tea-party back in England. The women's interests were really no different though the formalities—like emptying bottles of scent over the guest—were.

The visit to the Shereef's second wife was not so easy and pleasant. This ex-wife, also a cousin, was tall and rather plump. She was the mother of the Shereef's two eldest sons and suspicious of Emily as it was common knowledge that he preferred his two sons by the Englishwoman to any of his other children. Her expression was fixed and unfriendly when Emily was ushered into her presence. She was surrounded by her women whose demeanour was equally remote. She extended her hand and muttered phrases of greeting in such a low voice that Emily had to lean forward to hear her in order to make the correct replies. In her sitting room there were very few guests, and none spoke. The atmosphere was chilling and Emily sat trying to make conversation, surrounded by cold, curious faces of the women of the household, bundled into their fine silk haiks. She felt slightly hysterical; they looked as if they were all just about to get up and go out.

She took the first opportunity of handing over her presents of fine cloth, a necessary part of Moroccan etiquette, and fled, mopping her brow once she was out in the warm, scented air again. The ordeal was not over. Wife No. 3 was waiting.

This woman was the youngest of the Shereef's ex-wives, younger than Emily herself. She was a rounded girl with fine dark eyes and a soft, intelligent expression. Her skin was very clear. This girl had cried bitter tears when the Shereef had divorced her, probably because her chances of marrying another man or bearing any children were completely gone at the age of about twenty-two. She may even have loved the Shereef in spite of being chosen for him, yet she greeted his new wife with warmth and kindness. The fatalistic streak which dominated the thinking of the Moroccan people had probably helped her to learn to live with her situation.

She hugged and kissed Emily, her breastplate of jewellery digging most uncomfortably into Emily's bosom, had bottles of scent brought to pour over the head and hands of her visitor, served tea and asked sweetly and genuinely after Emily's children. Her women, taking their cue from their mistress, were jolly and friendly, and though almost exhausted with suspense and embarrassment Emily enjoyed the visit and felt she had met someone who could become a real friend.

'How did you get on?' the Shereef said, when he found her relaxing in the cool of the Sultan's garden later that day.

'Quite well,' she said. 'How pretty and charming the youngest wife is.'

'Yes,' he said. 'I always preferred her myself.'

* * *

Emily was not able to remain in Wazan for the long drawn-out wedding festivals. An epidemic of measles had broken out and the children of Wazan lacking resistence to the infection, were dying. The Shereef insisted that she return at once to Tangier, taking Moulay Ali and Moulay Ahmed for fear they might catch it. He was beside himself with anxiety about his sons, and though Emily found it difficult to take measles *that* seriously, she agreed to go home and said her farewells to the divorcees, all of whom pressed her to return again soon—including wife No. 2 who seemed to have mellowed a little. She wept a little over Lalla Heba, whose face was already grotesquely painted for the wedding ceremony in such a way that she hardly recognised her little girl under the doll-like mask of red and blue. But the girl seemed happy—which was all that mattered.

She missed her eldest daughter, as she always thought of Lalla Heba once back in Tangier, but she had plenty to do with all her various causes and interests. The European population was growing in the town and it was about this time that the Shereefa began to acquire her healthy disrespect for the missionaries who were beginning to flock to Morocco in the hope of making converts.

The first to arrive in 1882 on behalf of the Protestants was a Mr. Mackintosh, accompanied by his wife. He had been appointed agent for Morocco by the British and Foreign Bible Society. Early in 1883 the North African

Mission came into being, founded by an earnest and hard-working gentleman called Mr. George Pearse, who was assisted by a Pastor Lowtiz and a Mr. Edward Glenny. By the end of 1883, the North African Mission was flourishing, though claiming few converts, with five stations throughout the coastline of the country and with twenty-two eager and willing helpers, mostly single women.

Emily thought them all rather tiresome. Though she was a devoted Christian herself, she had become knowledgeable on the Moslem religion, and had time for its beliefs. She slept with a book of the sayings of Mohammed at the bedside, generally reading one or two before going to sleep. Her opinion was that it was a great impertinence to attempt to convert a good Moslem.

She was always friendly and helpful to the preachers, inviting them to tea, giving them advice about the customs of the country, but ignoring any requests for help to influence the 'poor, ignorant heathen'. The long-standing European residents who mostly considered the religion of the Moroccans was their own affair and agreed it suited the national temperament, still laughed over the story of a determined British man of God who had decided to take upon himself the conversion of the Moors. He offered to pay a local Tangier man who spoke reasonably good English to go with him to the market place and translate into Arabic the words of Christ. The Moor was somewhat taken aback at this request, knowing that should they be so foolhardy the chances were that both he and the Englishman were likely to end up dead at the worst and stoned at the best. But he was reluctant to turn down the fee; more than he could earn in a month. He agreed, and with the money tucked away under his robes, led the Englishman to the market place and called for attention.

The Englishman spoke first. The Moor followed. The crowd gradually ceased business and settled down to listen. For half-an-hour the duet between the two men went on to an enthralled audience. The sermon over the Englishman left the Soke, delighted with his success, eventually writing an article for a British newspaper describing his experience and saying he was convinced that the conversion

Moulay Ali heading a group of Riffian tribesmen.

Emily with her two sons photographed on their visit to London.

A portrait of Emily, painted not long before her death in 1944 by James McBey.

of the Moors would be no problem at all to any determined missionary.

Had he spoken or understood Arabic, he would have realised that his translator was telling stories from the Arabian nights. But then, had he spoken or understood Arabic, the incident might not have had such a happy ending,

Both Emily and the Shereef had their problems over the difference in their religions. While Emily fobbed off the missionaries, the Shereef's troubles came from his many relatives who really felt that it was time Emily embraced their faith, though they were far too polite to suggest such a thing to her directly. The Moors had better manners than the missionaries, who could not see that the good Emily was doing in the town by her help and the people's affection for her far outweighed the doubtful value of a few reluctant or even genuine converts.

The Shereef had his own way of coping with the problem of nagging relatives. He dealt with them Solomon fashion when tentative suggestions regarding the Islamisation of Emily were proposed. Majestically he would send for a slave to remove the carpets from the floor before bidding the tea-maker to pile a cone of sugar on his tray before placing it in the most conspicuous spot in the middle of the teaparty. This effectively halted the conversation. The guests, all seated Oriental style on the floor on a pile of mattresses would look from the sugar back to the Shereef. Words would falter; it was not polite to ask questions of a Holy man, and he was ignoring the sugar and continuing with the conversation. Nothing seemed to happen except that scampering purposefully across the tiled floors, from all directions, came a regiment of ants, who busily climbed the mountain of sugar, tumbled down again and hurried back to their respective nests, carrying the small white grains. When the sugar was a seething mass of insects, the Shereef would say ponderously: 'Now—witness all these ants. They had arrived from various quarters and all have reached the mountain and attained the good. Such is the case with Moslems, Christians and Jews.'*

* *Appointment to Fez,* G. H. Selous, Richard Press, 1956.

Emily was enchanted by this Biblical handling of the situation when she first learnt of it, and occasionally used the same method when the missionaries began to bore her beyond endurance. She enjoyed its effectiveness even more on witnessing their discomfiture at the invasion of the ants, who when disturbed could sting quite nastily.

She conducted a running battle with the missionaries all her life. Once when they had managed to acquire themselves a foundling, a little girl aged about eight,* they took her off in triumph, clothed her in European clothes and started to pound the word of the Christian God into the child's puzzled little head. Having been brought up on the Koran, the girl was terrified, believing that if they did manage to bully her into Christianity paradise would be lost for her. At the first opportunity she escaped from their mission and holding up her skirts ran as fast as her skinny legs would carry her, through the town and up to the home of the Shereef to beg the protection of *es-Senora*. Too young to appreciate the irony of the situation, she burst in on Emily crying: 'Help me! They are trying to make me a Christian. Oh, help me.'

Emily soothed the child and sorted out what the trouble was. She then put the girl in the kitchen with instructions that she was to be given a good meal. The child's sobs ceased at the sight of the food being cooked, and Emily put on her hat and riding habit, sent for her horse and took herself off to the mission. She was angry at the missionary's presumption and Emily angry was formidable. When she had finished with the gospellers, not only were they chastened, but it would be a long time before they tried to convert another child.

* This woman, now very old, is still living in Tangier

Chapter Eight

A PETITION AND A WARNING OF PRISON

It was in 1882 that Emily's marriage began to disintegrate completely. She had been married nine years. Her troubles were not caused by any of the normal situations which break up relationships. They were brought about by the Moroccan political situation, and in particular, a Monsieur Ordega, who was French consul in Tangier at the period. In 1881 France had added Tunisia to her North African colonies and were even more eager to spread their boundaries to the Atlantic. Ordega, a cunning and ruthless man, was determined to obtain *la glorie* as the man who opened up Morocco for the French to take over.

Like other Consuls before him, Ordega had settled upon the Shereef as the key to his ambitions, and in 1882 he badly needed the Wazanni family's support. Feelings were running high in Morocco against France since members of a French Trade Mission to the court 'got into a row' as Sir John Hay Drummond Hay put it in a letter to his family, 'and had a great many Moroccans arrested and flogged'.

The citizens of the country had enough difficulties with their own Government without added interference from France. Sir John wrote: 'The state of this country becomes daily more hopeless, and I do not see even a glimmer of hope for the future ... I am sick of Morocco and its affairs and am thinking seriously of taking off the galling collar; for I pull and pull and the vehicle only backs....'

However, the Sultan was not weak. He kept his subjects downtrodden and kept also his country's independence, much to the chagrin of the Quai D'Orsay. Even so, the knowledge that Ordega and the Shereef were so close did not please him; it constituted a threat. Also the Shereef's drinking bouts were becoming a public scandal. The pious still believed that the liquor turned to milk when it touched his lips, but the Sultan knew better, and as a religious man disapproved.

In 1883, the Sultan's position strengthened. He paid off the balance of half-a-million pounds sterling which Morocco had been loaned by the British Government in 1862 at the rate of 5%. In that same year he published a decree, a special copy of which was sent to the Shereef. It said, in effect, that the Sultan's authority should take cognizance of all crimes, faults, etc., of the person of each and every district of his company *without distinction of class or category.*

For the Shereef of Wazan this was a personal humiliation. The declaration had reduced him to becoming an ordinary Moorish subject instead of a privileged Prince. He could now be called in front of an ordinary Caid (judge) like anyone else. Even more damaging to his status, the law would also apply to his followers. He could no longer safeguard them from taxation or from the primitive justice of the country.

The decree had exactly the same result as the declaration the Sultan's father had put out at the time of the Shereef's marriage to Emily. Immediately on receiving it, knowing there was no chance of assistance from Sir John Hay Drummond Hay, the Shereef went to the French Consulate and requested French protection. This was immediately granted.

The situation was timely for Ordega whose policy was now to attempt to push the Sultan into such a position that as Sir John wrote acidly, 'when anarchy takes place, La Grand Nation hopes to be asked by the civilised world to step in and protest'. At the same time the French Company Moroccaine was quietly buying up as much land as possible. In connivance with Ordega, they too had chosen the Shereef for the kingpin of this operation. The Wazannis were not only great land owners, but also could help smooth the way to buying other property. Between the Consul and the Commercial gentlemen, the Shereef was so flattered and fêted that Emily began to find him impossible to live with.

His new friends were not averse to bribery and lies. They put Mahmoud, the Shereef's head negro slave on their payroll—a bitter disappointment to Emily who had respected the man. Usually a good judge of character she disliked her husband's latest companions, saw through their plotting and tried to warn her husband who then accused her of jealousy. She wrote that he would not even give her the credit for feeling anxiety on his account.

The turning point in their marriage came one evening when she and the Shereef were relaxing at the house she had bought from her husband with her own savings. This had become necessary in order to obtain some security for herself and her sons. The Shereef was selling off sections of his property to the Company Moroccaine and spending money so wildly—even the house at Wazan was denuded of its treasures—that Emily was afraid of finding her home sold over her head.

He still spent most of his time with her, and on this particular evening she was reading to him when they were interrupted by a servant who asked if Mahmoud could be admitted to see them.

The head slave entered, bowed, and explained in Arabic that one of the directors of the Company Moroccaine had sent him to arrange a private interview with the Shereef at 11 o'clock that evening in Emily's home.

The Shereef looked enquiringly at his wife.

She put down her book. 'He may come here,' she said, 'providing he comes alone and not with that mistress of his. I will not admit individuals of that class into my home.'

The Shereef looked disturbed. 'He will not come here without her,' he said. 'You know that.'

'In that case,' said Emily, 'they had better both stay away. Tell them we have dinner guests, Mahmoud.'

Mahmoud repeated the conversation, with Emily suspected, embellishments to the Company Moroccaine director who swore that he would repay the insult. With Mahmoud's help, he played on the Shereef's constant fears of assassination. The head slave passed the word that there were fifty emissaries of the Sultan's court, all of whom had vowed to cause the Shereef's death. Already depressed by the Sultan's decree, and knowing that his people referred to him as the Shereef Française, the Shereef believed the story.

Eventually one early morning when the Shereef was leaving Emily's house for his office in the town, a charade with a cast of four men was put into play. The men, stationed along the road had been paid to fire over the Shereef's head as he went along his route into town. After the third shot had whistled around his ears, the Shereef, quite terrified, abandoned his usual road and galloped into Tangier in a state of shock, convinced that Mahmoud and the Frenchmen had been correct about the assassination plot.

A director of the Company Moroccaine professed great concern and persuaded him that it would be safer to live in Tangier and that the remoteness of the road to Emily's home made him far too vulnerable a target for the Sultan's assassins.

The first Emily knew of the charade was when Mahmoud arrived with a message to say that 'Nothing would induce the Shereef to live at his wife's home again, as the shock had struck into his soul.'

He added that his master had suggested that Emily came into town to dine nightly with her husband as he knew she did not care to live permanently in the town. She accepted. There was nothing else to do. And for four months that became the pattern of their lives. The Shereef still went for his daily ride, but after the incident on the road he never went near her home.

By November the Sultan's decree was beginning to have effective results. He was 'eating up' the Shereef's followers around Wazan, and in the Riff, and so many pleas for help came via the Moulay Taieb messengers that the Shereef wrote to the Sultan to ask that his people be left in peace.

The only result of the letter was that the Sultan repeated his declaration and also, with some truth, threw doubts on the Shereef's loyalty.

Emily did not know what to do. Her husband was completely under the influence of Ordega and the Company Moroccaine and had turned into an abject coward. He would only sleep with a knife under his pillow and two loaded revolvers at his bedside. Nothing would induce him to return to the house on the Marshan and she was torn between caring for her children and trying to care for him. Painfully she came to a decision. The children must come first. She would spend most of her time with them.

The Shereef's behaviour was causing great dissatisfaction amongst his own people. They felt he was wanting in patriotism at a time when France was becoming more aggressive than ever, chipping away at the borders between Algeria and Morocco and threatening to invade the strip of Moroccan land down near the Sahara where the boundaries had never been properly defined. The Sultan's Government was making urgent representations to the European powers to settle the border question, but the French continued to whip up incidents between the Moroccan tribes and their soldiers, claiming aggression on the part of the Moors.

And in the meantime, the French Consul had also agreed to extend his country's protection not only to the Shereef and his sons, but to thousands of Wazanni dependants—an arrangement which, had it been effective, would have completely nullified the Sultan's declaration.

While this situation was building up Emily was in mourning for her father. He had died of cancer of the throat in February 1884, after retiring young—much younger than her grandfather. Aged 52, John Keene, junior, moved out of London to Wallington near Croydon after the Surrey County Gaol had been closed down in 1878 and settled down to the life of a country gentleman. Like his father he was not to have long to enjoy his leisure.

She was not excessively grieved by his death—she had not seen him for six years, and their relationship had never been close after her marriage. After a brief conventional mourning period she set off for Wazan to attend the name-day ceremonies of her step-son, Moulay Alarbi's first son. The journey, taking place in the early spring when the rain was falling in torrents was a difficult one. The ditches had become streams and the streams were swollen into vicious rivers. Emily, as usual, took the dangers of the ferry crossings, in her stride—though the messenger who had been sent on ahead to tell Moulay Alarbi of the Shereef's choice of name for his first grandson never arrived. He was drowned en route.

She returned to find the political situation more dangerous than ever. On May 20th, 1884 Sir John Hay Drummond Hay wrote the following letter to his sister explaining exactly what was going on in Morocco.

'You will perhaps have seen in the papers contradictory reports about the state of relations between France and Morocco—telegrams asserting that relations are broken off and the flag hauled down; then telegrams declaring that the most friendly relations exist. The fact is Ordega has been blustering here and threatens to break off relations, to march an army across the frontier, to send a fleet and encourage the Shereef (of Wazan) to raise the standard of rebellion and march upon the capital, and that a French force would cross the frontier and support him. All this to obtain the dismissal of Jebar, the Khalifa of Wazan who was unfriendly to the Shereef, the protégé of France. Some one of Jebar's dependants had called the Shereef's son an infidel for accepting French protection; upon which the latter seized the Moor and had him flogged and poured boiling water on him. Naturally, a few days afterwards he died. Then Ordega sent a Secretary of Legation to inquire about this, and the Shereef's son brought his witnesses to prove that Jebar had poisoned his own dependant. (Though Ordega acknowledged that the dead Moor had received two hundred lashes.)

'The Sultan refused to dismiss Jebar without inquiry. Then followed menace upon menace, and finally Ordega left for Paris. The French flag was hauled down, and all letters from Moorish authorities were returned by the Chargé d'Affaires. The impression of course left on the mind of everyone (except myself) was that war was imminent. I telegraphed my Government and so did my other colleagues . . . In the meantime the Sultan appealed to the Austrian, British, German, Italian and Spanish Governments against the proceedings of Ordega in affording protection to the Shereef, his sons, and thousands of dependants, and complained he was fomenting insurrection by sending emissaries to all parts of the Empire to call upon the population to rebel against his Sherifian Majesty's authority. No reply has yet been given to his appeal, and the conspiracy continues, backed by the French. I think it probable however, that Ordega has misled his Government and declared that he has not done what he had done; for he took care not to write his threats, and when a letter was addressed to him containing a repetition of all he had menaced, he would not receive it....

'...Our days of Quixotism are passed; but my fingers tingle to box the fellow's ears. I do not know how he can return here amidst the nest of hornets he has roused....'

Emily's fingers also tingled to box the fellow's ears when she discovered all that had been happening. She realised why the Shereef had sent her to Wazan alone. He had been plotting. She was ambitious enough for her sons' future to contemplate for a moment the possibility of her husband taking over the throne, but she knew (and he knew) that the old prophecy—'ye to rule and we to consecrate your rule'—was against him. There had been times in the past when they had discussed the chances of him taking over the country when difficulties with the Court had arisen, but it was too late now. The man she had married could have attempted the *coup d'état* and won. The man her husband had become under the influence of Ordega and the commercial Frenchmen of Morocco was a different proposition. He was no longer brave; he drank too much, his mind was fuddled at times and he was full of phobias and anxieties. The strength of character needed for such an adventure had gone. Ten years previously his qualities of tolerance, forward-looking and intelligence would have made him a fine Sultan for his country. But not in 1883.

She also had to come to terms with Moulay Alarbi's behaviour. Her earliest assessment of him had been correct when she had remarked he 'looked all things unspeakable'. But on her last visit to Wazan he had seemed changed; greeting her with kindness and courtesy. She had noticed that he, too, was drinking, but even so he appeared improved. In fact, before she left he had made her a present of a fine horse and pressed her to visit Wazan again soon. The sudden relapses into barbarity of the Moors who were so charming and gentle most of the time no longer surprised her, but it was difficult to adjust when such a brutal deed had been committed by someone from her own family.

'What will you do, Sidi?' she asked the Shereef.

'Do? I have to make myself look entirely uninvolved in the whole affair,' her husband said. 'Ordega says I must make it clear to the world that I do not approve of such behaviour. I shall bring Moulay Alarbi here, and I shall flog him as he flogged that man. The correct punishment for the crime and one that will signify my disapproval of the entire matter.'

'Have you told Ordega of this?'

'No—he says he does not want to know how I deal with the affair as long as I do deal with it. My son is a fool. Who can take his family's ambitions seriously when he does such things.'

Ordega understood her husband better than Emily had realised. He had guessed how the Shereef would react. The father would appear as barbaric as the son, and the Consul would have no blame attached to him because he would not know what had been planned. The Shereef was being lead into a situation that could end only in him having no choice whatsoever other than to completely throw in his lot with the French.

The Shereefa was no politician. Her interests were entirely bound up in the prosperity of her family and originally she had been as interested as the Shereef himself in joining forces with the French who could do so much to make their lives more comfortable. But the French had lost her alliance when Ordega's confrères had threatened her son's inheritance. Her thinking had swung to the viewpoint that the British way was best—the line of non-interference that Sir John Hay Drummond Hay followed.

She knew that she must find some way to stop her husband dealing with Moulay Alarbi in the way he proposed. Perhaps the punishment would put the Shereef's position straight with the French. Probably Moulay Alarbi deserved no better treatment, but she knew that if her husband flogged, possibly killed his son, his own people and the rest of the civilised world would never forgive him. She knew enough of Moroccan custom to understand what she must do. She threw herself at the Shereef's feet, and pulling the mass of her hair from its pins, wound it around his feet. She lay on the floor, silently, in the traditional Moorish supplication—a gesture which no true Moslem could ignore.

The Shereef knew he had to give in. Centuries of custom defeated him. He may well have been glad of the excuse not to act, for under normal circumstances, he was not a cruel man. He agreed to forgive his son.

The incident was not quickly forgotten. When it became clear that the Sultan would not dismiss Jebar, French pressure was promptly increased. There was fighting around the borders of South Eastern Algeria and more of the small oases in the undefined areas fell to the French.

It began to look as if war was imminent, and Tangier was in a turmoil of speculation. Emily had moved up to the Shereef's mountain villa for the summer months. Early in June together they watched an ironclad of the French Navy, the *Redoubtable,* steam into the harbour and lay anchor. The Shereef could not be dragged from the cliff; he was certain that Ordega had returned with news from the Quai D'Orsay. Some hours went by, and then a twenty-one gun salute boomed out from the guns of the fort as a boat put out from the *Redoubtable*'s side. Then the Shereef's curiosity and anxiety became so great that he insisted they should ride down into the town to discover exactly what was happening.

They found Tangier bordering on a state of siege. The *Redoubtable*'s heavy guns had been swung to face the town. Ordega had refused to land until the salute had been made, had demanded that all the Moorish notabilities of the town came to the pier to meet him, and no one had dared to refuse. The development pleased the Shereef. 'Now the Sultan will see that we mean business,' he said.

The following morning a squadron of eight French ships appeared in the harbour and there they stayed, guns lined to face the town. The Shereef had been to see Ordega and returned in high humour. It was almost time to move, he said.

His hopes were quickly dashed. He paced about all that day waiting for word from the French Legation, then the next morning, watching from the Mountain, he saw the Squadron get up steam and slowly depart from the bay. A little later a message came to go to the town immediately. Ordega wanted to see him.

He returned crushed. The French Government had ordered by telegraph the return of the Squadron and worse, protection for the Wazanni's dependants was not forthcoming. Ordega had said that he was not permitted to support the Shereef against the authority of the Sultan. France had promised not to disturb the frontier after pressure from the European powers. The plan had collapsed.

'Your friend, Sir John Hay Drummond Hay and his spy, Caid McLean have won,' the Shereef said, 'but Ordega said only the battle. We shall win the war.'

His disappointment with his French patrons made for a small period of happiness for Emily. For the rest of the summer on the mountain the Shereef turned to her. Ordega had let him down, the Sultan was 'eating up' his tribes and he was helpless to strengthen his position. She remained steadfast and loving—a good mother to his sons, and a good wife to him.

Her happiness was to end with the summer. As the colder Atlantic winds began to blow across the mountain, the Shereef decided it was time they moved back into Tangier. She returned to her own home on the Marshan but to her disappointment he returned to the Zowia, nearer the town, without even telling her of his plans. She spent a bitter and bewildering winter. Nearly every day Mahmoud, or another of the slaves, would arrive with a message that the Shereef wished to see her. Obediently she would ride to his home. Sometimes he would keep her waiting for hours in his office and then send her back without seeing her. Other times he would demand to know why she had left the children alone or some days, startlingly affable, would have her sit and talk to him as if there were nothing wrong between them.

Emily began to think that perhaps his troubles were not entirely caused by drinking. She began to suspect that he was going insane.

The sad, cold winter of 1884 dragged to its end and Christmas was not the same with the Shereef away from the house. It was the first Christmas he had not spent with his family and she and the boys missed him. Emily's sister Helena, had come to stay which cheered the atmosphere a little, and then in January 1885 a message arrived from Wazan. Lalla Heba's first baby was due and she wanted Emily to be with her.

As usual, without thought or question, Emily organised the expedition and set off on the difficult winter journey into the mountains to be with her step-daughter, leaving the boys in Helena's care.

At Wazan she found Lalla Heba almost hysterical with fear about the coming birth and was concerned at how pale and ill the girl looked. She decided that a brisk and efficient approach was best, treating Lalla Heba in her best nurse-manner, encouraging her to rest and relax, telling her there was nothing to fear, and no need for self-pity.

Lalla Heba seemed reassured by her step-mother's presence and after a few days was looking better. Emily hoped that the nervous state and genuine ill-health was only a passing indisposition, but after she had been in Wazan a fortnight, the girl became much worse and spent four days and nights in real agony. Emily sat beside her bedside, bathing the hot forehead, holding her dry hands, trying to cool and calm the girl. She knew it was a case for a skilled doctor—but from where? Wazan had no such thing; the roads to Tangier were impassable, and besides, it was as much as any European doctor's life was worth to visit the town. Had anything gone amiss he would have been blamed for the death of a Shereefa. There was little Emily could do. If the traditional Moroccan methods of accouchement were not followed and either child or mother should die, she, too, would be considered responsible in spite of her position in the family.

Poor Lalla Heba went through the ordeal of a Moroccan birth as Emily had witnessed it years before in the house outside Tangier. The son was still-born and the mother unconscious for 24 hours afterwards. Emily was distraught. She needed skilled help, but there was none. She did her best; little enough for there was no medical aid she could give. It was after a day and a night of anxious watching that Lalla Heba's long brown eyes opened and she grasped at her step-mother's hand.

'The baby?' she said. 'How is the baby?'

'Don't worry about him,' Emily said.

'Him!' said Lalla Heba. 'It is a boy. Good,' and fell into a quiet sleep.

Emily stayed at the bedside without a break for eight days, dozing in her chair at night. She only told Lalla Heba that the baby was dead when she judged her strong enough to break the news. As she watched she sewed a warm and practical flannel jacket for her step-daughter to wear when she was well enough to sit up. On the eighth day conscious, with colour in her cheeks, and looking recovered Lalla Heba tried it on and gave Emily a kiss in thanks.

'Now, mama,' she said, 'please have some sleep yourself. I am better now.'

'Are you sure?' Emily said, her hand on the girl's forehead. It seemed cool. There was no fever.

Emily suddenly realised she was very tired. Her back and eyes ached, but she was still reluctant to leave the girl, yet she found herself yawning at the very thought of rest. 'If you are sure,' she said, and gathered up her sewing things, leaving behind the flannel jacket. It was close on midnight, and she leaned over to kiss the girl tenderly before going back to her own house.

It was three a.m. when she was awakened by a tremendous banging at the door of her room. 'Come quickly. Come quickly,' a voice was calling in Arabic. Half-asleep, she hurried out of bed and searched blindly for her dressing gown and heavy coat to put over it if she was to go out into the cold night air of Wazan. At first she thought that the tribes in the hills were attacking the town—there had been rumours of disturbances all week—and then she heard the screeching screaming death dirge of the women reverberating through the streets and narrow alleys of the town. She stopped. Who were they mourning? Her husband? Her children? Could news have come? It could not possibly be Lalla Heba who had seemed so well just a few hours since. She hurried from her room into the narrow hallway to find women waiting for her. Anxious hands grabbed at her and dragged her away to Lalla Heba's home, and she knew that her step-daughter must be dead.

The scene in the death house was chilling. Women were strewn in corridors and doorways, faces contorted and bleeding where they had torn at themselves with their own long nails. A high hysterical wail filled every corner, bouncing back on the air, unstoppable; the dreadful voluble sound of grief. All swayed where they stood or lay, clinging to doorways beating their bare breasts where they had torn away their clothing. Emily picked her way through them while they clung at her skirts and eventually managed to reach the upstairs room where Lalla Heba had lain since the birth of her baby. The immediate family waited there, more controlled than the women below, though even they occasionally broke into the Arab dirge—the first few bars of which sounded like a mad laugh, then sliding into a heart-rending minor key, back to the hideous laugh and finishing with a shriek of pure despair at the end.

The curtains were pulled around the bed in the room, green candles burnt a melancholy light, and two women sobbed, one at the foot and one at the head of the bed. Lalla Heba had died peacefully. She had admired her new bedjacket, drank a glass of milk and slept for an hour. Then she woke and drank some broth, and quite suddenly, threw up her arms and had gone. Peritonitis had been the cause of death.

The girl was buried within a few hours, according to the rites of the Moslem religion. Her nostrils and ears were plugged with camphor wrapped in cotton wool with more of the same placed under her arms. They washed her three times from head to foot with warm soap and water and arranged her in a shroud made from twelve yards of new calico. Her two big toes were tied together and her body turned to face the East. Two thousand people attended the funeral in bright sunshine walking over ground like a fresh green carpet put down for the occasion where the new grass sprouted tenderly after the heavy rains. It took two hours for the burial procession to reach the mausoleum at the Mosque—a distance of a little more than a mile. A few prayers from the Koran were recited over the ready-dug grave, and the grave-digger covered the remains of Lalla Heba.

Emily did not attend the funeral, though she watched from the roof of her home and heard the moans and cries of the mourners. There seemed little point in her entering into a ritual so different from the one of her own church; she was not even sure that she would be welcome. And besides, what did it matter? She had lost her daughter. She would mourn her own way.

She remained in Wazan for another week and then made the journey home. The Shereef was genuinely grieved by Lalla Heba's death, and their combined sorrow seemed for a while to bring them together again. Emily moved to his house on the mountain, earlier than in the last few years and she began to feel that perhaps their marriage might now settle into a steady companionship, althought events had killed much of the romance they once shared. Another helpful development was that Ordega had been suddenly recalled to Paris, having gone too far in his ambitions to be the man who delivered Morocco to his Government. The new minister who arrived early in 1885, M. Feraud, was a different type more intelligent, friendly and with great charm. He was also a first rate Arab scholar, a poet, an artist and an archaeologist. Possessed of more subtlety than Ordega, Sir John Hay Drummond Hay believed he might prove more dangerous in the end, but admitted with relief, that it was a happier prospect to battle wits against a man of Feraud's calibre.

In July Moulay et-Touhami came home from school. He had done well, gained several prizes and learned to speak French perfectly. He began to teach the language to Moulay Ali who, by invitation of the French Government, was to go to the same school at the start of the next term. It was decided that Emily should accompany the boys back to Algiers. They left rather earlier than necessary; the Shereef was becoming restless by the end of the summer, and had resumed his dealings with the representatives of the Company Moroccaine, except that now, instead of one man to influence him, there was now a syndicate of five. Emily realised things were deteriorating again when he disappeared into town at every opportunity and began pressing her to travel, taking the boys with her.

She left for Oran by steamer with her three boys, the Shereef and a large entourage seeing her off at the harbour. He had suggested that she took the boys on a trip to the South of Algeria and South East Morocco before they enrolled at the Lycée in Algiers.

'You have always wanted to see more of the country,' he said. 'Let this be an opportunity.'

She agreed, knowing his reasons were not entirely unselfish, but thinking that perhaps a spell away from him might have the same results as her visit to Fez when he had missed her and been glad to have her home again.

It was an incredible journey that she and her sons made. Moulay et-Touhami had been keen to get back to the Lycée and declined to travel with them, and she with Moulay Ali, Moulay Ahmed, Mohar and a small entourage of servants and guards, set off plunging deep into the South, almost to the borders of the Sahara. She met the tent dwellers for the first time; travelled over vast mountain ranges and across desolate plains where nothing grew but prickly scrub. Most of the time they lived under canvas in areas where European women had never been. It should have been dangerous, but word of her work with vaccination, and respect for her husband and sons as descendants of the Prophet were protection in themselves. Everywhere she and her retinue were welcomed and entertained.

At an encampment near the town of Aflou she joined in a gazelle hunt dining off the meat afterwards and then, when riding towards the town, Moulay Ahmed who had 'borrowed' a spur from one of the guards, tried it out on his mare who resented the application and promptly took off at a mad gallop. The horse thundered past Emily and her first impulse was to follow, but her retainers all shouted at her and Moulay Ali to stop as the animal vanished at speed into the distance her son clinging on for dear life.

'Lady,' Mohar said, 'the mare will stop if she does not hear hoofs coming behind her. You must wait.'

He and several of the other men took off their boots and ran on foot after the runaway as quietly as possible, leaving Emily behind in an agony of mind, uncertain whether her son would still be alive once the silently running figures ahead caught up with him. She had to bear with half-an-hour of apprehension before they heard a shout, and the men who had remained motioned her to ride on. She was white and trembling when she saw Mohar and the others standing in the distance. Reaching them, she found Moulay Ahmed still in the saddle, Mohar hold-the reins, teetering on the edge of a precipice where the mare, still trembling and restive, had ended her flight.

'I made him stay mounted, lady,' Mohar said, 'so that you could see he had not fallen. He is a fine horseman.'

Emily was off her horse and had her child in her arms in a second. The boy was white as a sheet and trembling as much as she was. She fed him a little brandy and water to calm him. They rested for half-an-hour until he was reassured enough to set off again.

'Mama,' he said, as he remounted. 'Shall we now call Aflou "I flew"?'

'Indeed you flew, darling,' she said. 'But how did you manage to keep your seat?'

'Well, mama,' he said gravely, 'you always call me a little monkey, and by acting as such I was able to cling on. So in future when you call me a monkey, you will be perfectly right.'

The journey was to stretch on for nearly three months of constant wandering while Moulay Ali and Moulay Ahmed were introduced to the tribes who acknowledged their father as their leader and they finally returned to the nearest railway line at Tieret where they caught a train back to Algiers. Emily recorded that they then moved to the Hotel l'Oasis and enjoyed the luxury of a good bed, 'for although fairly comfortable in the Arab encampments, the difference is very perceptible and acceptable after a month or two'.

New Year's day 1886 was spent in Algiers. It was wet and chilly and Emily knew no one in the town. She sat in her room at the Hotel l'Oasis watching the Europeans of the town go off to parties in their carriages. In four days time, Moulay Ali would be taken to his school and it would be time for her to return to Tangier with Moulay Ahmed—to what? She had received word that the Shereef was not very well. This probably meant that he had been on another drinking bout, for his enchantment with alcohol was beginning to affect his health. She was still also concerned that he had periods when his mind was deranged, and she was not certain as to the cause. Her problem was that she still loved him. He still fascinated her as much as he had done when she was twenty-two, but her pride had taken so many knocks in the past few years, that her emotions were dulled. She had never felt quite so depressed. It was not her nature to be buffeted and bruised by circumstances and she was angry with herself that her mood was so melancholy. She hated, too, the thought of leaving Moulay Ali behind. She adored both her children, and their presence, love and dependence on her had kept her going through all her difficult days.

The morning after Moulay Ali had been enrolled at the Lycée, Moulay Ahmed also had a fit of the blues and she sent him off with Mohar to buy new toys, and then permitted herself the luxury of a really good weep until she could not squeeze out another tear. Then, she briskly got on with her packing for the return home in a more cheerful state of mind.

* * *

The journey took longer than was intended. Letters from the Shereef asked her to take messages to his followers at different towns en route and it was early February before she arrived again at Tangier.

The Shereef looked ill, Emily thought, when he met her

at the boat. He was suffering from gouty eczema and was beginning to look his age. Her heart went out to him as she saw his eyes fill with tears when Moulay Ahmed ran to meet him, with no older brother running ahead.

He hugged and kissed the child and said over his head: 'I almost think you should go back and fetch Moulay Ali —how we will miss him!'

Emily was half inclined to agree.

Moulay Ahmed was also miserable for a few days but he soon settled down, and Emily got down to the task of trying to nurse the Shereef back to health. On her return his drinking ceased and he began to recover but progress was slow, and the constant irritation and pain of his leg made him bad tempered. Finally the doctor suggested that it might be as well to take him up to the sulphur baths at Hammam Bougrarah near Marnia in Algeria. It was a difficult journey. The Shereef was ill and often delirious. Emily nursed him patiently until gradually his health began to improve. Their stay was fairly quiet as very few of the faithful knew that he was in Algeria, but once word of his presence did seep out letters came from the leaders of the tribes in the Riff Mountains asking if the Shereef would visit them on his return to Tangier. Their crops had been poor for several seasons and they wanted the benefit of his *baraka*. The Shereef agreed. It was his duty for one thing, for another the hunting was good, and then there was the matter of *Yiasa*.

The Shereef was at first reluctant to take Emily on the journey but he finally agreed to take her with him. There were good reasons for his reluctance. Christian faces were unwelcome in the Riff, but Emily was determined not to miss the opportunity to see the mountain fastness that was still the most impenetrable part of the country.

'Oh, don't *fuss*, Sidi,' she said. 'I am not in the least afraid and the opportunity might never occur again. Please let me come. You know perfectly well that I shall be quite safe with you.'

The Shereef looked at this wife; she was smiling the cajoling smile of her youth, her eyes bright and blue in a face tanned from their last journey. She was still an attractive woman at the age of thirty-seven, her figure fuller, but the waist slim, and the hair richly massed about her head. As the chestnut faded a little she had taken to using a touch of the henna that Moroccan women used to dye their hair and the deeper colour made it appear even more luxuriant. As for him, his beard was greying and his leg hurt. Sometimes her vitality and energy made him feel tired. And without any more argument he agreed.

They set off on the 21st of May and by the 24th they had reached Oujda, which Emily considered as dreary a little town on the second visit as it had been on the first. But at least it was quiet now. The inhabitants had other problems than fighting between themselves since the Sultan's decree reducing the powers of the Shereef.

They stayed in Oujda for six days and during this time various chiefs arrived from the outlying tribes to plead with the Shereef for his intercession for French protection for them and their people to prevent the Sultan determinedly eating up their land.

The Shereef realised that he would have to make some attempt to their behalf or his influence would be reduced with the tribes. He decided to go to Marnia in Algeria to talk with the military authorities there to see if anything could be arranged.

The French commandant in Marnia was delighted by the request. It gave him bargaining power. For some time the French authorities had been wanting to survey the terrain of the Riff Mountains in preparation for the time when the opportunity came to move in Morocco. The Riff Mountains, glowering along the Mediterranean coast, would be the first natural barrier that any force invading from the sea would have to meet and they had never been surveyed. Some kind of knowledge of the land would be essential, the Riffians were fierce; a problem to their own Sultan. Assisted by mountains as wild as the men who lived in them, they were almost impossible to defeat in war. They had fought the Spanish many years before, led by the Shereef and inflicted heavy casualties on the Spanish troops. Europeans had left them severely alone ever since.

'We will try to help in obtaining protection for your

people,' the French commandant said, stroking his moustaches, 'but perhaps you could help us in a small matter. On your journey through the Riff would you take one of our most celebrated travellers, M. Duveyrier? He is interested in exploring the mountains, but we realise he would not be safe without escort and under your protection.'

The Shereef regarded him quizzically, quickly understanding the reasons behind the request.

'And will M. Duveyrier be undertaking any surveying work?'

'Oh, a little. Nothing very important, of course. Perhaps you could explain him away as your medical attendant.'

The Shereef accepted another drink from the Commandant absentmindedly. He knew exactly what was in the man's mind but clinging as he was to the last shreds of his own French protection while asking for the same for his tribes, it was difficult to refuse.

'I will take him,' he said slowly, turning the brandy glass in his hands, 'but it is impossible to guarantee his absolute safety. No European is safe in the Riff. Sir John, perhaps, but then he has made friends and the Riffians respect him for his prowess at the hunt. Anyone else....'

'You are taking your wife,' the commandant pointed out.

'My wife is a different matter entirely.'

He sat staring moodily into the glass. The French were always asking the impossible and when it came to the pinch, they let him down. He understood the reasons behind this particular request only too well and was reluctant to be involved.

Emily was quite happy to take Duveyrier along with them, not sensing the political motive. A keen traveller herself, she accepted his interest in the Riff on its face value but she was rather disconcerted to find that the Shereef appeared to be resentful of the man's presence, particularly as no sign of protection for the Oujda tribes seemed to be forthcoming. To signify his disapproval he rode on ahead of the party every day to hunt, leaving her to cope with Duveyrier. Emily did not object particularly, but she became positively alarmed when the Frenchman suddenly brought out a very comprehensive set of surveying instruments and got to work with them. He was so totally engrossed that he never noticed the angry and anxious looks of the Riffians accompanying the expedition. Emily did.

She knew how the Moroccans' keen intelligence immediately spotted anything that threatened their country's independence and though she could control her own personal slaves and servants, was uncertain that one of the local escort might not choose to murder M. Duveyrier in his bed one night.

She had other problems. The journey was proving to require enormous physical endurance. The mountain ranges were wild, with huge crevasses and mere apologies for footpaths, so that most of the journey had to be done on foot. Mohar carried Moulay Ahmed on his shoulders and she picked her way close behind to keep a watchful eye on the safety of the boy. Ever the housewife, she was delighted to find wild lavender growing in profusion and promised herself a grand store for her linen cupboard only to discover that the plant was entirely without scent.

Her organisation was also upset when a camel laden with kitchen utensils ran amok, tearing down the moutains with more than a dozen excited and shouting Arabs chasing him until he finished up on a plain in a valley below. There the animal bucked like a horse as the men tried to catch him and at every new bound another pot or kettle went flying into the air until the entire retinue and Emily herself were weak with laughter. The camel was finally brought to a standstill after the last piece of equipment had gone and the animal stood trembling but on four legs, surrounded by a battery of broken plates and kitchen equipment.

At the coastal town of Melilla M. Duveyrier's expedition came to an abrupt end. A letter from a local Caid arrived for the Shereef saying that he could not be responsible for the safety of any European travelling deeper into the mountains.

The Shereef became very royal and sent back a reply saying that if the ban included his wife he would return immediately to Tangier by way of Oran, cancelling his visit to the Riff people. Another letter was returned stating that there were a thousand welcomes for Moulay Ahmed's mother, but that M. Duveyrier was a different matter entirely.

'You can tell him,' said the Shereef flinging the letter towards her. He had never thought the scheme would work, but was annoyed at being baulked. 'You've seen more of him than I have.'

It was the open use of the surveying equipment that had caused the trouble. The Riffians had realised that M. Duveyrier was no medical man. Emily though still unaware of the political aspects thought privately that their fellow traveller had behaved very carelessly. She was sorry for his disappointment as well as being concerned that the Shereef would be unable to keep his promise to the French. But in any case, there was nothing to be done. M. Duveyrier was returned to Oran by sea from Melilla, like a wrongly addressed parcel.

They then pressed on deeper into the mountains. It says much for Emily's iron constitution that at the age of thirty-seven she was able to make the journey, wearing the hampering and uncomfortable clothing of the period. Their route skirted the Mediterranean for most of the way, but involved climbing mountains so high that the people and animals on the seashore below looked like inhabitants of a toy world. Much of the ascent was so steep that the only way to move upwards was on hands and knees, painfully inch by inch. The animals, eyes rolling fearfully, had to be hauled up by the Riffians, who quite unconcerned by the dizzy drops and chasms formed human chains along the edges of the most dangerous precipices so that the Shereef and his party could pass without being too aware of the alarming way the land fell to nothing.

The scenery, uncorrupted by road or rail was superb. Great snow-capped peaks towered all around, catching fluffy clouds like wisps of veiling. Sunrises and sunsets were technicolour spectaculars of green, blue, orange, pink and red. Emily thought it the most magnificent scenery she had seen yet in North Africa.

She was very taken with the people of the area. They

were often blue-eyed and fair skinned, belonging to the indigenous Berber race of Morocco who had settled the country long before the Arabs arrived bringing Mohammedism with them. In these remote and inaccessible highlands, the Riffians had managed to keep their national identity clear; Islam sat on them lightly, just as Christianity had done at the time of the Romans. They clung to many semi-pagan customs, but were more advanced than the Moslems in the treatment of their women who were not kept in seclusion and went about unveiled. It seemed to Emily that their life was nearer to that of a European woman, though they worked considerably harder. Often they would be yoked to a plough with a horse at their side. At first Emily was shocked, but then remembering the drudgery of charwomen in London, thought perhaps there was not much in it. And these Riff women looked fit and healthy and enjoyed life in their periods of relaxation.

They were fascinated by Emily who was the first European woman they had ever seen, giggling as discreetly as possible behind their hands at the odd way she dressed. But they were friendly and brought her many gifts which they offered shyly and with timid smiles. At one village a quantity of honey was offered and Emily recalled in her memoirs the fuss that the gift caused.

'The Shereef had, as usual, preceded us,' she wrote, 'as he preferred hunting on the road. The heat was too intense for me to take part and I feared it might affect my little boy, so I followed with the baggage animals. When I reached this village (Monstaza) I found that some delightful, cool cabins had been set apart for us, small but comfortable. My camp furniture was brought in, and the women crowded round inside and out, depositing their offerings, honey and honeycomb being predominant. Some, more bold than the rest, thought a close inspection of me would be interesting, so with due respect I was approached and my habit, gloves, boots, etc., were in turn commented upon, favourably or otherwise I cannot say, as they spoke the Riffian language. To avoid carrying an umbrella, I provided myself with an Algerian sun hat as worn by the men when travelling. They are identical in shape to that worn by Mother Goose in children's picture books. Made of light straw, in red and natural colours, the broad brim and high crown are great protection from heat. I was able to arrange my hair pyramid fashion inside the crown, and thereby cover the whole of my head with a fine muslin kerchief to keep out the dust before donning my elegant headgear.

'On the floor was a large dish of fresh honey just arrived, and as I thought the investigation of my person had been sufficiently prolonged, I made signs to my visitors of dismissal, at the same time removing my hat. One woman noticing that some honey had overflowed from the dish turned to remove the little stream with her hands. At the moment I dispensed with my headgear she was so overwhelmed at that sight, that before I could prevent her she clutched at my top-knot with her honey-smeared hands, and beckoned her companions to return. I pushed her away as quickly as possible, and my Moorish maid came to my rescue, too late to prevent the trickling of honey all down my face and habit, fortunately a linen one. The women scampered away, and the Shereef from his cabin opposite wondered what was the cause of all the hilarity on my side, but when he saw the object before him he joined in the mirth with his jolly and hearty laugh.

'Meantime a large basin was found and some water heated for my hair to be washed. As I possessed rather more of that commodity than most people have, the difficulties can well be understood in a confined place, and I am afraid that I did not feel charitable towards the woman who caused the disaster in her surprise at seeing such an unusual mop.'

It took until July 14th before they reached home in Tangier after a journey consisting of less light moments. Moulay Ahmed was nearly lost in a deep pitfall, only the quick thinking of the Riffian men saved him and his pony. A horse fell hundreds of feet to the shore below. Emily had taken all the dangers and discomforts with remarkable *sang-froid* and after a trip that would have exhausted a coal heaver, dressed up and went out to a ball at the French

Legation at 11 p.m. on the night of their return. She was indefatigable.

In September she was off again, taking her boys back to school after the holidays. Moulay Ahmed was starting at the Lycée and while they were away, the Shereef went on a visit to Wazan. On his instructions she took a letter to Tlemcen on her way back to Tangier. The plan was that she would stay at her home for a day or two to rest before setting off again to join her husband at Wazan. But at her home to her great disappointment, she found a letter from him telling her to wait his return in Tangier. Puzzled and unhappy she wandered around the house wondering why he did not want her with him. It seemed very quiet and empty with no husband and no children to greet her. She had hoped as she was always to hope right up until the time of the Shereef's death, that perhaps their marriage had been mending, and that they would be happy again. He had been so pleasant and loving on the long trip through the Riff, but now it seemed that the pattern of behaviour that had plagued her for the past three years was recurring. All manner of thoughts as to why he did not want her in Wazan went through her mind. Perhaps it was simply the opportunity to drink without her to prevent him but perhaps it was the youngest and prettiest of his ex-wives. She realised that his great love for her two boys had held them together more than anything else over the difficult times, but now the boys were away, it seemed that he, too, would stay away from her. A sense of complete desolation came over her. She had never felt so alone and unhappy in her life. She wandered from room to room, seeking consolation from their familiarity, while the servants uneasy and anxious at her unhappiness, followed her. They were frightened by her despair—normally she was always so calm and happy, never permitting anything to upset her. Finally she flung herself on her bed, so big without her husband to share it, and sobbed for hours.

The women of the house crowded round, cooing, patting her gently, trying everything they knew to comfort her but it was only when she had cried herself out that she fell into an uneasy sleep, broken by unhappy thoughts of what her future might be.

* * *

She had been right to be concerned for her future. An explanation for the Shereef's decision for her not to join him in Wazan finally came. The tribes, he said, were in a turbulent state around Wazan, and it was not safe for her to travel. He stayed away much longer than usual and on his return moved into his house near the town, leaving her alone on the Marshan.

Her life could have been worse. The European residents of Tangier were fond of the Shereefa, having quite forgiven her for once having embarrassed them. Everyone rallied around to make sure that she was entertained and had company. It was not a chore; she was a pleasant guest, always amusing and warmly friendly, never bothering others with her problems. That the problems existed everyone knew, though she never spoke of them.

She was sitting at home quietly one day when one of her women came to see her in the long living room. Emily had done many small services for this particular servant's grandchildren at different times, and the old woman was devoted to her mistress.

Now she looked troubled; hovering in the doorway, a shapeless bundle in her striped skirt and loose blouse, her hair tied up in a cloth. She came into the room hesitated as if she were about to speak and then in a half-hearted manner bent over from the waist, legs planted firmly apart on the ground, and began to rub over the tiled floor which had already been cleaned an hour before, swinging her body from side to side as she polished.

Emily was amused.

'The floor is clean, Fatima,' she said.

The old woman straightened, embarrassed, and stood indecisive.

'Did you want to speak to me?' Emily said.

'Oh, yes, lady. But it is a delicate matter. You will not be angry.'

The woman had come to warn her and to beg her to bring 'our revered master the holy Shereef home'. In Tangier the servant said, the people were plotting against him. They were taking their revenge for his friendship with the French. The mother of one of his servants had gained possession of a herb named tartshah and they gave it to him when there was the opportunity.

Emily stared at the old woman, appalled. Tartshah was found in the Riff mountains and if fed regularly to a person would slowly destroy their entire system. It could take months or years to kill depending on the amount administered. If the old woman was speaking truthfully it would explain a great many things; the Shereef's continual maladies; his uncertain temper; his odd behaviour; the doctor's bafflement at his ill health.

'Oh, Fatima,' she said. 'What shall we do?'

The woman moved closer. 'You must bring him home,' she said urgently. 'Persuade him to come here. Only you can do it.'

'I will try,' Emily said.

Early the following morning about the time she knew her husband came home from his morning shoot, she carefully piled up her hair, put on her most becoming riding habit and rode into town. She found her husband at his office, surrounded by papers. He looked up, irritated, as she came through the door. By then he preferred that she was announced before coming to see him.

She thought there was no point prevaricating. She begged him to come home. Told him he needed her care.

'But I am perfectly all right,' he said testily.

It was obviously true. His dark eyes were clear, and his beard and hair, though greying, grew vigorously around his face. He was a little too heavy, but his frame was strong and his movements decisive. Looking at him, so different from the suffering man who had met her from the boat, Emily wondered if Fatima could be right.

'Why will you not live with me?' she asked.

He fidgeted uneasily in his chair.

'You know perfectly well that I cannot live at your house. Remember what happened last time. They nearly killed me on the road. It is too dangerous.'

She decided to play her last card.

'Have you never thought that all your illnesses and

problems might not be something to do with poison? Could it not be that someone is poisoning you? At my home that would not happen.'

He looked outraged, took the glasses he wore for reading off his nose and flung them on the table.

'Who would try to poison me in my own home? My servants and people are loyal to me. Besides, poisoning me would be a sin against God and Mohammed. Remember *I am* the Grand Shereef of Wazan.'

'You believed that someone was trying to shoot you. Would that not be a sin against Mohammed and God?'

'That was different. They were not my own people.'

Logic never did have much effect on the Moslem temperament she thought. There seemed to be nothing more to say, but she tried one last plea.

'Oh, Sidi, *do* come home. It is all so empty without you....'

His dark eyes met her blue ones, and to her surprise she saw that his had filled with tears.

'I cannot live with you,' he said. 'But I will come to your home sometimes—perhaps for tea or for lunch. And you can come to my house whenever you wish.'

He had risen and was busily scraping a handful of papers together. His movements jerky, he grabbed his djelabah, pulled it on and hurried towards the door.

'I have to leave you,' he said. 'We will meet soon for lunch or dinner.'

He went, leaving her alone in the room.

She sat there for a little while, collecting her composure. She was near to tears and confused by his behaviour. He must be guilty about something; either some new dealings with the French syndicate, or, a much worse thought—another woman. The one consolation was that he did not appear to want to banish her from his life entirely, but maybe that was only because he did not want to be separated from his sons. He understood her very well, and would realise that whatever happened to their marriage she would never part with them.

The problem was that she did not want to part from him either.

Chapter Nine

DIVORCE

Tangier 1887. The town was changing. Sir John Hay Drummond Hay had retired and was living quietly at his out-of-town home, Raven's Rock. He still remained in a position of trust with both the Sultan and the British Government on Moroccan affairs, and at the Court, his protégé, Harry MacLean, known now as Caid MacLean, had become one of the Sultan's most influential advisers. The Sultan continued pro-British; he had even chosen an Englishman as his personal doctor—a situation which continued to infuriate the French Legation in Tangier, who had never succeeded in planting a man of their own at Fez.

William Kirby-Green, soon to become Sir William Kirby-Green, had taken over the British Legation and was as respected by the Moors as his predecessor had been. Hadj Hamed, veteran of a thousand boar hunts was slowly dying in his bed and the first wheeled vehicle—a gig—ever seen in the town had been brought to Tangier by an enterprising Spaniard from Oran. At first the contraption terrified the Moors when they saw it drawn across the beach by a spritely horse wearing bells around its neck. The Spaniard hired out gig and horse for rides along the beach and once the Moors got over their original fear, he began to have a great commercial success.

Tangier was beginning to acquire a small tourist trade and a stream of contemporary writers arrived and left to write breathless books about their adventures in darkest Morocco. Emily, the Shereefa of Wazan had become something of a local curiosity as far as the writers were concerned. She saw those who asked for an interview, entertained them and sent them on their way with a few more paragraphs to add to their experiences. The town had become well-known enough for the London *Times* to acquire a correspondent there. Walter Harris, who was to write many fine books about Morocco, had settled in and had already become a close friend of the Wazanni family both in Tangier and Wazan itself.

The Hotel de France had increased its accommodation and could now take more than fifty guests. The Hotel Continental, a rambling new hotel with a magnificent view of the bay was being built and was soon to open. The British residents were pressing for a Protestant Church to be built—they still held services in a room at the Legation, but in the meantime, the British community upheld the old country by forming a cricket team. And in the local jail languished Fatmah, a Turkish negro illegally sold when a boy, who had been in the prison accused of no crime for over a year. He was offered by his 'nominal master' in the Tangier newspaper '*The Times of Morocco*' for about £24 and would be handed over by the Governor of Tangier on receipt of the sum. He could be examined daily at the Tangier jail on application to the gaoler.

The Perdicaris family were still very much the hub of European society, though it seemed as if Walter Harris might well succeed them. One wet, but warm spring evening they were relaxing at the El Minzah Palace in their big, elegant living room. The atmosphere was cool and pleasant; the room blazed with candles, lighting the fine tiled floors, rich carpets and magnificent silk decorations. Ellen Perdicaris was still dressed for dinner and enjoying a glass of Madeira with her husband. They were discussing the wedding of Hebe Varley, Mrs. Perdicaris' daughter to young Gianatelli Gentile, the first dragoman at the Italian Legation. He was a charming young man whose prospects in the Italian diplomatic service were good, and both families were delighted with the match. The marriage was to take place on the 30th of July, and they wanted the occasion to be one that would be a day to remember for both the young couple and their many friends in Tangier.

Their discussions were halted when the wife of their

major-domo hurried in the room to tell them that there was a lady to see them.

Before the Perdicaris could ask who their visitor was, a tall figure pushed the major-domo's wife aside and almost fell through the door. There, to their astonishment standing in their withdrawing room, her train muddied, her hair tumbling in long wet strands, her face the colour of green chalk, was the Shereefa of Wazan. She swayed on her feet, put out a blind hand and then collapsed on the Persian carpet.

For a moment neither Ellen or Ion Perdicaris could quite take in what had happened. There had been no communication between them and Emily since Mrs. Perdicaris had precipitated her from their home fifteen years previously—only a cold nod when they passed on the street or met at a reception.

Ion Perdicaris was the first to recover. 'Get a doctor and send in your husband,' he said to the major-domo's wife who hurried from the room.

With the help of the major-domo they managed to lift the Shereefa to a bedroom. She opened her eyes, vomited, and the green pallor began to fade a little from her face.

'Poison,' she said. 'They tried to poison me.'

She had been alone in her own home. Both her boys were at school in Algeria and Moulay et-Touhami was back in Wazan where he was causing the family considerable concern by his wild behaviour. It was already dark when a messenger arrived from the Zowia where she had spent the first months of her married life to say that a servant was sick. Would she come?

Emily never refused a call for assistance when someone was ill. She changed into her riding habit and rode the short distance across the Jew's River and once at the Zowia went straight to the servants' quarters. The servant did not appear to be very sick, but she administered to her as best she could and prepared to leave for her own home. The Shereef was living in the Zowia and she was uncertain as to whether he was in Tangier or not and did not wish to meet him unexpectedly in case he thought she was searching for excuses to bump into him. She was just looping up the train of her old-fashioned riding habit when another servant appeared and offered her a cup of coffee. The poison, immediately obvious by the burning pain and overwhelming feeling of nausea, had been put into the drink.

The Italian doctor who attended her at the Perdicaris' said that the dose had not been great enough to do any permanent damage. She was extremely fortunate, he added. He had seen examples of poisoning before. The irritants used in Morocco were usually untraceable and worked slowly, killing after several days. He was sure that whoever had put the dose into the coffee had merely intended to frighten or make her ill.

That was small comfort. After finishing the coffee and realising what had happened, Emily had been terrified. She, too, knew about Moroccan methods of poisoning, probably in greater detail than the doctor, and she was convinced that she was going to die. As well as terror, she felt a great sense of outrage that anyone should do such a thing to her. The people of the town, as she remarked in her memoirs, had always professed the greatest affection for her.

She had panicked. She needed to be with Europeans. She knew she did not have sufficient strength to get to her own house and the nearest house was the one below the Zowia—the home of the Perdicaris.

She had no idea whether or not they would be at home, but the major-domo was European. She dragged herself on to her horse, and clinging to its neck somehow managed the rough road to the house below.

One happy ending came as a result of the near tragedy. The long breach with the Perdicaris family was healed, though it was never discovered who tried to kill her. Gossip was that it was one of the women of the Shereef's unofficial harem who wanted her out of the way—but they would have been more thorough. Unkinder gossip said it was the Shereef himself, but the attempt was more likely to have been a continuation of the complicated series of plots and intrigues put into action by Ordega four years previously.

It could not have been the Shereef personally. He had left for Paris just prior to the attempt on her life, having originally promised to take her with him. At the last moment he had changed his mind and left with a professional interpreter and a group of men from the Company Moroccaine.

Almost certainly they had put pressure on him to leave her behind. Emily was still a constant thorn in the flesh of their ambitions. Her mind unclouded by alcohol or flattery, she was more wide-awake than her husband, and tiresomely far-seeing when it came to money matters, and she still had a surprising amount of influence over him.

Shortly after his return from Paris, the reasons for her exclusion from the trip became clear. The Kirby-Green family warned her that the Shereef had been talked into selling every acre of land he owned in Morocco in return for an income of £5,000 per annum.

Seeing her sons' inheritance vanishing and her own security jeopardised, Emily went into action. She busied herself with more enquiries and discovered that the deed of conveyance had not been signed, and more important, that the syndicate making the purchase had no capital. She sent a trustworthy servant to inform the Shereef of her knowledge, and also to say that she proposed protesting to the Moorish authorities if he persisted in going through with the transaction. She knew she had a good case, and that the Moroccans would not welcome large tracts of their country being sold to France. The Shereef listened to her message without comment, but the sale did not take place. The incident was never mentioned between them.

He was, though, in financial difficulties. Since the Sultan's restrictions on his authority, the *Yiasa* was not so forthcoming as it had been. The people still kissed the hem of his robe, but as his tribes were now forced to pay the Sultan's taxes, it left little to give even for the privilege of his blessing.

Later in 1887 he sold property around her house on the Marshan to a French business man, the sale being handled by one of the same syndicate who had nearly managed to buy all his land. Wiser this time, the Frenchman kept the proceedings secret so that no word should leak back to the Shereefa whose militancy in money matters they now appreciated. She learnt nothing about the transaction until it was too late, but had the pleasure of turning away a party of people who came to take possession of her own house, informing them without mincing her words, that the property was not the Shereef's to sell.

This caused confusion and recriminations back at the French Legation, and finally the Shereef was forced to take a lesser price for the remaining land and a smaller house which stood beside her own.

He was still living apart from her though they continued their social engagements as though nothing were amiss. The event of the year was the wedding of Mrs. Perdicaris' daughter, Hebe Varley, at the end of July to the dragoman at the Italian Embassy. The old feud now over, Emily and the Shereef were amongst the sixty guests, the élite of Tangier, who were invited to the reception which took place in the Moorish portion of the El Minzah Palace.

The Perdicaris had erected a splendid altar in one of the rooms opening on to a patio where all the guests gathered to watch the wedding, conducted by the Reverend Padre Jose Lerchundi and several Franciscan friars. The Shereef, apart from the members of a Moorish band, was the only Moor present. He was in a good mood, and enjoying himself. He ate heartily of the European meal that was served and tried a little Moroccan food that was being served to the orchestra. Three sheep had been roasted and there was unlimited kous-kous. He extravagantly complimented Mr. Perdicaris on his Moorish cook, threatening to lure the man to his own household.

The new Mrs. Gianatelli Gentile and her husband were going to Europe for their honeymoon and the entire wedding party accompanied the couple to the harbour where the old *Hercules* waited to take them to Gibraltar on the first stage of their journey. It was just the kind of procession the Shereef loved—six Moorish soldiers in new uniforms provided by Mr. Perdicaris led the way, followed by the band who marched behind them playing, and then came the couple with the wedding guests who followed throwing confetti and rice. The Shereef enthusiastically pelted the young couple, and Emily may well have remembered her own wedding day when the same custom had so puzzled him. Together they ran with the other guests through the streets down to the harbour, watched all the way by a big crowd of local people. The Shereef held her hand, and seemed closer to her than he had been for some time.

But he went back to his own house immediately the wedding was over.

By January of 1888, Emily was exhausted and ill with the worry and confusion of the past months. She asked William Kirby-Green to see her husband to try to discover exactly what his wishes were regarding her, but the Shereef would tell him nothing. Eventually he announced that he wished her to live in Algeria, near to the children. She agreed, feeling that the separation would be a relief, but almost the next day he refused to permit her to go. Bewildered, she consulted the French Consul with reference to her financial position, as the Shereef was still so involved with the French, but to no end. Finally she took herself to a Moorish 'savant' who talked her problems over with the local Caid (judge) with the result that they wrote a letter to the Shereef reminding him of his responsibilities to his wife.

Surprisingly, for a man so Europeanised, this was the only move that obtained any results. Her husband sent for Emily and asked her to move from the Marshan and take a small house in Tangier itself. She did as she wished.

Her illness in January 1888—a bad attack of bronchitis which confined her to bed for several days—changed their relationship again. The Shereef hurried to visit her, sat at her bedside every day holding her hand, and crying as she struggled to breathe.

'You must not die,' he would say over and over again. 'The children need you.'

'Don't fuss, Sidi,' she said painfully. 'I assure you I have no intention of dying.'

Immediately she recovered, they set off travelling again. The Shereef's leg was troubling him, and he wanted to visit the Sulphur Baths at Hamman Bougrarah where he had now purchased an estate. By the time they arrived, he was seriously ill and she nursed him for six weeks. He was grateful, and they stayed away for several months, perfectly contented together. But eventually the Shereef had to return to Tangier for business reasons, and it became obvious that forces at work in the town were the cause of their marital troubles. Immediately they returned any kind of rapport vanished, and the Shereef became unpredictable and evasive again. His health failed in Tangier; his drinking increased. He was subjected to pressures from the Sultan, pressures from the French commercial business men, pressures to some extent from Emily. Perhaps, not surprisingly, he would retreat to his own home and surround himself with his own servants.

Equally unsurprising, Emily could not understand him. As her bewilderment grew and her funds diminished, she tried to get her life into a settled pattern of some kind or another, by this time almost wishing that she could completely break with the Shereef for the sake of some peace of mind. Her difficulty was that she still loved him, and she had a strong suspicion that if he did not love her, he could not quite do without her. She was certain that most of his unkindness was caused by guilt. He might avoid seeing her, but he was never impolite when they met. She had been told that one of his cousins had remarked it was curious that she remained in Morocco, and that the Shereef had replied: 'God forbid that she should do otherwise, and grant her long life with our sons.'

And so she resigned herself to the situation for the sake of her children.

It was in the summer and he was living in the house on the mountain when he sent for her on a matter of great importance. She rode immediately to his home, and found him hovering, waiting for her to arrive. He hurried forward and helped her to dismount and then led her into the pretty summer-house in the garden where several people were with him. Gradually all left and when they were alone, the Shereef seated himself opposite her and sat staring at her silently.

'What was it you wanted to see me about, Sidi?' she asked.

He got up and began to pace the room, pulling his robes about him. The proposition came articulately. He had obviously been preparing what to say. He did not wish to live in Tangier. He wanted to leave Morocco. He was tired of insults from the Sultan, and the French appeared powerless to stop them. He wanted to go to Algeria where he was appreciated by both his own people and the French Government. He had decided to live in Oran and wished her to live there with him. But—there was no money to be had.

There was a slight hesitation in his manner before the point of the proposition came. He wanted her to sell all the furniture in her home to raise ready cash. It might even be necessary to sell the house. And once this was done, he wanted her to go on to Oran to find a home, while he went to Wazan to arrange matters with Moulay Alarbi before joining her in Algeria.

She heard him out and then considered what he had asked. It could be another move to separate them permanently; once her home in Tangier was sold there would be no point in returning, or the suggestion could be genuine. It would be the best possible move for him to leave Morocco—the difference in his health and stability was marked once they were away from Tangier. If the move would effect a reconciliation it was well worth taking the chance. But if the offer were not genuine....

'I must think about it,' she told him.

'It would set my mind at rest if I could have your answer now.'

She shook her head. 'I am sorry, Sidi, but I must think it over. There are the boys to consult, and I must be sure in my own mind that it is the right thing to do.'

She got to her feet and busied herself arranging the train of her riding habit. He watched her moodily before walking with her out of the summer-house and helping her mount her horse. She rode off without looking back.

Moulay Ali and Moulay Ahmed were both home for the holidays and neither were happy at the suggestion that they should give up their home in Tangier.

'Papa should not ask it of you,' Moulay Ahmed said. Though only eleven, he was intelligent and perceptive, his thirteen-year-old brother, tall and slim with a grave expression, equally so.

Both boys were adamant that the move was not a good thing. They pointed out that should their papa leave the family alone in Algeria, their mother would have no friends at hand and they spoke in a way that suggested they completely understood her problems of the past few years. She was perturbed by this. She had never spoken of her difficulties with their father and tried to be certain that they respected and loved him, but it was difficult to hide from a thirteen-year-old boy all that was going on.

Word came the following day from the Shereef that the house would have to be sold. This helped Emily make her decision. She would go half-way—selling the furniture and moving to Oran, but she would not sell her home. It was her lifeline with Tangier and her friends, and asking too much to expect her to part with it.

She went to Oran, and very quickly realised it had been a mistake. The Shereef did not follow her.

The months dragged by and she felt abandoned in a town where she had few friends and only two women to attend her. She was very short of money, the Shereef not having sent her any, and lived for the time when her boys would be with her again. She was not yet forty, and still a handsome woman, but it never occurred to her to contemplate divorce or remarriage. Her circumstances were complicated by the fact that whatever happened, she remained in love with her husband.

In December 1888 at one o'clock in the morning a carriage drew up outside her rented house, followed by a tremendous banging on the door. Her two women pushed into her room, their hennaed feet bare, clutching haiks about their night clothes. They were frightened and begged her not to open the door.

Emily being Emily ignored the warning and with the women creeping behind her she moved swiftly from her bedroom and down to the door, removing the chain that secured it for the night.

'Who is there?' she asked.

'Lady—it is I—Mahommed, the guide. The Sidi is on board a ship in the harbour and is dangerously ill, God grant that he live. The commander has asked that I bring you to him.'

She thought for a moment, her hand on the door chain. It could be a ruse to get her out of her house and the streets of Oran were not noted for their safety after dark. But she knew Mahommed and recognised his voice. She did not think he would be involved in any plot to harm her. She told him to wait.

Her two women burst into wails, protesting the risk. Both were convinced that some mischief was planned. Emily disregarded them. She had said she would go, so she would go. She dressed methodically then went to the kitchen to put on some meat for beef tea, her panacea for most ills.

Mahommed was waiting for her with a carriage. She climbed in and he whipped up the horses and set off through the dark town as fast as he could go as if he were not happy himself at being out so late. Oran was rather sinister at night. The narrow alleys were voids on every side, only a very rare cloaked and hooded figure was to be seen, slipping into the darkness. But Emily, never one to be afflicted with nerves, was more concerned about what she would find on the ship.

Twenty minutes later Mohammed was helping her aboard and she arrived rather breathless on deck to find the Commander was ready to receive her. He was obviously relieved that she had come, and explained that her husband had locked himself in his cabin and refused to come out. Diffidently he explained that it seemed as if the Shereef was a little demented as well as ill.

Emily knew the Captain's embarrassment meant that her husband had been drinking.

She was led to his cabin and after her knock the door opened slowly and cautiously and the Shereef's face and greying beard appeared around the jam.

'Come in. Quickly,' he said, catching at her arm to drag

her inside. 'Thank God you have come. I can trust only you.'

'What is the matter, Sidi?' she asked calmly, taking off her hat and placing her gloves neatly on the dressing table.

He leaned towards her, his mouth close to her ear.

'It is Mahmoud. He is trying to poison me. He is in league with some of the crew. I dare not eat. I have not eaten for two days.'

Emily considered. It was possible that he was right. She would believe anything of Mahmoud, being very well aware that his cupidity and disloyalty had added considerably to her marital troubles with the Shereef. On the other hand, the Shereef's present condition was more likely to be one of his all too frequent delusions, following a heavy drinking bout. Logically it was absurd to suspect Mahmoud of murdering his master. She still believed that Fatima had been telling the truth about the tartshah, but she was certain that Mahmoud was not the poisoner. The slave made money from the French who had bribed him to spy on his master. He received his board and lodging from the Shereef. If the Shereef died, he only stood to lose.

But regardless of whether her husband was suffering from a delirium or not, she had the opportunity to take him home with her.

Firmly she dressed him, packed his bags and took him to the little rented house and put him straight to bed. She was content. He was in her care, again.

He stayed with her at the house in Oran until after a diet of beef tea, nourishing food, no alcohol and constant nursing, she had brought him back to health. Restless, perhaps bored with the constant attention and babying, he then said he must leave for his estate at Hammam Bougrarah, insisting she stayed in Oran to wait for him to return. He would, he said, be away for a fortnight.

She recorded their parting ruefully, writing: 'I was much struck with the excess of cordiality in the railway carriage as he was leaving he seemed as though he could not part with me. Again and again he took me in his arms; fortunately there was no other passenger at the time. On starting he hung from a window until a curve took the train out of sight. He wrote to me from Tlemcen, and sent a messenger from Bel Abbes. I could not imagine why he went there. Then the money he promised me never came, and there was no more news except from outsiders, that he was at Hamman Bougrarah. No reply to telegrams, but at last one came: 'Shereef suddenly decided to return to Tangier; embarked at Nemours; do not follow.'

She heard no more of him for some long time; there was no money and she was faced with doctor's bills from his illness. Enough was enough, she decided and refused to settle his debts.

Uncertain what move to make she waited for some word. When it finally came in a telegram to the French authorities she suffered a bad shock.

The telegram requested that the authorities inform her she had been divorced.

A very unhappy employee of the Legation came to break the news, and she stared at his embarrassed face unbelievingly. She could not credit it possible. Under the marriage contract drawn up all those years before the Shereef had no grounds to divorce her. She had done nothing to give him cause.

'Run along,' she said absently to the young Frenchman, putting him out of his misery. She wanted to be alone to think and was remembering how badly she had felt about the unromantic aspect of the clause in her marriage contract which said the Shereef must pay her £800 if he divorced her without reason. Now, it seemed, he had done just that. Yet, she was reasonably certain that he did not have £800 to pay her. And she had no money herself. Her father had left nothing for her in his will, believing her to be well provided for, but any small savings that she had managed to acquire had completely gone. She was practically destitute.

There was no point in sitting down and crying under the situation. She packed a bag, called a carriage, and with her last money bought a railroad ticket to Algiers where she went straight to see the French Governor General of Algeria, M. Firman. They were old friends—his daughter was Madame Feraud, the daughter of the French Consul in Tangier—and he was highly sympathetic to her plight. He advanced her 1,000 francs, and solvent again, she decided to go home to Tangier to find out exactly what was going on.

What was happening was that the Shereef had been almost constantly drunk since he left her in Oran. His drinking was now to some extent motivated by despair. His life was in chaos; he had lost most of his power and a course of action, originally meant to try to help improve his country had become twisted into unravellable knots. He felt no one respected him; Frenchman or Moor. In his lucid moments he could see exactly how he had been manipulated by successive French consuls and business men. He understood where he had gone wrong, but it was too late to salvage his pride, his power or his marriage. He had very few coherent hours. His mind was fuddled both by drink and by illness and possibly even the insidious doses of tartshah if Fatima were right. He was facing ruin. He had hardly any money left, much of his Tangier property had been sold off, and somehow he had to get more cash. One painfully hungover morning when he had started drinking early to make himself feel stronger, the answer came to him. He would remarry. The gifts from the tribes and relatives would come pouring in to save him. But who could he marry? He decided the identity of the bride was relatively unimportant, and he picked upon the first servant girl he saw of his household; one who had always been kind to him, and who looked presentable enough to become the new Shereefa of Wazan. The girl, unable to believe her good fortune, even though the Shereef was nearing sixty, accepted immediately.

He dreamed up the scheme when drunk; carried it out without thought for the consequences when drunk, and was left with time when sober to reflect upon what he had done.

It cost him £800 of the *Yiasa*. Emily with her son's future and her own security in mind extracted her due from him through the Caids. It appeared that he had not actually divorced her, but merely exercised his prerogative as a Moslem to marry again. He paid £800 for the privilege of exercising that prerogative. Had he also divorced her, it would have cost him another £800.

He awoke one black morning just after she had reappeared in Tangier to realise exactly what he had done. He felt ill, old and tired and wanted to be with Emily. He was frightened of treachery and she was still the only person he really trusted. He sent his servants to see her to beg for an interview, but they came back with word that she did not wish to see him. Time and time again he tried, always asking for her to come to him—he could not quite swallow his pride sufficiently to go to her—and every time she refused. Then he found she had returned to Oran, without a goodbye. He felt she had failed him, too. He thought she should have understood.

Her friends in Tangier had urged her to apply for divorce, but Emily would not. She decided that her sons were safer while she still remained the Shereef's wife, even if there was another. On her return to Oran she was seriously ill, her health breaking under all the strains of the past years, and even when she had recovered her troubles were not over. The Shereef, raging in Tangier, decided that he would put his sons under the guardianship of the French Government and take them away from their mother. A punishment for refusing to see him.

But he was no longer as important to the French. His authority was so diminished by the Sultan and his own personal habits that the Governor General in Algeria came down on Emily's side, to the extent of using guards of soldiers to deliver the children to their mother so that the Shereef's few remaining loyal followers could not make any attempt to kidnap the boys.

But then, a year later, for some unknown reason the French refused the Shereefa permission to go to Algiers to take her sons back to school.

Her entire life fell into a series of similar unpredictabilities. When she took her sons home to Tangier for their first holidays after the Shereef's remarriage, he was waiting at the newly built pier to greet the boys and professed surprise that she was with them. But was so affable towards her that a stranger would have thought them a devoted and happy couple. He persuaded her to take the boys with him to Wazan, and she agreed—on condition that she had separate caravans.

Wazan was not the same. The Shereef's excesses had stripped the pretty house of all valuables; even the charming fountain of marble and tiles which had made the centre-piece in the Sultan's garden had gone. On his last visit he had arrived with a clockwork steam-boat with which he played in the pond. It had run into the stonework and smashed, and furious he had the fountain removed and smashed, too.

Worse, Moulay et-Touhami had become completely uncontrollable. He was drinking very heavily, and when drunk, became violent. There was no friendship between him and his brothers, and he complained to Emily that they kept him short of money. But his condition was so bad that Emily could see little hope for him. Had all been well between her and the Shereef she would have taken him home with her, but it seemed an impractical thing to do, the way her life was progressing.

In December of the year, Moulay et-Touhami went quite mad. Walter Harris, the *Times* Correspondent, who was in Wazan visiting the Shereef's younger son at the time, chronicled the event.* Moulay et-Touhami had been locked in his house after a series of incidents. Harris wrote:

'In a fit of madness he fired from a window of his house upon people passing to the mosque to prayer. Several were killed, but his sanctity (as a son of the Grand Shereef of Wazan) rendered him immune from any punishment. The townspeople stated it was the "Will of God", manifest through the Holy Shereef, and some even envied the people who had found death at his hands. All that was done was to warn the passers-by that there was a risk of being shot! The same night Moulay et-Touhami wrote me a letter. It is undated—it was December 1889—and is written in French: —

* *Morocco that Was,* William Blackwood & Son, 1921.

'"My Dear Friend—I beg you to tell my brothers that I thank them very much for having sent still another soldier to kill me, for today I went up to my couba (upper room) for a little air. As I looked out of the window I saw a soldier armed with a rifle. I was afraid and I aimed my rifle at him, but as he told me he would do nothing I let him pass quietly. He at once went to my brothers to say that I had wished to kill him. I swear to you on the head of our Prophet Mohammed that if I had wished to do so I have other places from which I could kill everyone who passes, only I am not mad. I killed those men because I was drunk, and also angry on account of a journey and on account of a story between me and a Shereef. I swear to you, my dear friend, that I was off my head.

'"Now, dear Friend, ask Moulay Alarbi to return me my mules and that he send me some money for my family and I are starving.

'"I beg you to do your utmost with my brothers, so as to save my life and that of my poor mother. The shot that the soldier fired missed me.

'"Is it thus that brothers should be?

'"Moulay Touhami."'

'He omitted to state in this letter that he had, as well as killing the people he speaks of, attempted to murder the two sons of his brother Moulay Mohammed, by firing on them inside the mosque!

'On Christmas night, a few weeks after these incidents, I went to see Moulay Touhami, who had been sober and in his right mind for some time. We were to go hunting the next day at dawn, and a few details of our excursion still remained to be settled. I had supper with him, but on leaving the supper-room in which we had spent the evening I was treacherously attacked by the Shereef and his slaves. In the struggle I fell down the steep flight of stairs. My call for help had alarmed some passers-by, and the Shereef's retainers heard voices in the street. They fled and their master disappeared into the inner part of the house. After a short period of unconsciousness I was able to open the door and get into the street—a pitiful figure, my clothes torn to rags and stained with blood from a wound on the head, happily only skin deep, and much bruised.

'Moulay et-Touhami was imprisoned. After a period of incarceration at Wazan, he was taken to Tangier but he had become quite insane, and on being brought into the presence of his father, Sidi el-Hadj Abdeslam, who still lives in Tangier, he wanted to assassinate him.

'He was at Tangier and some little time later was sent to a lunatic asylum in France, where he lived for several years, suffering from the strange delusion for a Mohammedan—that he was Jesus Christ.'

The whole of this episode was painful for Emily. She had a hand in bringing up Moulay et-Touhami, and she wondered if she could be responsible in any way for his fixation on Jesus Christ as Touhami loved and admired her. Until the end, she was the only one who could control him in any way, and he would listen to her even when at his most dangerous.

She wondered, too, if some form of insanity could run in the family. Nobody, thank God, she knew, could be more stable than her own two sons, but their father's behaviour continued irrational and erratic. For the next two years she moved backwards and forwards between Oran and Tangier, always treading on egg-shells when in Morocco, as sometimes the Shereef was cordial, and at other times would revert to his old habit of sending for her and then refusing to see her. She noticed, too, that many of his European tendencies were vanishing with age. As his beard grew greyer, he moved more and more to the comfort of childhood-based Moslem thinking and custom. As a woman with deep religious feelings of her own, she could understand this return to his earliest source of reassurance.

In February 1890 she was living in Oran and received word that the Shereef was dying. If this were true she knew it was necessary to be at hand with her boys in order to guard their inheritance.

In a strangely calm mood she telegraphed the Governor General in Algiers to send the boys to her at once, sold up her furniture and made the decision then and there to live in Tangier permanently. All the to-ing and fro-ing was becoming far too expensive, and besides, she was happier in Tangier. Her friends were there, and she felt that she had done quite enough to disembarrass the Shereef of her presence. Whether he was dying or not, it was time to think about her own life. She was forty-one, and the last seven years had been unbearable. It was time for change. She left Oran feeling free. The decision had released her. She made another. If the Shereef did live no longer would she permit him to humiliate her. She planned to start a completely new life.

The Shereef nearly died. He was clinging to a thread of existence which was strengthened when Moulay Alarbi, waiting by the bedside, suggested that notaries be brought in to make certain of the Wazan properties passing to him and his children. This suggestion so enraged the Shereef that he made a remarkable recovery shouting at his eldest son: 'Do you consider me a dying man? Remember you have brothers and the law gives equal portions. Aha! You want to inherit from a live man; can't you wait until I'm dead!'

Moulay Alarbi was packed off home to Wazan in disgrace.

The improvement lasted a few days, and the doctor, an Italian, asked to see Emily to explain that the Shereef must be removed from Tangier and taken away from the entourage who constantly surrounded him.

Tactfully the doctor explained that though they both knew the Shereef drank too much, there were other symptoms that were inexplicable. He feared there was some treachery afoot.

'Can you not take him away from here?' he said.

Emily was adamant that he was no longer her responsibility.

'I will look after him in Tangier, but nowhere else,' she said.

But as always her sense of duty defeated her commonsense. The Shereef sent for her and begged her to find him a nurse who spoke Arabic, a secretary and a courier to travel with him as the doctor had said that he must not take any of the present staff.

They were the services that she had always fulfilled for him. It was obvious what was in his mind—he wanted to travel with her but did not dare ask. Emily struggled with her conscience. She did not wish to go with him—if he died en route, the Tangier entourage would say that she had been at fault, and her chances of settling in the town would go. On the other hand, she felt she could not abandon him after so many years. He was the father of her sons. They were at school and she was free, with nothing to do. She decided to compromise with her conscience. If she could find the three people he needed, she would hire them for him and forget the matter. If she could not find anyone suitable—she would go herself.

No one suitable was available, and reluctantly she told him that if he wished it—she would travel with him.

His relief and delight were flattering and they decided to leave in four days, taking only two servants. The trip was to be around the Mediterranean, taking in Southern France, Southern Italy and coming back along the North African coast from Tunisia.

It might, she thought, her unquenchable optimism rising, even be enjoyable.

The next morning while she was busying herself with the preparations for the journey, the servants announced that the Italian doctor wished to see her. He was a most un-English fellow, she thought, for not knowing of her decision to accompany her husband, he had come to beg her to do just that. His method of pleading was somewhat dramatic. He flung himself on his knees before her, so agitated that he forgot to take off his gloves, and folding his hands in supplication begged that she would take the Shereef away.

'I am convinced, madam, that he is being poisoned. Only you can save him.'

And save you, too, Emily thought. The Moors were always difficult if a Moslem died when under the care of a Christian doctor.

'I have already arranged to accompany him, sir,' she said tranquilly. 'Do let me help you to your feet.'

He seized her hand in his.

'Madame—you are an angel of mercy,' he said. 'How can I thank you enough.'

She sighed.

'I am only doing my duty,' she said. 'But I shall do my best to bring him home well again.'

That was exactly what she did. But the trip was not without anxious moments. The Shereef was first desperately ill and then suddenly rudely healthy. His case puzzled doctors from Marseilles to Palermo and on to Constantine. But by the time they were in Gibraltar Bay, the mountains of Morocco breaking into the sea across the water, he was well again and had been for over a week.

They stood together on the deck, and he asked her the question that she had asked him so many times without receiving any reply—what was their relationship to be?

She looked at him—still an impressively handsome man, his colouring deepened by the sun of the holiday, his beard and hair, though grey, thick and vital about his face.

'Your friend and your nurse for as long as I live,' she said slowly, 'but I can never be anything more to you now.'

'I understand,' he said.

That was how the situation remained. Emily lived in her own house in Tangier with her sons at home with her permanently. Moulay Ali had caught typhoid in his last term at school. He was very close to dying but she had nursed him back to health. Unfortunately he was not strong enough to return to the Lycée and she was reluctant to let Moulay Ahmed stay there alone. So they both returned home and private tutors were engaged.

She spent time in Wazan, where the oldest and the youngest of the ex-wives had become her good friends, and again was called to nurse the Shereef through what looked like a fatal bout of illness. His one fear was that he would die away from Tangier. This would have meant that he could not be buried at his mother's side, and he constantly begged Emily to promise that she personally would see that he was buried at the Mosque of Moulay Tiaeb in the family grave there.

But his behaviour remained as eccentric as ever. In her

memoirs Emily wrote of the early days of his last illness when he was still able to humiliate her.

'Three weeks before my husband's death I was startled out of my sleep, very early in the morning, by hearing his carriage driven up to my door. It was the only one in Tangier then. He was carried into the drawing room, while my bedstead was quickly brought down to the dining room for his convenience. He was rather delirious, and begged me not to let him be poisoned, to lock up everything, even the water, and prepare his food myself. Then he fell into a comatose state and nothing could rouse him. I sent for a doctor, he said he could not account for his state; the only thing to be done was to administer beef essence, and this he would swallow from a teaspoon when I put it into his mouth. Towards afternoon he again revived, but would not hear of seeing a medical man, and I naturally did not tell him one had been summoned. Towards evening he insisted upon being propped up; then he tried to play draughts with Moulay Ali and Mannie and would not part with them until the children could not keep awake any longer. After extracting a promise from them to get up early and go to the mountain to shoot him a wood-pigeon, he let them go. Several people called, but only those who were not of his entourage would he see. He remained awake all night, towards morning he dozed, and I went to take my bath. I had scarcely commenced to dress when I heard a tremendous scuffling downstairs, and found my house invaded by servants and retainers from the Zowia. Poor things, I thought, they are anxious about their lord and Master; little did I guess the real cause of the army of women. I heard the Shereef talking and hastened to take him the coffee I had prepared for him. Then what did I see; a woman dressing the Shereef as quickly as she could while others held him up on the bed. I asked the meaning of this, and the reply was "Sidi's orders". He refused the coffee, and I remonstrated with the women on their procedure, but all to no purpose. Presently the carriage came, his men hoisted him in their arms, and he was driven at a furious rate the short distance to the town. When the boys came back and found their father fled, it was piteous to see the children's distress. They went to their father's residence, only to be refused admittance.'

She was not to have very much longer to be baffled and bewildered by the behaviour of her husband and his followers. It seemed most likely that the new Shereefa, backed by the servants to whom she had belonged so recently, had removed the Shereef from Emily's home. The Shereef himself was not in any condition to argue about what was done with him. After the precipitious departure from her home his mind seemed to have gone and once Emily finally managed to get a doctor to her husband, he said that his malady defied diagnosis. In his lucid moments, the Shereef told Moulay Alarbi that he was to be guardian to Moulay Ali and Moulay Ahmed and that he expected the older step-brothers to behave fairly towards the younger boys. He grasped Emily's hand one day as she sat by his bed and whispered with difficulty: 'Do not permit the children to go anywhere without you to guard them.' He told his youngest sons that they would never go wrong if they followed their mother's advice.

He was very near to death and he knew it. The last years of drinking had caused attacks of D.T.'s which had been the reason for so many of his fears. His health was ruined and the doctors warned him that there was little time left. Emily never left his side.

On September 27th, 1892, his mind cleared and he sent for Emily's sons, his other sons, his secretaries and as many relatives and members of the household as could be gathered together.

'I have something to say to you all,' he whispered. He was lying on a mattress, facing the East, his face sunken and pale. Speech was not easy, but he struggled on: 'I appoint my wife, Emily, Shereefa of Wazan as my principal nurse while I live, and guardian to all my sons, including Moulay Alarbi and Moulay Mohammed. I declare that my *baraka* shall pass to her on my death, and I ask that all shall respect her as a "born Shereefa".'

A buzz of amazement went around the room as his voice faded. Emily took his hand. She was finding it difficult not to cry for she knew that what he was saying would ensure a sheltered position for her in the Moroccan community for the rest of her life.

'That is all I have to say. My estates must be divided according to the law.'

His eyes closed and the doctor moved forward to look at him and disengaged the Shereef's hand from Emily's.

'Why not go and sleep. You must rest yourself,' he said to her. 'He will be all right for a while.'

She was struggling with her emotions. She was dreadfully tired but she did not want the Shereef to wake and find her gone, but the doctor insisted he would not wake until the morning.

She took the carriage and was driven to her house where, half-undressed in case of emergencies, she laid down on her bed. She wanted to think about the incredible compliment he had paid her; she a Nazarene woman to be given guardianship of her own sons and even adult male stepsons. It was an unheard of honour in Morocco for any woman. Also to style her 'a born Shereefa' and to pass to her his *baraka* was, she knew, an extraordinarily significant event in Moroccan history. There was no doubt that what he had said would be observed. In spite of all the last years of debauch he was still the most holy man in Morocco and his death-bed wishes would never be disregarded.

More important, she thought, as she dropped off into sleep, her sons would be safe, too.

The Shereef did not sleep throughout the night. About midnight he awoke, struggled to sit upwards and shouted: 'My mother beckons me. I must go. Bring my wife.'

It took both Moulay Alarbi and Moulay Mohammed to hold their father down on the mattress and he called again and again for Emily until finally, Moulay Mohammed, the younger and gentler of the two boys insisted that she was fetched.

It was just 1 a.m. on September 28th, 1892, when Emily heard a heavy knocking on her door. She knew immediately the reason, and was on her feet, pulling on her top garments and chivvying the servant to get the children dressed. The carriage was waiting outside and the three of them, the children sleepy-eyed and rather fearful were hurried back to the Zowia.

He was as she had left him, again unconscious. A place was made for her at his side while the sons and servants stood around. The room was very silent, though faintly from outside came the sound of a crowd who walked in circles chanting 'Allah, Allah, Allah' in a last effort to save their Shereef's life.

'It is useless to speak to him,' Moulay Alarbi said, 'He is already a dead man.'

'No. Try,' Moulay Mohammed urged.

'Yes, try,' said one of the secretaries, 'he may respond to your voice.'

She leaned over him.

'MacDuff, MacDuff, I am here,' she said.

His hand groped for hers, and she took it. His fingers tightened over hers. He opened his eyes and said: 'You are here, my darling.'

'Yes,' she said, 'I am here.'

It was the end, and Moulay Mohammed's secretary moved forward to release her hand from the dead man's clasp.

Chaper Ten

THE NAZARENE SAINT

Just off the broad, modern main road that runs through the Marshan area of Tangier there is a small turning which leads down to two pretty villas, an up-to-date hospital faced by a few tumbledown shacks and a small walled garden.

In the garden, shaded by dusty fig-trees are a jumbled collection of graves, some childsized, others for adults. The most impressive is a large raised tomb with a small grille set high at the side. From the railings of the grille flutter a few wispy rags that were once part of a petticoat or a handkerchief.

Even in the 1970s, this part of Tangier holds many memories of Emily, Grand Shereefa of Wazan. The villas were hers—one of them the house where she began her marriage and where she died sixty-eight years later. The shacks she built to house her slaves. The hospital, appropriately is just a few yards from the spot where for many years she vaccinated the Moroccan people against smallpox.

The garden graveyard contains the remains of some of her children and her grandchildren, but the imposing tomb is her own. Today the simpler women of Tangier and from the Riff mountains believe Emily to have been a Saint, and the fluttering rags tied to her tomb are there as petitions for a husband, a baby, more money or a better life.

She lived for nearly 50 years after her husband's death, dying herself at the age of 92 years, 2 months and 8 days on the 10th of December, 1941.

'She was nursed night and day by her grandsons and daughters,' her son, Moulay Ali, wrote to her relatives in England. 'No outsiders were needed.

'I was with her on the last day. She was unconscious for three or four days before she died and I think she recognised me for she put out her hand and held mine for a while. She died the next morning at about a quarter to six, local French time. I was with her about a quarter of an hour afterwards. It was my last look at her as I could not stand all the burial preparations. This took place on the 11th of last month and by her repeated recommendations she was buried in a plot of ground in front of my house which I had reserved as a private cemetery at the death of dear Minni (his daughter) and exclusively reserved for members of the family.

'We were able to do this as we found a late will witnessed by Miss Ferida Kirby-Green and Miss Wheeler—the former her oldest friend among the European colonists actually in Tangier. This will annulling all previous wills gave my brothers and myself full powers as sole legatees and executors of her last wishes.

'Having communicated the same to Her British Majesty's Consul General, Mr. Gascoigne, we came to the conclusion that it would be more convenient that she should be buried in our own private cemetery instead of the English one, and this because of the convenience of the family, the female portion of which could never visit the grave, and to prevent a possible riot by the Moslem people who consider her one of their Saints, which would have been very awkward at this time for all concerned.

'On the evening of her death, HBM Consul General and Dr. Anderson of Hope House accompanied by numerous lady friends had a burial service in her bedroom. Next day she was put in a semi-Moorish, semi-European carved coffin with a deep green pall (she had mentioned to several members of the family that she objected to black or flowers being used at her funeral or a carriage and that she would be exclusively carried by Moors). The last item was solved by her grandsons who requested the honour of bearing her to her last resting place. This satisfied all concerned.

'The funeral was very impressive and cosmopolitan. There was never such a gathering of all the Moorish authorities, all the diplomats of all nations, (Axis excepted)* with every class of European and Moorish

* It was of course wartime.

population. The sight was unique in Tangier, especially the complete mixture of all present without distinction of class and creed and most impressive of all was the respectful silence observed by all. The farewell ceremony was very much proof of the affection shown by all classes.

'As the members of the family stood in a line to receive the condolences of all present (which took a long time) no order was observed. For instance, first the Basha, next a European lady and Israelite, a military attaché, and so on, and the respectful silence; no bustling or murmur. "She belonged to all and all felt her loss. She was in death as in life a friend and benefactor."'

But Emily's death caused almost as much controversy as her marriage had nearly seventy years before. The British of the town felt very strongly that she should have been buried in a Christian graveyard. The Moors wanted her for their own. Moulay Ali's compromise was the only answer and eventually the Forces Chaplain came from Gibraltar to consecrate the ground in which she lay.

One feels she would have approved of her son's decision. In 1936, when she was still a surprisingly vigorous 86 year old, she wrote home to her niece, Margaret Williamson, saying:

'People seem to think that I have done so much for Morocco. I have never laid myself out for same. Gave advice when requested, that's all. I have always been treated with the utmost respect; never insulted or asked to change religion or dress or asked why I retain all English mannerisms and customs; never interfered with theirs. All know I am a Protestant as I have never hidden same. Am treated as one of their own people and what more do I desire? And it has ever been the same. Whether Morocco, Algeria or Tunis in my past travels. Yet in 1873 the press predicted I should be *poisoned* in two months ! ! !'

But she had done much for Morocco. After her husband's death, she had raised a fine tomb to him in the Mosque where his mother was buried, knowing that his grave must become a Holy place to the people. Then she went on with the task of seeing that her sons' inheritance and educations were taken care of.

She chose their wives—according to custom—with many heart-searchings, picking for one the very fair-skinned little girl she had known many years before in Tetuen. And when their children were born, she took them, and the children's children under her capable, maternal wing.

Emily lived on in her own Victorian furnished home, with a photograph of her husband on the wall near a little painting of the spot where they first met. And she continued to give vaccinations against smallpox; worked on a project to house freed slaves, and was at the beck and call of anyone who needed her help in any way.

The habit of service was too ingrained for her ever to change.

She also managed the money affairs of the family, and being remarkably thrifty as well as intelligent, by clever usage of their land replaced and increased the family fortunes without having to resort to *Yiasa*.

But at the end of her life she must have been missing her old friends. John Hay Drummond Hay died in Scotland in November 1893 and by a strange coincidence the rope on the flag at the British Consulate in Tangier broke so that the flag was at half-mast at the time of his death.

The Perdicaris family left Tangier for the safety of Tunbridge Wells in 1904 after Mr. Perdicaris had been captured by a bandit, Raisuli, and held to ransom in considerable discomfort in the Riff Mountains. The kidnapping came near to causing a war between America and Morocco, but it was the diplomatic intervention of Emily's sons that brought Perdicaris back to Tangier in one piece.

Later, in 1907, Raisuli also captured Caid Harry MacLean and the British Government were finally forced to pay out £20,000 for his release. Nevertheless, Caid MacLean probably owed his life to the careful handling of the negotiations which were again undertaken by Emily's sons.

The long-standing, edgy feud with the Sultan Moulay Hassan was to end with the Shereef's death. Not long after her sons were presented at Court and received with great honour. She herself was subsequently decorated by the Sultan.

But the King, too, died long before her. In 1894 he set out to repress a rebellion that had broken out in one of the further corners of his Empire, and while in camp, on enemy territory, he died from an internal complaint.

His death at that time and place could have put the entire country in a state of civil war with rival factions battling for the throne while the warring tribes descended to wipe out the Royal army.

It was imperative to keep his death a secret until the army was able to return to Rabat. A plan was made by the High Chamberlain, who kept the fact of the King's death from everyone but his master's personal slaves. In forced marches the army returned home. Food was taken in and out of the Sultan's tent; the troops were told that he was too tired to appear. *The Times*' correspondent Walter Harris was told the story by Moulay Hassan's son and recounts how there was another day of forced marches —'But Moulay Hassan's death could no longer be concealed. It was summer. The state of the Sultan's body told its own secret.'

By the time the Army returned to Rabat, two day's later and five days after Moulay's Hassan's death the body was terribly decomposed, and the King's escort constantly sick, in spite of scarves tied over their faces. But the plan had worked. The Sultan's son, Moulay Abdul Aziz, was pronounced Sultan.

Unfortunately for Morocco Abdul Aziz was not a strong king. It was during his reign that the thing the Shereef had worked for, and Sir John Hay Drummond Hay had fought against, took place. The French took over Morocco.

They came in 1912. Emily did not live to see their going in 1956.

Once France had taken over the country as a Protectorate the Tangier Emily had known for forty years began to change. Roads were laid. A railway line was started to Fez in 1917 and eventually extended to Taza, not far from the Algerian border.

By the 1930s, the European population of Tangier alone had grown to over 500 from the 54 who had been in residence when Emily arrived. And the town had been declared an international zone, harbouring financiers, smugglers, criminals and carpetbaggers.

None of it meant a great deal to the Shereefa. She kept herself busy late into old age, sewing, writing letters—she corresponded with 40 people in all parts of the world—and caring for her grandchildren and great grandchildren.

The visiting authors still came. V. C. Scott O'Connor went to see her in the early 1920s and wrote of her in his book 'Vision of Morocco'.*

'The Grand Shereefa of Wazan came to Morocco fifty years ago, an English girl, the companion of Mrs. Perdicaris. The Shereefa carries her 73 years with a gallant air, and still bears out her statement that when she married the Shereef she was a hearty and vigorous girl.

'Much has happened since then. The Sultans of Morocco have ceased to rule, as such, resting now chiefly on their spiritual descent. The Shereefs of Wazan still remain the heads of the confraternity of the Taibiya, in its day one of the most powerful (sects) in Islam, whose chiefs bore the proud motto: "No Sultan for us: Without us no Sultan." They retain their material possessions their farms scattered over Northern Africa and their convents affiliated to Wazan. But their spiritual influence is dying, their wealth is no longer sustained by the rich offerings of the faithful. Their pact with a Christian power has damaged their sanctity. The future, it may be, is with those who shall one day rise up against it.

'The old Shereef whose picture is on the wall (in Emily's home) is long since dead. One of his sons holds an office bestowed on him by the French at Wazan; a grandson is being educated at the school for nobles at Meknes and will go to St. Cyr and great grandchildren frequent the old house where the Shereefa still lives, holding her place alike in the esteem of her Moslem family as well as in the regard of her own people.

'I see her seated there in the midst of her chandeliers and mirrors and old-fashioned chairs, her photographs of

* Thornton Butterworth, 1923.

Princess Beatrice and other visitors upon the wall and upon a multitude of tables; with a red woollen wrap on her shoulders, cheerful, unaffected, kindly, brave.

'She told me that fear never came into her life; that she could always enter into and understand the point of view of other people and take life as it came. "Perhaps," she said quietly, "that is why I have been able to keep my place so long."'

Morocco changed, but Emily did not. In 1956 G. H. Selous, who got to know her when he worked for the British Embassy in Fez, wrote in his book 'Appointment to Fez': 'Riffis seeing her passing on her mule, shrouded and swathed in her outer Moorish raiment would dash up to kiss her shoulder or the hem of her garment with all the signs of veneration. I can still visualise it as if it had taken place yesterday, the occasion when I myself witnessed such an incident. I could not tell that the recipient of this remarkable attention was not a Moorish woman, but even so such a reverent homage towards a seemingly Moorish woman struck me as so odd that I could not rest until from one of the Ambassador's daughters I had ascertained the key to the mystery.'

The last letter that Emily wrote to her English relatives was in 1940, just two years before her death, and she was still articulate as well as interested in world affairs. But her health was failing.

'Unusually cold weather here,' she wrote, 'and even extra clothing does not seem to provide the warmth required. I have been obliged to keep to my bed the last four days and stay there with an old petrol-can stove in the room to warm the cockles of one's heart.

'As for arthritis, it flies all over my body at times from head to toe, but I tell myself to grin and bear it and be thankful it is nothing worse.

'Am glad to hear of your mother's remarkable recovery. My love and congratulations to Elizabeth (Margaret Williamson's daughter, who became a missionary) she must be a very clever girl, and no doubt John (Elizabeth's brother and Emily's great nephew) will do his share when the time arrives, (He did. He was killed on active service in Sumatra.) which may never be if that mad man (Hitler) passes over to the majority and his seven companions join him. Local press news we have daily and the wireless is also very interesting. The whole clan (the Nazi party) must be a set of Atheists of a very degraded class.

'My mail has been heavy. Forty-seven letters to date coming from Australia, America, the Cape, Denmark, Italy, England and Scotland. Housekeeping almost double the usual monthly expenses. On Friday the prophet's birth, hence the season of the yearly pilgrimage to Mecca. Moulay Ahmed's eldest son is joining the number this year. He will be presented to the King of Mecca.

'My hand says "down tools" so with much love to all and best wishes for 1940 to all. It may interest you to know that 314 prophets in the Old Testament are also prophets of the Moslem.'

By then it was many years since her last visit home to England, but she never lost touch with her family nor ceased to reassure them that her Christian belief was as strong as ever. But her eldest grandson, Shereef Moulay Hassan, who was the Pasha of Ksar el Kebir up until his retirement believes that towards the end of her life she turned more and more towards Moslem thinking, reassured by the similarities between the two creeds.

She would have been pleased that her funeral combined aspects of the ritual of both.

Another account of the ceremony survives.

'Her burial was unique. First there was the burial service in her home read by the British Consul General. Her sons and grandsons formed a guard of honour around the coffin, which was draped with the Union Jack. The whole British colony and personal friends took part in this moving ceremony. The interment took place next morning. The coffin was carried shoulder high by her grandsons in dead silence through a dense crowd of all nations and their official representatives and tenderly placed in a garden tomb. In the absence of the British Chaplain the British Governor General read the committal service. Later the Chaplain General of the Forces came especially from Gib to consecrate the tomb and give a final blessing. For weeks afterwards processions of Moors came from all parts of Morocco to pray and give thanks for the Christian woman who devoted herself to their welfare.

'The English woman, the *Roumi* (Christian) sleeps in a Moorish tomb, in a Moorish garden, beside her Moorish grandchildren, consecrated and blessed by the English church. To the Moors she is a Saint, and my Lord's wife, and the women especially offer up their prayers for her.'

If there is a life after death, one likes to think that Emily would have found the Moslem ideal of Paradise.

'In Paradise there are rivers of incorruptible water and rivers of milk the taste whereof changes not; and rivers of wine pleasant unto those who drink and rivers of clarified honey; and in Paradise the faithful shall have all kinds of fruits and pardon from their God.'